Old Age Pensions and
Policy-Making in Canada

CANADIAN PUBLIC ADMINISTRATION SERIES
COLLECTION ADMINISTRATION PUBLIQUE
CANADIENNE

J. E. Hodgetts, *General Editor/Rédacteur en chef*

The Institute of Public Administration of Canada
L'Institut d'Administration publique du Canada

This series is sponsored by the Institute of Public
Administration of Canada as part of its constitutional
commitment to encourage research on contemporary
issues in Canadian public administration and public
policy, and to foster wider knowledge and understanding amongst practitioners and the concerned citizen.
There is no fixed number of volumes planned for the
series, but under the supervision of the Research
Committee of the Institute and the General Editor,
efforts will be made to ensure that significant areas
will receive appropriate attention.

L'Institut d'Administration publique du Canada
commandite cette collection dans le cadre de ses
engagements statutaires. Il se doit de promouvoir la
recherche sur des problèmes d'actualité portant sur
l'administration publique et la détermination des poli-
tiques publiques ainsi que d'encourager les praticiens
et les citoyens intéressés à les mieux connaître et à les
mieux comprendre. Il n'a pas été prévu de nombre de
volumes donné pour la collection mais, sous la direction du Rédacteur en chef et du Comité de recherche
de l'Institut, l'on s'efforce d'accorder l'attention voulue
aux questions importantes.

Canada and Immigration:
Public Policy and Public Concern
Freda Hawkins

The Biography of an Institution:
The Civil Service Commission of Canada, 1908–1967
J. E. Hodgetts, William McCloskey, Reginald
Whitaker, V. Seymour Wilson

Old Age Pensions and Policy-Making in Canada
Kenneth Bryden

Old Age Pensions and Policy-Making in Canada

KENNETH BRYDEN

The Institute of Public Administration of Canada
L'Institut d'Administration publique du Canada

McGill–Queen's University Press
Montreal and London 1974

©McGill–Queen's University Press 1974
International Standard Book Number 0-7735-0206-8 (Cloth)
International Standard Book Number 0-7735-0221-1 (Paper)
Library of Congress Catalog Card Number 74-75972
Legal Deposit second quarter 1974
Bibliothèque nationale du Québec

Design by Anthony Crouch
Printed in Canada by John Deyell Ltd.

Contents

Tables

Preface

THE STUDY OF POLICY-MAKING PROCESSES is still in its infancy in Canada. The study of the processes involved in making policy on income redistribution has hardly even begun. Yet, the issues generated by income redistribution have probably the greatest salience of any domestic issues in advanced societies. As Lowi has observed: "Issues that involve redistribution cut closer than any others along class lines and activate interests in what are roughly class terms. If there is ever any cohesion within the peak associations, it occurs on redistributive issues, and their rhetoric suggests that they occupy themselves with these most of the time."[1] This book, which is based on a Ph.D. thesis submitted to the University of Toronto in 1971, explores the politics of income redistribution through a case study on old age pensions. Such pensions have at least two characteristics to commend them as the subject of an exploratory study: (1) they have been a recurring issue in Canadian politics since the beginning of the twentieth century; (2) more governmental resources are now devoted to them than to any other single public program.

I am especially indebted to the Laidlaw Foundation of Toronto and to my thesis supervisor, J. S. Dupré, chairman of the Department of Political Economy of the University of Toronto. The generous financial assistance granted to me by the foundation greatly extended the range of research which it was possible for me to undertake. Professor Dupré's penetrating criticisms of successive drafts were most important to me in sharpening my presentation. F. W. Peers of the Political Economy Department also made valuable suggestions.

Ruth M. Bell, chairman of the Board of the Macdonald Cartier Library, established and operated by the Progressive Conservative Women's

Association, granted me access both to the collection in that library and to the records of Conservative leadership conventions now in the Public Archives of Canada. Allan O'Brien, former national director of the Liberal Federation of Canada, allowed me to avail myself of the primary and secondary sources in the federation's library, and his staff was most helpful in locating material in which I was particularly interested. Clifford Scotton, federal secretary of the New Democratic Party, authorized me to consult the files of the Cooperative Commonwealth Federation (now in the Public Archives) and NDP records. George Home, political education director of the Canadian Labour Congress, gave me access to congress records and his own extensive knowledge of trade union legislative activities, and representatives of other major associations were more than helpful. J. W. Willard, former federal deputy minister of welfare, permitted me to see certain departmental files in the Public Archives and assisted me in other ways. J. I. Clark of the same department offered useful criticisms of the manuscript. Staff members of the Public Archives were unfailingly cooperative in helping me find my way through the King and Bennett Papers and other collections in their custody.

My thanks are also extended to about fifty federal and provincial politicians and public servants who took time out from their crowded schedules to submit to lengthy interviews. Finally, I express my appreciation to Hugh Whalen of Memorial University of Newfoundland, who got me started on this project while he was a professor at the University of Toronto and whose criticisms of the manuscript led to several important improvements.

Chapter One

Framework of the Study

THIS BOOK IS A CASE STUDY on the politics of income redistribution, the focus being on income maintenance for the aged in Canada. As a result of the high degree of urbanization and industrialization in Canada in the past century, powerful pressures arose for public policies guaranteeing economic security for the growing urban work force, including old age pensions. Resistance to such income redistribution was grounded in a deep-rooted set of cultural values, referred to as the market ethos, which reinforced dominant economic interests. The central theme of this book is that public pension policy in Canada has been the product of this conflict between the emerging environmental want and the market ethos.

These underlying forces are placed in juxtaposition and examined in chapter 2. Chapters 3 to 8 show how the conflict between the two forces was resolved in the political system. Chapter 9 organizes the information presented in this study within the theoretical framework outlined in the rest of this chapter, the essential finding being that, in the process of being incorporated into tradition, public pensions in Canada were unmistakably stamped with the market ethos. The general reader, whose interests may lie more with the background and development of public policies on old age pensions than with the theoretical framework, may prefer to start his reading at chapter 2, after perusing the comments and definitions contained in the next few pages.

It has often been assumed that there has been a levelling of income disparities in western democracies since the 1930s. Titmuss and Miller have cast serious doubt on the validity of that assumption with regard to the United Kingdom and the United States, respectively.[1] Although some redistribution among groups has occurred, there has been little or no net vertical redistribution. The general level of income has risen with increasing productive capacity, but it is doubtful if disparities have been significantly affected. Podoluk has produced similar findings for Canada.[2] Public policy can be regarded as the ultimate determinant of distribution patterns only in the formal sense that it has established the legal framework within which social, economic, and political interactions occur. In that sense, all public policies could have redistributional implications: indirectly by affecting the rules under which the competition for resources occurs or by giving to some access to benefits denied to others; directly by transferring income or the equivalent from some groups or individuals to others.

To explain distributional patterns in those terms, however, would require an analysis of public policy in its historically accumulated totality and in all its ramifications. Since that is hardly possible, a more practical strategy could be to focus on policies designed to effect transfers to those with little or no income and perceived by the relevant actors in the political process as having that design. Western democracies have produced many such social welfare and social security policies in the last 100 years, with strong emphasis on income maintenance, and these now account for substantial proportions of public expenditure. Yet, many students of poverty are convinced that they have done little to solve that problem.[3] A possible explanation is that they have effected downward redistribution which has been offset in other ways. This too is open to question. Gordon's study of welfare policies in the United States, for example, led her to this generalization: "To the extent that vertical income redistribution occurs as a result of welfare programs, it tends to be largely from average workers to families whose capacity to participate in the labour force is, for some reason, impaired. Or, as it has sometimes been put, most of it occurs within the income groups under about $5,000."[4]

If the principal effect of policies apparently designed specifically for downward redistribution has been merely to reshuffle income among lower income groups, then an understanding of why this is so should increase understanding of why public policy generally has not affected overall distribution significantly. It is proposed here that a study of the political processes relevant to such policy designs will contribute to that understanding. This study, however, does not propose to deal with welfare policies generally, but with one policy only in one country only, namely, income maintenance for the aged in Canada. If one is to believe that such a study will contribute anything to the understanding of the question under consideration, one must accept two major assumptions: that case studies can throw important light on political processes and that such processes are significant determinants of policy designs. Since both these assumptions fall well short of universal acceptance, I will discuss them more fully later in the chapter.

In public discussions of income maintenance for the aged, certain key terms have often been used imprecisely and inconsistently. I have attempted to arrive at definitions which are reasonably exact without violating popular usage more than necessary.

Annuities and Pensions. An annuity is a series of regular payments either for a specified period or for life. Only life annuities are relevant here so that *annuity* will mean the life variety. *Pension* will designate an annuity resulting from a formal group arrangement—whether undertaken by the state, by an employer or group of employers acting on their own initiative or in conjunction with a trade union, or by a voluntary association. What are called *group annuities* are really pensions. Pensions as so defined may be paid in consideration of conditions other than old age, for example, disability and widowhood. My concern here, however, is with old age pensions, and unless otherwise indicated, *pension* will be used in that restricted sense.[5]

Public and Private Pension Plans. The distinction is between plans providing pensions under conditions applicable to the entire population and those providing them only to specified groups which are segregated by virtue of their employment by a common employer or group of employers or of their common membership in an association. The former plans can readily be described as *public*, since it is obvious that only governments can undertake them. There are certain disadvantages in referring to the latter as *private*, since superannuation plans sponsored by governments and government agencies for their own employees are important in this area. A more satisfactory term is not available, however, and no confusion should arise if it is borne in mind that public and private refer to the coverage rather than the sponsorship of the plans.

Old Age Pensions. There is no reason in logic why pensions provided because of age under private plans should not be called old age pensions. This, however, has never been an accepted popular usage. When people have referred to old age pensions, they have almost always had public plans in mind. To depart from this widely accepted usage would lead only to confusion. Therefore, whenever the term *old age pensions* appears in this study, as in the title, it is to be taken as meaning public pensions.

The question might arise as to why the term old age should be used at all since it is ambiguous and sometimes pejorative. Here again one must bow to popular usage. Notwithstanding periodic attempts to promote the euphemism senior citizen, old age has been used well-nigh universally in this context for more than half a century, and it appeared in the short titles of all relevant Canadian statutes before the Canada Pension Plan, as well as in the long title of the Canada Pension Plan. Moreover, there is no satisfactory alternative. For example, retirement pensions would be misleading since no public pension legislation in Canada before the Canada Pension Plan imposed a retirement test as such. In this study, as in the legislation, *old age* and *the aged* will be used in the neutral sense as referring simply to the age at which public pensions are payable. This has varied over the years, with sixty-five and seventy having particular relevance in Canada. The context will make it clear what age is being referred to. There is no implication that a person suddenly becomes old at sixty-five, seventy, or any other specific age. It is simply a case of the exigencies of analysis, as well as of legislation, requiring an arbitrary line to be drawn somewhere.

Contributory and Noncontributory Plans. A *contributory* plan is one in which payment of benefits is conditional on previous contributions by the beneficiary. It does not necessarily follow that those are the only contributions—on the contrary, there are usually others—but if they are not a condition of benefits, the plan is *noncontributory*. Public plans of a contributory nature throughout the world are based in many cases on tripartite contributions—from prospective beneficiaries, employers, and the state. In some important plans, contributions are restricted to prospective beneficiaries and employers, and there are also examples of plans to which only prospective beneficiaries and the state contribute.

Flat-Rate and Earnings-Related Benefits. Benefits may be on the same basic level for all participants or they may be related to previous earnings and/or contributions in some identifiable way. The former will be designated as *flat rate* and the latter as *earnings related*. Other factors, such as length of service or participation, age, and means, may modify the level of benefits, but that does not affect the underlying distinction drawn here.

Means and Related Testing. In social welfare plans of many kinds, payment of benefits may be subject to a means, income, or needs test. Under the *means test* as it has been applied to old age pensions, eligibility for pension and the level of benefits are determined by income or lack of it from other sources. Income is attributed to assets according to prescribed rules, and some types of income in kind may be included at imputed cash values. The usual method over the years has been to place a limit on allowable income and to reduce the pension by the amount by which outside income exceeds that limit. What is called an *income test* is now gaining some currency in Canada. It is similar in principle to the means test but is applied less rigorously. The *needs test*, which is coming into favour in some welfare programs but which is only of marginal significance in relation to public pensions in Canada, differs from the means test in that an assessment of need is substituted for the arbitrary income ceiling.

Types of Public Plan. The great variety of public and private pension plans which have been established throughout the world can be classified in many different ways. For the purposes of this study, it is not necessary to classify private plans. It is useful, however, to distinguish three basic types of public plan, which will be designated as *contributory*, *means-test*, and *universal* plans. The meaning of the first two designations should be clear from the definitions above. The third requires some explanation. In strict logic any public pension plan could be described as universal, since the conditions under which pensions are paid are universally applicable by definition. It is more useful to reserve the term for plans which are neither contributory nor based on a means test. In other words, pensions are paid to everyone who meets stipulated conditions regarding age, residence, and sometimes citizenship. On the basis of the broad distinction between contributory and noncontributory plans, both means-test and universal plans are subtypes of the latter. Their importance in the public pension field has been such that it is more meaningful to treat them as separate types on a par with contributory plans. In means-test plans, benefits are necessarily flat rate, and in universal plans they are usually so. They are more likely to be earnings related in contributory plans, but this is not always the case. It has often happened that more than one type of plan is in effect in the same jurisdiction at the same time. Where this is so, the totality of the plans will be described as a *program*.

1. THE HISTORICAL DIMENSION

With the growing emphasis on comparative and quantitative analysis associated with the behavioural approach to the social sciences, the case study has fallen into disfavour. Salisbury stated the argument against it as applied to policy-making: "Policy is necessarily an abstraction . . . to be approached through aggregative or summarizing analytic procedures. It is *patterns* of behavior rather than separate, discrete acts which constitute policy. The concept of policy is thus anti–case study in its implications for research strategy and encourages controlling for idiosyncratic variables."[6] Case studies, it is commonly alleged, contribute nothing to the development of a science of politics. Since they deal with unique confluences of events, they are not cumulative. They do not provide a basis for rigorous testing of hypotheses with a view to the formulation of valid generalizations of increasingly broad applicability, of scientific laws even.[7] Therefore, case studies lack predictive and *ipso facto* genuinely explanatory power. At best they have produced intuitions and insights of varying degrees of interest and provocativeness. To date, however, more rigorously designed comparative and quantitative studies have not been noticeably cumulative either, in the strict sense in which that word has just been used. They have produced a myriad of intuitions and insights, many of them interesting and provocative, but the contribution they have made to the articulation of "a new more surely scientific paradigm"[8] is not apparent to one who is not a true believer in the method. On the other hand, both these comparative and quantitative studies and the benighted case studies have had a certain cumulative effect: both have provided an expanding body of those tentative (loose) generalizations which are the stock-in-trade of political science. In Canada one can justify either approach on the ground that basic research into political processes, other than those of a constitutional-legal nature, is still in its infancy. Almost anything will provide grist for the mill, and case studies can make a contribution. They will prove nothing, but if undertaken in sufficient volume and variety, they will give rise to more informed though loose generalizations about the political system. They may even be useful to the more positivist analyst by generating testable hypotheses.

There is no substitute for the case study in one vital aspect of policy study. Policy-making is a historical process, not merely in the narrow sense that any policy output has a time dimension even when viewed in isolation from its antecedents, but also in the broader sense that it *has* antecedents: it is an outcropping of a historical development that may be extended. In the present state of knowledge, these antecedents can only be regarded as "idiosyncratic variables," and it is by no means certain that anything more will ever be possible. Controlling for such variables is essential for certain research strategies. Controlling for them to the extent of consigning them to oblivion, however, can only lead to the impoverishment of understanding. As Mills put it: "To fulfill their tasks, or even to state them well, social scientists must use the materials of history. Unless one assumes some trans-historical theory of the nature of history, or that man in society is a non-historical entity, no social science can be assumed to transcend history."[9]

A recent interesting line of inquiry into policy-making consists of quantitatively designed comparative studies of policy outputs in the United States, to which further reference will be made later in the chapter. Although they have enlarged our understanding of the determinants of public policy, one of their limitations is that they tend to obscure qualitative differences in policies. For an elementary illustration of how this can happen, I will take the example of public pension policy in Canada and the United States. Both countries have well-developed policies with many similarities along measurable dimensions, such as proportions of community resources devoted to them, extent of coverage, and average benefit levels relative to general income levels. The policies are far from identical, however, though it is perhaps possible to detect a long-term tendency towards convergence. Contributory pensions constitute the core of the U.S. design, as they were intended to do at its inception in 1935, but means-test pensions continue to form a not inconsiderable part of the whole. In Canada, contributory pensions were grafted onto a universal plan less than ten years ago, and the universal plan continues to be the base of the program. The reasons for these differences are embedded in history, and neither design can be adequately understood except in its historical dimension. In both cases, policies implemented at given points in time were among the determinants of subsequent designs. I will use the term *developmental process* to designate this historical accumulation. An understanding of that process is essential to an understanding of the relationship of public pension policy to income redistribution. The process has been extended in Canada, covering almost the whole of the twentieth century. Its significance within the total policy-making framework is suggested by the steadily increasing volume of resources devoted to pension payments, as is shown at the end of this section.

The developmental process of policies on public pensions can be divided into three distinct stages. The first centred on the Old Age Pensions Act of 1927. That act authorized the federal government to participate with the provinces in a shared-cost plan to pay means-test pensions. The maximum pension payable was initially $20 per month but it reached $40 in 1949. Complementary action at the provincial level was necessary before the pension became payable in the province concerned, and some provinces required financial participation by the municipalities. In the second main stage, a two-level program was established by the Old Age Security and Old Age Assistance Acts of 1951. At the upper level, the federal government assumed full responsibility for a universal pension at age seventy, called old age security. The lower old age assistance level consisted of a shared-cost plan under which means-test pensions were paid to the sixty-five to sixty-nine age group. The amount of the universal and the maximum of the means-test pension were set at $40 a month at first but were increased periodically. The third stage culminated in the enactment of the Canada

Pension Plan in 1965. A contributory plan was superimposed on old age security and assistance, thus creating a three-level program. While the Canada Pension Plan was under consideration, however, a decision was made to phase out old age assistance, and it disappeared at the end of 1969. There is now a new two-level program, radically different from that established in 1951. A basic pension (old age security) is paid universally at age sixty-five, and is supplemented by a contributory pension bearing some relationship to previous earnings and contributions. The federal government is solely responsible for the universal pension, as well as for the contributory plan in all parts of Canada except Quebec. The Quebec government has established a contributory plan of its own which is basically the same as the Canada Pension Plan. Finally, by legislation first passed in 1966, a guaranteed income supplement is now added to the universal pensions of those who qualify under an income test.

The 1927 act was a policy departure whose full significance can be appreciated only in retrospect. Apart from the special case of plans adopted during and after World War I for the benefit of veterans and surviving dependants of soldiers killed in action, the 1927 act was the first significant and continuing federal intervention in the social welfare field. It was also the first significant and continuing shared-cost program.[10] As such it foreshadowed the regime of joint federalism which attained large proportions after World War II. Public pensions, however, have been removed from the area of joint action. After 1951 the federal government alone undertook almost the entire responsibility for them, and its responsibility is now complete except for contributory pensions in Quebec. Since Confederation there have been three amendments to the British North America Act affecting the distribution of powers between the federal and provincial governments. Two of them (described in chapters 6 and 8) arose in connection with public pension plans.

The result of this government intervention has been federal spending of major proportions. In 1937, the first year in which pensions under the 1927 act were paid in all provinces, expenditure on benefits was $37 million, which amounted to 2.9 percent of all government spending. The federal share was $28 million, or 6.1 percent of its spending. In 1952, the first year in which old age security and assistance were in effect, expenditure on benefits was $365 million, or 5.3 percent of all government spending, with the federal government contributing $341 million, or 7.8 percent of its spending. Preliminary figures for the 1973–74 fiscal year indicated payments of $3,000 million for the universal pension and guaranteed income supplement. The federal government was entirely responsible for these payments, which represented 13.3 percent of its total spending.[11] In addition, more than $300 million was spent on old age benefits under the Canada and Quebec Pension Plans, an expenditure which will increase rapidly in coming years. These huge expenditures were exclusively for income maintenance in old age. It may well be argued that there are other important elements in the total well-being of the aged, but in political terms the burning issue has always been income maintenance. As a Senate committee put it: "The universal need, which only a small minority of people can provide for themselves, is a floor of income security to maintain self-reliance. Organizations servicing older people understandably concentrate on the need for services and on plans for improving the administrative structure, but the elderly themselves equate money with freedom."[12]

2. POLITICAL AND SOCIOECONOMIC POLICY DETERMINANTS

The relative importance of political and socioeconomic variables in policy-making has been a matter of some controversy. Studies by Key and Lockard of the U.S. southern and New England states, respectively, attributed major importance to the political variable of interparty competition in the formation of taxation and welfare policy.[13] Key's position was that, though such competition may not be significant for many policies, it will have substantial impact on policies mediating the conflict between the haves and the have-nots to the benefit of the latter. Lockard added an economic dimension, arguing that a high level of economic development induces interparty competition, which in turn leads to welfare policies tending to favour the have-nots. Dawson and Robinson, in a quantitative analysis designed to discover the interrelationship of interparty competition, economic development, and welfare policies in forty-six of the fifty states, found that there was indeed a correlation between interparty competition and welfare policies.[14] More significant, however, was their further finding that economic development was fundamental to both: it emerged as the independent variable and the other two as dependent covariables.[15] This finding was supported on the whole in further studies of American states by Hofferbert and Dye, the former directed mainly to welfare policies and the latter to a variety of policy types.[16] Cutright transferred the comparison to the international plane, focusing his attention on social security programs in seventy-six countries.[17] His analysis yielded similar results. Notwithstanding large differences in political representativeness among the countries studied, the most powerful correlation was with economic development.

9

The results of these studies are far from conclusive. The adequacy of their various measures of political competitiveness, economic development, and policy outputs could be the subject of an extended debate. Yet the cumulative effect of the studies has been to stress the primacy of socioeconomic factors rather than to eliminate political factors altogether as policy determinants. To take one example, Cutright found that when he controlled for economic development, there was a positive correlation, albeit of relatively small magnitude, between political representativeness and social security coverage. More recent studies have pointed to greater significance for political variables than the earlier studies seemed to indicate.[18] Cnuddle and McCrone tested the Key-Lockard and Dawson-Robinson models, as well as one of their own in which interparty competition was treated as an intervening variable transmitting socioeconomic influences to policy-making and modifying those influences, against selected policies in the American states. Their findings suggested that different models were the more appropriate inferences for different policies and that interparty competition was significant for policies arising out of the struggle between the haves and the have-nots. Sharkansky and Hofferbert rejected the isolated variables used in earlier studies and turned instead to factor analysis. They too came to the conclusion that "different social and economic characteristics have different relevance for policies, and their relevance varies between substantive areas of policy. Furthermore, central features of state politics are important for some policies, even when socioeconomic variation is controlled."[19] Fry and Winters criticized earlier studies for concentrating on *levels* of public revenue and expenditure, an area where political influences were likely to be minimal. Using multiple regression analysis, they focused their attention on the net redistributive effect of revenues and expenditures in American states, and concluded that in this area politics not only "makes a difference" but "plays a dominant role." Sullivan, on the other hand, argued that the Fry-Winters methodology was biased in favour of political variables. Reworking their data on the basis of a more neutral selection of variables, he suggested that politics was not dominant though it probably made a difference. He cautioned against hard-and-fast conclusions, however, since in his view the selection of variables is likely to affect the result.

These studies and others like them serve as a caution against excessive preoccupation with political structures and processes in the study of policy-making. Clearly, economic development has profound implications for the society in which it occurs. It gives rise to an ever-widening range of new problems and old problems in more urgent forms, not least of which is the economic security of a work force detached from previous life styles. As a result, new patterns of demand on the political system appear and require policy responses from it. Since the nature and range of the problems to be dealt with will be similar at given levels of economic development regardless of the nature of the political system, it is hardly remarkable that there are also significant similarities in policy outputs among societies with different political systems. There is, however, no simple determinism. The processing of demands through the political system can influence policy outputs both in their historical development and in their current shape. Quantitative studies have tended to confirm what Key hypothesized in the first place, namely, that a system's competitiveness will have a bearing on welfare policies. This has *a priori* credibility: it seems logical to assume that competitiveness will usually open up channels to lower income groups which would otherwise be closed to them.

Canadian federal politics have substantial competitive characteristics. Elections are held regularly, and there has been universal adult suffrage during the entire period of policy-making on old age pensions. No significant formal constraints have been imposed on the formation and activities of political parties or other voluntary associations. Wide freedom of expression and assembly is permitted. Prolonged periods of one-party dominance in the House of Commons reduce the system's score somewhat in some measures of political competitiveness. This dominance, however, should not be abstracted from the system's multiparty context of competition among structured, cohesive parties. A party in office for a long period no doubt tends to develop a sense of security of tenure, but the election of 1957 indicated that tenure can be terminated abruptly precisely when the sense of security is highest. In any case, in only two elections since World War I (1940 and 1958) has any party received as much as 50 percent of the votes cast. Given the complexity of interest configurations in Canada, the fact that more than two parties have consistently had some degree of electoral success since World War I has meant that there have been direct channels into the House of Commons for interests which might otherwise have received little recognition. In particular, the fact that one of these "third" parties has a moderate socialist orientation is a guarantee that redistributional questions will be regularly aired in the House. Some interests are of course substantially more influential than others, but the system is competitive enough overall to provide considerable scope for interest articulation.

The socioeconomic factors operative on public pension policy in Canada are referred to briefly at the beginning of this chapter and are discussed in detail in chapter 2. To summarize, Canada has experienced rapid economic development in the last century, with the result that there have been profound structural changes in the society, which can be embraced within the terms urbanization and industrialization. These changes have given rise among other things to persistent demands for income redistribution in favour of the aged. An equally persistent resistance to downward redistribution has been grounded in the market ethos. Those who could gain from old age pensions and other redistributional measures outnumbered those who might lose. Because of its wide acceptance in the society, however, the market ethos softened conflict, delayed action, and modified policy designs.

3. THE POLICY SPIRAL

Abstracted from its historical dimension, policy-making can be visualized as a cycle consisting of three components: "policy process," "policy design," and "policy outcome."[20] Though interwoven in the real world, the components are nevertheless conceptually distinct, a factor which is analytically useful. The focal point is the policy design, which is often described and will be described here simply as *the policy* or *the design*. This design refers to a course of action deliberately chosen and implemented to effect desired consequences in some designated part of the relevant environment, which in the case of a public policy is the society at large. The design may be but is not necessarily embodied in whole or part in a formal instrument or instruments (acts and regulations in the case of a public policy in Canada). The policy process and policy outcome components are the links between the policy design and the environment: the policy process determines the nature of the policy design, while the results produced by that design in the environment are the policy outcome.

Some of the concepts of systems-derived analyses are useful in expounding the nature of the cycle.[21] In such analyses the political system is conceptualized as a complex set of interacting variables in continuous interaction with their environment. Boundary exchanges between the system and the environment are classified into inputs and outputs, and inputs in turn are subclassified into demands and support. To an extent both of these subsets are autonomous in that they may be affected by environmental changes occurring independently of the political system. To an extent also, however, they are affected by the system's outputs through the changes these produce in the environment. In Easton's model, what I am calling the process phase of the cycle consists of (a) the conversion of environmental wants into demands, (b) the reduction of these demands at the boundary of and within the system through

12

winnowing ("gatekeeping"), collection and combination, and issue formulation, and (c) their conversion by "the authorities" into "authoritative allocations" (policies), which are the outputs of the system.[22] In similar vein, the process is broken down by Almond and Powell into interest articulation, interest aggregation, and rule-making and application.[23] In the reverse phase of the cycle, outputs necessarily alter the environment, and it is to this effect that I apply the term outcome (following Easton). As already indicated, outcomes affect inputs—both the nature of future demands and the level of support—and the cycle is complete. Communication flows are an inseparable part, though only a part, of the cycle. Feedback from the environment to the authorities as to expectations, opinions, beliefs, interests affect outputs, and the feedback loop to the environment affects inputs.

Only a fraction of the vast range of environmental wants which characterize a differentiated society are articulated as demands on the political system. Many articulated demands are not processed through the system and those which are rarely emerge unmodified. Reduction is effected by the system's structure, its communication patterns, and its culture, of which the last mentioned will be dealt with later. Interest articulation and aggregation and communication of relevant information are performed by actors—individuals and organizations. A demand will not enter the system unless it is articulated by an actor or actors with some capacity to make themselves heard and unless there are channels through which relevant information will be communicated. As the demand enters the system, it will typically meet resistance from other actors. Thus, if it makes any progress at all, it will likely become an issue. It is in response to issues that policies are commonly made. Moreover, several issues and their originating demands will inevitably be to the fore at any given time. It is necessary to emphasize this rather obvious point in a case study because of the artificiality which can arise from looking at one case in isolation. For the single issue or demand, aggregation consists basically of fitting it into the larger framework of policies. In the case of public pensions in Canada, aggregation revealed itself primarily in the recurring debates over the cost factors involved—notably coverage, including age of eligibility, and level of benefits—and the manner in which those costs were to be financed.

The authors of the two models referred to suggest a certain specificity of structure to the articulation and aggregation functions. Thus, Almond and Powell argue that articulation is preeminently the function of interest groups and aggregation of political parties.[24] They emphasize, however, that this is far from a one-to-one relationship. In actuality, parties and their spokesmen often contribute to articulation, and interest groups, especially large peak associations with multiple objects, to aggregation. Contribute is the key word here in view of the multiplicity of actors involved in the system's total policy process. Even the authorities may articulate interests on occasion, while their part in aggregation is pervasive and decisive. It is they who ultimately must take responsibility for the volume of societal resources devoted to public purposes and the allocation of these resources among competing demands. The question of the specific functions performed by specific actors is an empirical one to be determined for each individual policy.

Support can be divided into two categories for the purposes of this study: support for the system as such[25] and support for the incumbents of authority roles at any given time. To the systems analysts, concerned as they are with systems in their totality, support for the system is the significant variable to the extent that support for the incumbent authorities is largely subsumed under it. In this study the order of priority is reversed. During the period under review, the Canadian political system was stable on the whole, and certainly pension policy by itself was not seen to be crucial to its survival. There was only one instance where systemic support had any relevance to policy-making in this field. Stress arising from cultural-linguistic conflict reached a relatively high level in the 1960s. The federal authorities' desire to reduce this stress was a determinant of policy on contributory pensions in 1965. Of more continuing significance, however, was support of the incumbent authorities. In a competitive system such authorities can hardly be indifferent to that support. Concern about it was a recurring influence in the specific case of pension policy in Canada. To an extent, the influence of support in both of the above meanings will be *ex post facto*: feedback about the effect on it of previous policy outcomes will influence new policy outputs. There is also an *ex ante* effect, since the authorities can hardly avoid advance assessment of probable outcomes.

This leads to a consideration of public opinion as an environmental influence on policy-making. It is doubtful if public opinion can be entirely ignored even in an authoritarian system, and it is undoubtedly a continuous influence in a competitive system. Its relationship to policy-making, however, is by no means direct and immediate. Empirical evidence on the state of opinion on any given issue is not usually available, is often inconclusive when it is available, and was not available at all before the advent of survey research. Thus, the authorities rarely have objective information on the state of public opinion and are reduced to assessing it subjectively. Active and vocal groups and individuals can no doubt create an illusion of stronger public support than actually exists, but the authorities may also dismiss such groups and

14

individuals as unrepresentative. In any case, the state of opinion is only one of the variables the authorities take into account. They may themselves be convinced of the rightness of a policy and may even equate this with a high level of public support. Even if they do not, they may nevertheless proceed to an authoritative allocation in the expectation that it will then command increasing support or at least will not provoke substantial opposition.

A society's culture is a basic determinant of opinion within it. The culture is particularly significant in reducing the demands made on the political system. Articulation and aggregation will be severely inhibited in relation to wants which are widely regarded as inappropriate for political action. Culture, however, is not static. Changes occurring elsewhere in the environment will impinge on it, and the political system itself will react on it as on the rest of the environment. This reciprocity is illuminated by Hennessy's schema of the opinion variable in policy-making as a progression from "sacrilege" through "idea (private)," "proposal" and "policy (public)" to "tradition."[26] A policy germinates as an "unthinkable thought" or "latent idea" which is "proscribed by the culture."[27] It can become more than that only if it is formulated and voice is given to it as an idea. If sufficient support coalesces around it, it can in time become a proposal and ultimately a public policy. It is then on its way to becoming a tradition, to the point where in time the unthinkable thought will be to undo it. Public support for the policy will increase from close to zero at the sacrilege stage to near unanimity if it is eventually incorporated into tradition. It is not necessarily or perhaps even usually the case that the proposal will command majority support at the point of conversion into policy. Its salience as an issue, however, will usually maximize at about that time. Salience is negligible at or close to the sacrilege stage, while its decline after a policy is implemented is the other side of the coin of growing acceptance of the policy. Articulation could be said to occur in the Hennessy schema between the idea and proposal stages. If cultural resistance is strong, an extended time interval can be involved. On the other hand, an idea corresponding to widespread and important wants in the society will probably be pushed across the boundary of the political system sooner or later.

The gradual incorporation of a policy into tradition will provide a base for further interest articulation. *Prima facie* it seems logical to assume that at least a possible outcome of the conversion of a demand into a policy will be to extinguish the demand. This, however, is not universally accepted. Edelman, for example, has argued that "success in achieving a political objective leads to demands for larger amounts of the same benefits or to new goals different in manifest content but like the old in respect of a latent dimension."[28] The actual development of pension policy in Canada is consonant with this hypothesis. Edelman's explanation is that, notwithstanding the apparently rational forms demands may assume, what is actually sought is "symbolic reassurance," which is a recurring need. Without denying the significance of the non-rational in behaviour, it is perhaps possible to add a more pedestrian explanation. Policies rarely take the precise form of the demands which gave rise to them. The demand is often that "something" be done; the policy is only one of several possible somethings. For many it may satisfy the original want only in part, and for both them and others it may give rise to new wants by raising expectations. In other words, the policy is inseparable from the developmental process.

The incrementalist model, of which Lindblom has offered perhaps the most complete and systematic formulation,[29] is widely accepted as offering a valid explanation of the developmental process in competitive systems. Development is here represented as continuous "mutual adjustment" of conflicting interests, which results in an endless sequence of small accretions to and adaptations of existing policies. The model has both descriptive and normative dimensions. Its proponents argue not only that this is a realistic description of how policies are actually made but also that it is how they should be made. The major criticism levelled at the model at the descriptive level is that it can take account of policy innovations only as exceptions,[30] and therefore it explains only part of the developmental process.[31] Etzioni argues that though innovations may appear to be exceptional because of their relative infrequency, their importance makes them fundamental to the entire process. Incremental changes may prepare the way for them but, on the other hand, they are often the departure points for such changes. This insight is relevant to the case of public pensions in Canada. Here the developmental process was quasi-dialectical rather than linear. The policies of 1927, 1951, and 1965 were leaps to a new plateau from which incremental changes were then made. When these changes proved inadequate to meet rising demands, the next leap was made. In developmental terms, policy-making resembled a spiral more than a cycle.

In an attempt to explain this phenomenon, we will turn to the resistance which demands commonly meet at the boundary of and within the political system. Those which do not represent strongly felt environmental wants will simply be screened out, thus protecting the system from overload. Where a demand is solidly grounded in such want, however, it is unlikely to be screened out permanently. It may meet strong resistance which will delay its conversion to an output, but prolonged delay will result in a leap forward when resistance is finally broken down. Resistance is likely to be strongest when a basic cultural norm is at stake. In the realm of old age security, meeting the environmental want of the urbanizing and industrial society required redistribution of income. Such redistribution was in flat contradiction to the market ethos, which was an elaborate justification of the distribution patterns and especially the wide disparities in them produced by the play of the market. The environmental want was so powerful that opposition to public pensions as such was overcome eventually. The market ethos, however, was far from being reduced to inefficacy. Instead, it was adapted to impinge on aggregation. Outright opposition gave way to conflict over the degree and nature of the redistribution which was to occur. This transmutation continued to have a delaying effect, which resulted in the leaps already mentioned. It also influenced the nature of the policy innovations which were finally adopted.

If as I have argued many actors are involved in policy-making, then it is logical to describe them all as policy-makers. Obviously there are some at the centre—called "the authorities" by Easton and "proximate policy-makers" by Lindblom—with decision-making power. In the system which Canada inherited from the United Kingdom, the power centre is the Cabinet—the federal Cabinet where federal policy outputs are involved as in the case of public pensions—and this body is appropriately referred to as "the government" in daily discourse. It need hardly be said that it necessarily shares power with other actors. As with interest articulation and aggregation, the identity of these actors and their precise roles vary from case to case and must be determined empirically. In general the actors can be identified as (a) the federal public service, (b) provincial governments and public services especially where joint programs or shared jurisdiction are involved, and (c) investigatory bodies such as commissions of inquiry, task forces, and parliamentary committees. As for elected members of parliament, they can hardly be regarded as proximate policy-makers. The party cohesiveness required by the cabinet system has led to executive dominance over the legislature. It does not follow, however, that the policy-making function of M.P.'s is inconsequential. They participate in interest articulation and aggregation, and their closeness to the government makes them an important link between it and the environment. This is so whether they are on the government or opposition side of the House. The government cannot lightly ignore strong representations from its own supporters, and it is rarely willing to let the opposition monopolize a popular issue. Moreover, M.P.'s may on occasion move into the circle of proximate policy-makers through their work on parliamentary committees.

It is in the conversion of demands to outputs, which is the culmination of aggregation, that the authorities are the central actors and the design phase of the policy cycle comes into focus. This phase can be divided conceptually into four elements: (a) commitment by the authorities to the attempt to effect specific environmental changes (outcomes); (b) information processing, often but not necessarily on the initiative of the authorities, to discover a course or courses of action which will effect these changes; (c) choice by the authorities among courses of action where more than one is available; (d) implementation of the chosen course. This ordering of the elements has no necessary relationship to their chronological sequence in the real world. In fact, they are likely to be intertwined in the seamless web which constitutes reality. Information processing, for example, may be inseparable from choice, since it may point ineluctably to a single feasible or preferred course of action. It may also be a necessary prelude to commitment, and that in turn may create a need for further information processing. On the other hand, choice may be integral to commitment, since different courses of action will not have identical outcomes and the commitment may be to a specific outcome. Examples of the different ways in which these elements may be interconnected could be multiplied.

Furthermore, the developmental process cannot be overlooked. New information arising from implementation may be a factor in the incremental change of policy A to A_1, A_2, or in extreme cases, in its abandonment in favour of policy B. It is unlikely to be the only or even the most important factor. Development occurs within the framework of interest articulation and aggregation. A demand may be based on a strong environmental want, but it may also give rise to strong resistance. It will in any case be only one of many demands competing for a share of the resources allocated to public purposes. Thus, aggregation before conversion to policy may extend over a substantial period. Some precipitant or precipitants, often external to aggregation as such, may then be necessary for commitment. As will be shown in later chapters, such precipitants were significant at certain points in the development of public pension policy in Canada.

Chapter Two

Market Ethos versus Environmental Want

1. THE MARKET ETHOS

THE MARKET ETHOS is the cultural expression of the market economy which has moulded Canadian social, economic, and political development. Deriving originally from Europe and especially from England, the first country to emerge into the market economy, that ethos was adapted to the particular conditions of Canada. Its unifying principle was what Macpherson called "possessive individualism."[1] Society was seen as an atomized collection of individuals engaged in endless competition for material possessions. They were motivated to participate in productive processes by an innate drive to maximize their individual utilities. This they did by exchanges on the market. Those with no possessions other than their labour power could sell it; those with possessions could purchase that labour, which they used for productive purposes to the benefit of society and the greater glory of God. The extent of their material possessions was thus a measure of their worth to society. Those possessions were exclusively their own, having been earned by their own effort and enterprise. Subject only to very broad limitations, private property was sacrosanct and could not be transferred against the owner's will. Those who accumulated little or nothing in the way of possessions could carve out a respected if humble niche for themselves (and lay up treasures in heaven) by working diligently for those who could use their labour more productively than they could themselves. The slothful were execrated. Without labour there would be no production and without production there would be no exchange. The market would collapse and all would be reduced to the state of nature where life is "nasty, brutish, and short."

Those who stumbled and fell in the competitive struggle were the objects of stern scrutiny. The possibility was admitted that some of them might be "deserving" in that their condition could have arisen from circumstances beyond their control. The presumption which had to be rebutted in any individual case, however, was that poverty resulted from lack of diligence and foresight. Sentimentality in the treatment of the poor was deleterious both to them and to society. Labour had disutility, and thus most men would waste away in idleness if they could live without working. This would destroy their moral fibre and impose an injust burden on the industrious and thrifty members of society. Sustenance not earned by the sweat of one's brow was evidence of one's lack of moral worth. Investment income was justified, however, as the product of past work. Indeed, since capital was needed for production, thrift was to be admired and encouraged. The capitalist was entitled to reward whether or not he was also an entrepreneur or otherwise engaged personally in production. This was so even when his capital was derived from inheritance rather than personal saving. The man of inherited wealth, however, was expected to use his capital prudently and in a manner calculated to increase production. The spendthrift scion of a wealthy family was not highly regarded, though no doubt he had other compensations.

The destitute were considered to be more in need of moral exhortation and uplift than material assistance. Since they were numerous and sometimes prone to violence, their material needs could not be entirely neglected. The fundamental belief was that the family was responsible for those of its members, both children and adults, who were unable for any reason to provide adequately for themselves. When this line of defence broke down, as it often did, other devices had to be resorted to. The medieval approach had been to exalt Christian charity which, while incidentally conferring some small benefit on the receiver, was a source of merit to the giver. Charity was not displaced as the market economy matured, notwithstanding the strictures of some of the more severe Puritans on almsgiving as a form of personal vanity which demoralized the poor, but it was inadequate. In England the Elizabethan poor law as codified at the turn of the sixteenth and seventeenth centuries provided the guiding principles in the relief of distress for more than two centuries. The destitute could fall back on their local parishes for sustenance, but they were closely supervised, in theory at least and often in practice, to ensure that indolence did not pay. The objective of the poor law was to make the needy earn their keep by consigning them to workhouses where those existed, by creating work for them, or by farming them out to employers. In spite of the stated objective, outdoor relief was common, especially for those unable to work, though it was often casual, usually humiliating, and always parsimonious.

As urbanization and industrialization proceeded, this method too became unsatisfactory, especially after the Speenhamland revision of 1795. Property owners found the poor rates increasingly burdensome, while industrialists were thwarted in achieving a free labour market by the restrictions on labour mobility inherent in parish administration and reinforced by the Settlement Act of 1662. This coincidence of interests produced the poor law reform of 1834, a masterpiece of the scientific application of Benthamism to social problems. The basic principles of the reform, though not fully realizable in practice, were logical and straightforward. Outdoor relief was to be abolished, with institutional care (the workhouse) becoming the only acceptable method of relieving distress. Workhouse life was to be made as bleak and degrading as possible so that a job—any job at any wage—would be attractive by comparison, and there were not even to be exceptions for unemployables since there was always the presumption that they had brought their unfortunate condition upon themselves. Central direction of administration would both cut the tie that bound the poor to their parishes and ensure that the new principles were applied efficiently, uniformly, and remorselessly. On Polanyi's interpretation, the poor law reform was a calculated plan to reduce labour completely to the status of a commodity and thus remove the last impediment to the establishment of a full market economy.[2] Dicey saw the reform from the point of view of the champions of the market economy: "The object of the statute was in reality to save the property of hardworking men from destruction by putting an end to the monstrous system under which laggards who would not toil for their own support lived at the expense of their industrious neighbours, and enjoyed sometimes as much comfort as or even more comfort than fell to the lot of hardworking labourers."[3]

Life in Canada in the pioneer stage simultaneously reinforced the values of the nascent market economies from which the pioneers had come and sheltered some of the incapable from their worst consequences. A man wresting a livelihood from the wilderness needed no convincing of the virtue of hard work and self-reliance. Isolation and shared hardship knit the family closely together, a factor particularly important for those who survived after age had reduced their capacity to work. The farm of Upper and Lower Canada produced some wheat for the market, but mainly its produce was consumed by the farm family. In New Brunswick and in the Ottawa valley the staple export was timber; in Nova Scotia it was fish; but in those areas too the subsistence farm, supplemented in New Brunswick and Nova Scotia by

21

inshore fishing, provided many with a second line of defence. The self-sufficient family unit provided the only social security there was. Grand-parents were an integral part of the family, sharing in the subsistence which it provided and also, to the extent of their capacity, in the endless tasks to be performed. This way of life, however, was already in transition before Confederation. By the 1880s labour problems in industry were serious enough that a royal commission was appointed in December, 1886, to study them. In the course of its extensive inquiries, the commission noted the problem of the worker who was too old to work. It recommended a system of government annuities—modelled on one already in operation in France—which was not different in principle from that ultimately adopted in 1908.[4]

The Elizabethan poor law was not accepted in any of the Canadian colonies except New Brunswick and Nova Scotia where it was only indifferently applied, and the reform of 1834 was not formally adopted in any part of what eventually became Canada. English thinking and experience, however, affected Anglophone Canadians. In the ad hoc expedients devised to deal with welfare problems, one can detect the influence of the principles both of local responsibility (Elizabethan poor law) and of the efficacy of institutional care (reform of 1834).

Knowledge of welfare philosophy and policy in the nineteenth century is more adequate for Ontario than the other provinces, thanks to Splane's research.[5] Local municipalities in Ontario were authorized but not required to provide outdoor relief, and counties to establish homes of industry or refuge. The province gradually established institutions of its own for specific disabilities (mental illness and retardation, blindness and deafness), but it accepted no responsibility whatever for outdoor relief and not until 1890 did it offer construction grants for county homes. The municipalities for their part moved at a snail's pace in exercising the authority conferred on them. The void was partly filled by organized private charity, which emphasized institutional care but also provided some outdoor relief. It was not long before the private organizations were on the provincial government's doorstep asking for financial help, and such assistance (not available to the municipalities) was both given and gradually systematized. Provincial officials were far from happy with this development. They would have preferred a more elaborate system of county homes, with emphasis on industry rather than refuge, but they met resistance from the property owners who had to foot the bill. The underlying attitude continued to prevail that only a very few were genuinely incapable of providing for themselves, and in addition the belief in the primacy of family responsibility had if anything been strengthened by pioneer experience. Institutions, it was

22

argued, would be magnets for the slothful, attracting them even from overseas. Relief for the few who merited it could best be dispensed at the township and village level, for none knew better than neighbours who the slackers were.

The official view prevailed in 1903 when an act was passed requiring all counties to establish homes by 1906, either by themselves or by the cooperation of two or three contiguous counties. This statute was re-enacted in 1912 when the requirements were spelled out in great detail. As a result, institutional facilities expanded considerably, and some of the most yawning gaps of the nineteenth-century system were partly filled. Actually it was and continued to be a makeshift rather than a system. Many people in need fell through the net, but the relatively well-developed system of jails provided a certain reservoir of accommodation. Indigents often found themselves behind bars through mis-application of the charge of vagrancy, and the local authorities did not always distinguish between those who were unable to work because of age or disability and able-bodied indigents who, in the harsh moralism of the day, were considered to be in need of reformation or punishment even though they had been convicted of no specific offence.

Quebec's approach to indigency was inspired by the social doctrines of the Catholic Church rather than English poor law. It did not, how-ever, reflect the spirit of the papal encyclical *De Rerum Novarum*, but was an outgrowth of the antistatist position developed by the Quebec church after the conquest as a defence against the threat to French-Canadian culture posed by the dominance of the Anglophone, Protes-tant, commercialist minority. As late as 1938, a leading Catholic sociologist in Quebec averred:

> The Church lays on the faithful the personal duty of charity even unto the gift of one's self, and the performance of this obligation is essential to the attainment of their ultimate end. . . . it is the bounden duty of each individual to provide, according to his means, for assistance to the destitute and unfortunate, and the state should intervene only when private initiative finds it impossible to supply existing needs.[6]

Religious orders provided an organizational base on which to implement these principles on a considerable scale, and organized private charity in Quebec was quite highly developed. It is doubtful if the net result for the poor was significantly different from that in the rest of Canada. Institutional care, public or private, supplemented by handouts, munic-ipal or charitable, were the distinguishing characteristics of welfare policy in all of the older provinces.

It was in this context that the early advocates of public pensions had to state their case. They were regularly met by a standard objection. A pension paid by the state would reward shiftlessness and profligacy; it would thereby discourage thrift and initiative, virtues that were particularly needed in a new country. In the face of widespread hardship among the aged, this attitude could not prevail indefinitely. The market ethos did not, however, lose its vitality. Instead it gradually assumed the colouration of the rising philosophy of "social insurance." If the state had to provide income for substantial groups of its residents, and the need was inescapable, then the beneficiaries should be made in some way to earn their benefits. This could be done by a system of contributions or forced savings. When benefits could be represented as the product of savings, even if only in part, the essence of the received wisdom was preserved. Sir Wilfrid Laurier argued in 1907 that noncontributory pensions were nothing but public charity which would interfere with thrift and encourage fraud, as, he asserted, New Zealand's experience with its noncontributory plan of 1898 had demonstrated. "To ask purely and simply," he said, "that there should be an old age pension whether a man has been thrifty or the reverse, whether he has been sober or not, whether he has been a good citizen or a bad citizen, is going further than I would be disposed to go."[7] So pervasive was the influence of the market ethos that reformers who wanted redistribution of a kind not tolerated in that ethos were often leading advocates of social insurance. In their anxiety to remove from the poor the stigma of pauperism, they tacitly accepted the philosophy that income not "earned" within the conventions of the market ethos is the mark of the pauper. Benefits related to previous contributions were considered to be received by right, not charity: self-reliant men and women could accept them without disgrace.

2. URBANIZATION AND ITS CONCOMITANTS

As used here, *urbanization* embraces a highly complex set of interactions of which a unique manifestation has been a shift of population to cities, towns, and other built-up areas. It is not a purely post–World War II or even a post–World War I phenomenon in Canada. Stone identified the take-off point as the decade following Confederation. Since then the process has accelerated, with only two significant pauses, immediately before the pre–World War I flood of immigration into the West and during the depression of the 1930s, until Canada is now in the top fifth of the world's nations in degree of urbanization.[8] This long-term process has had continuing consequences for public policy.

In the 1961 census, population was classified as urban if it resided in centres (incorporated or not) with 1,000 or more inhabitants or in the urban fringes of centres of 5,000 and over. Definitions in earlier censuses varied from this, the most important difference being that the population in urban fringes was classified as rural before 1951. Stone reworked the census data back to 1921 on the basis of the 1961 definition, and he assumed that before 1921 the difference of definition was of no great consequence.[9] Table 1, derived from his work, shows the long-term increase in urban population relative to total population both nationally and provincially. At the turn of the century British Columbia and Ontario were leading the way in urbanization, and since then Quebec has moved up rapidly. These three provinces are all above the national average in degree of urbanization, with the rest being below.

In addition to the growth of urban areas, there has been a shift of the rural population away from the farm. The 1931 census showed that between 1921 and 1931 the male population aged 10 and over classified as rural had increased by more than 25 percent, while the increase in the same population gainfully employed in agriculture had been only 4 percent. As a result, the first effort was made to differentiate between farm and nonfarm rural population. The nonfarm percentage increased from 38 in 1931 to 45 in 1941.[10] Subsequent censuses are not directly comparable with those of 1931 and 1941 on this point, but they show the nonfarm population as 47 percent of the total rural population in 1951 and 63 percent in 1961.[11] The nature of farming itself was changing as the subsistence farm gave way to a less self-sufficient unit. Quantitative data on this change are not available, but a major aspect of it can be noted readily, namely, the growth in importance of prairie agriculture with its emphasis on mechanization and cash crops (often wheat only) which do not provide direct subsistence for the farm household. By 1911 the number of males gainfully occupied in agriculture in the three prairie provinces already amounted to 30 percent of the total for the country. It increased to 36 percent in 1921 and 40 percent in 1931. Remaining fairly constant through the 1941 and 1951 censuses, by 1961 it had again increased to 45 percent.[12]

Concurrently with the urbanizing process was a radical change in the industrial structure of the country. There is no way of measuring this for the period before the mid-1920s, but a few trends may be noted. The net value of manufacturing production increased from $96.7 million in 1870 to $1,687 million in 1920. Over the same years the number of employees in manufacturing increased from 188,000 to 610,000.[13] In 1920, when the Dominion Bureau of Statistics attempted its first (inadequate) survey of overall production, manufacturing was already

TABLE 1

Urban Population as Percentage of Total Population, Canada and Provinces, Census Years, 1871–1961

	1871	1881	1891	1901	1911	1921	1931	1941	1951	1961
CANADA	18.3	23.3	29.8	34.9	41.8	47.4	52.5	55.7	62.4	69.7
Newfoundland									43.3	50.7
Prince Edward Island	9.4	10.5	13.1	14.5	16.0	18.8	19.5	22.1	25.1	32.4
Nova Scotia	8.3	14.7	19.4	27.7	36.7	44.8	46.6	52.0	54.5	54.3
New Brunswick	17.6	17.6	19.9	23.1	26.7	35.2	35.4	38.7	42.8	46.5
Quebec	19.9	23.8	28.6	36.1	44.5	51.8	59.5	61.2	66.8	74.3
Ontario	20.6	27.1	35.0	40.3	49.5	58.8	63.1	67.5	72.5	77.3
Manitoba		14.9	23.3	24.9	39.3	41.5	45.2	45.7	56.0	63.9
Saskatchewan				6.1	16.1	16.8	20.3	21.3	30.4	43.0
Alberta				16.2	29.4	30.7	31.8	31.9	47.6	63.3
British Columbia	9.0	18.3	42.6	46.4	50.9	50.9	62.3	64.0	68.6	72.6

Source: Leroy O. Stone, *Urban Development in Canada: An Introduction to the Demographic Aspects*, 1961 Census Monograph (Ottawa: Queen's Printer, 1967), table 2.2, p. 29.

slightly ahead of agriculture in its contribution to total output as then defined—43.7 percent compared with 41.3 percent.[14] Industrialization, however, involves more than an increase in manufacturing output. Integral to it is the growth of a sophisticated structure of financial and other services to meet the diverse needs of a complex economy. Table 2 presents the percentage contribution to the gross domestic product of major industries in selected years since 1926, the first year for which figures are available. The importance of agriculture has declined sharply while that of the service industries has increased.

The ecology of the city and, to a less extent, of the nonfarm rural area, of prairie agriculture, and of other farming drawn more fully into the market economy is vastly different from that of the relatively self-sufficient subsistence farm. Sustenance has to be paid for with cash earned outside the family environment; young adults move to new locations in search of economic opportunity; urban living accommodation for most people is less commodious than on the farm of the past. As a result, the three-generation family becomes less viable. Data on the living arrangements of Canadians broken down by age groups did not become

TABLE 2

INDUSTRIAL DISTRIBUTION OF GROSS DOMESTIC PRODUCT AT FACTOR COST, CANADA, SELECTED YEARS, 1926–1967

(Percentages)

	1926	1930	1940	1950	1960	1967
Agriculture	18.1	11.6	11.4	10.4	5.4	4.5
Resource industries[a]	5.3	5.1	8.1	6.7	6.2	5.4
Manufacturing	21.7	23.1	26.7	28.6	26.1	25.1
Construction	4.2	4.7	3.1	5.3	5.4	6.1
Transportation[b]	12.9	12.5	11.9	11.0	12.2	11.9
Wholesale and retail trade	11.6	14.7	11.9	14.1	13.9	13.7
Finance[c]	10.0	10.5	8.9	8.2	10.6	10.2
Service	12.9	13.8	10.7	10.7	13.1	15.8
Pub. admin. and defence	3.4	4.1	7.3	4.9	7.2	7.3

SOURCE: DBS, *National Accounts, Income and Expenditure*, 1926–56, 1960, and 1967 (Ottawa: Queen's Printer, 1960, 1962, and 1968), table 21 in each case.

[a]Forestry, fishing and trapping, and mining, quarrying, and oil wells.

[b]Transportation, storage, communication, and electric power, gas, and water utilities.

[c]Includes insurance and real estate.

TABLE 3

LIVING ARRANGEMENTS OF POPULATION 65 AND OVER,
CANADA, 1956 AND 1961

(Numbers in thousands)

Living in	1956		1961	
	Number	Percentage	Number	Percentage
Own homes	871	70.6	1,002	72.7
Homes of relatives	211	17.1	208	15.1
Homes of nonrelatives	105	8.5	109	7.8
Institutions	47	2.8	59	4.3
TOTAL	1,234[a]	100.0	1,378[a]	99.9

SOURCES: 1956 Census of Canada, Bull. 3-6, *Analytical Report: Size and Composition of Households*, table 17; 1961 Census of Canada, Bull. 7.2-3, *General Review: Household Size and Composition*, tables 31, 32.

[a]Slightly less than the total population aged 65 and over because relationship to head of household could not be determined in all cases.

available until the 1956 census. Table 3 indicates the essential information which emerges from that and the 1961 census. Well under a fifth of the population aged 65 and over were living with relatives in both 1956 and 1961, and the fraction declined even in the five years covered. In Quebec and the Atlantic provinces the proportion of the aged living with relatives was larger than in the other provinces, but it was not large in any province. In 1961 the figure was highest in Newfoundland where it approached 25 percent, and next highest in Quebec where it was just under 20 percent.

It might be argued that the large and growing percentage of people 65 and over living in their own homes reflected an improving economic position for that age group. This is true to an extent. As we will see, income levels of the group are still low, but it is probably fair to say that in the last generation more people have been able to save at least enough to buy their own homes. Public pensions have made it more feasible for them to continue to live in those homes after a decline in earning capacity. It is to be noted that the amount of the old age security pension and the maximum payable under old age assistance increased from $40 to $55 a month between 1956 and 1961. This does not invalidate our basic argument. Whether the aged lived apart from their children by choice or necessity, the three-generation family unit was of minor and declining significance by the mid-1950s. A process which was then so far advanced must have started much earlier when neither the capacity for even minimum saving nor public pensions existed.

A growing disability of the aged was the steady restriction of their employment opportunities. Occupations in which they have often been able to carry on past 65 and even 70, notably farming and small business, have declined in importance in the total picture. The trend in factory, office, and commerce has been to the large bureaucratic establishment with personnel policies which permit a few individual exceptions. An arbitrary retirement age, usually 65, has become common, and many firms have been disinclined to hire new employees at 45 or even 40. Partly this has been due to prejudice or unnecessarily rigid personnel policies but often, too, it has been the product of the nature of employment in modern industry. Older workers often cannot adapt to the requirements of the large factory, not to speak of the even more rigorous conditions of construction or the resource industries.[15] Raw census and other data on labour force participation are difficult to interpret because of incomparability over time. A few years ago, however, Denton and Ostry produced new historical estimates on a definitionally consistent basis.[16] In the matter of age breakdowns, they were able to carry these estimates back as far as 1921. Table 4 summarizes their findings. The most significant series is that for males, because the labour force attachment of females in the age group was slight throughout the

TABLE 4

Labour Force Participation Rate of Population 65 and Over, Canada, Census Years, 1921–1961

	Total	Male	Female
1921	32.5	59.6	6.6
1931	31.9	56.5	6.2
1941	27.2	47.9	5.8
1951	22.3	39.5	4.5
1961	18.0	30.6	6.1

Source: Frank T. Denton and Sylvia Ostry, *Historical Estimates of the Canadian Labour Force*, 1961 Census Monograph (Ottawa: Queen's Printer, 1967), tables 3–7.

Note: Labour force participation rate is the percentage of the total population of the age group formed by the segment in the labour force.

Newfoundland excluded throughout.

TABLE 5
POPULATION BY SPECIFIED AGE GROUPS, CANADA, CENSUS YEARS, 1871–1961

	As Percentage of Total Population				As Percentage of Population 21 and Over			
	45–64	65–69	70+	65+	45–64	65–69	70+	65+
1871	11.1	1.5	2.1	3.6	24.6	3.4	4.1	7.5
1881	12.2	1.6	2.5	4.1	24.1	3.4	5.3	8.7
1891	12.9	1.8	2.8	4.6	*	*	*	*
1901	13.9	2.0	3.1	5.1	*	*	*	*
1911	14.1	1.8	2.8	4.6	25.3	3.3	5.1	8.4
1921	15.0	2.0	2.8	4.8	27.4	3.6	5.1	8.9
1931	16.8	2.2	3.3	5.5	29.6	3.9	5.9	9.8
1941	18.5	2.7	4.0	6.7	30.7	4.4	6.6	11.0
1951	17.7	3.1	4.7	7.8	37.0	5.1	7.7	12.8
1961	17.4	2.7	4.9	7.7	30.6	4.7	8.7	13.4

SOURCE: Census reports of various years.

NOTE: Newfoundland included 1951 and 1961.

*Breakdowns in 1891 and 1901 census are by five-year age groups only.

period. Male participation in 1961 was hardly more than half of what it had been in 1921. In short, not only the protection of the family but also the opportunity to earn a living (even where the capability existed) came to be less and less available to the aged.

At the same time, the size of the older age groups was increasing both absolutely and in relation to the rest of the population. This is illustrated by table 5. For more than half a century, 65 has been the age which supporters of old age pensions have most often advocated as the appropriate pensionable age. In legislative programs, however, age 70 was for many years preferred. Both ages have been selected in the preparation of the table. The 45–64 age group has also been segregated on the assumption that people in that range have a more immediate concern than their juniors with problems of old age security, both because they have reached the age where they are developing a lively awareness of the need for such security in their own cases and because they constitute a substantial part of the population on which falls responsibility for the maintenance of aged parents. Table 5 shows the population in these three groups as percentages of the total population and of the population aged 21 and over. The latter category was chosen because a universal franchise at age 21 was established in federal elections in Canada in 1922.[17]

From 1871 every decennial census showed both the 65–69 and the 70-and-over age groups increasing as percentages of the total population, except in 1911 and 1961. The decline in 1911 resulted from the substantial immigration of young adult males in the decade preceding World War I. In the main, that of 1961 was a product of the high birthrate during and immediately after World War II and of immigration consisting predominantly of young families and young adults in the postwar years. The older age groups have also increased as a proportion of the population of voting age. By 1931, four years after Canada's first public pension legislation was adopted, the 65-and-over group was just under 10 percent of the 21-and-over group, and with the 45–64 group added, the percentage was close to 40. By 1961, it was approaching 45, notwithstanding a substantial falling off from 1951 in the relative size of the 45–64 group.

Regional variations in the changing patterns of age composition are shown in table 6. In the three traditional maritime provinces the ratio of the 70-and-over group to the total has always been higher than the national average. This was particularly so in the period between 1921 and 1931 when public pensions were first under active consideration. It is probably to be explained by continuous emigration of young adults from that region. By contrast, the ratio in the four western

TABLE 6

POPULATION 70 AND OVER AS PERCENTAGE OF TOTAL POPULATION,
CANADA AND PROVINCES, CENSUS YEARS 1901–1961

	1901	1911	1921	1931	1941	1951	1961
CANADA	3.1	2.8	2.8	3.3	4.0	4.7	4.9
Newfoundland						4.0	3.8
Prince Edward Island	4.3	5.3	6.0	6.5	6.3	6.5	7.0
Nova Scotia	4.2	4.7	4.7	5.1	5.2	5.5	5.7
New Brunswick	3.5	3.8	3.9	4.2	4.4	4.8	5.1
Quebec	2.9	2.8	2.7	2.9	3.1	3.4	3.6
Ontario	3.4	3.5	3.5	4.1	4.9	5.3	5.3
Manitoba	1.3	1.4	1.7	2.6	3.6	4.9	6.0
Saskatchewan	1.5	0.9	1.2	1.9	2.9	4.6	6.2
Alberta	0.9	0.8	1.2	1.9	2.9	4.0	6.4
British Columbia	1.3	1.2	1.8	3.0	4.7	6.3	7.1

SOURCE: 1961 Census of Canada, Bull. 7.1-4, *General Review: Age and Sex Composition*, table 3.

provinces was well below the national average in the early part of the century. These provinces were the main destinations of migrating young adults from both outside and inside the country. As these people grew older, the age composition of all four provinces changed markedly. The high percentage of the 70-and-over group in British Columbia in the last two decades is to be explained at least in part by the attractiveness of the more moderate climate of that province for retired people from the prairies. Quebec's ratio has been below the national average from the beginning of the century, and the discrepancy has widened over the years—a reflection of the high birthrate which prevailed in that province until recently.

Related to, and in part an explanation of, changing age composition has been a steady rise in life expectancy. Not until after the 1931 census were the first comprehensive and reliable calculations on this subject produced for Canada. Table 7 shows the trend since then. It is reasonable to suppose that the trend to higher life expectancy extended back at least to the turn of the century, a supposition supported by the trends shown in the tables for England and Wales which date back to 1838.[18] By 1931 the average life expectancy of both 20-year-old males and females in Canada extended well beyond age 65. It is doubtful if this was true at the turn of the century. Life expectancy of people at or approaching pensionable age steadily increased (more rapidly for females than for males). It is impossible to assess precisely the effect of

TABLE 7
Expectation of Life at Selected Ages, Canada, 1930–32 to 1965–67

| | At 20 Years | | At 45 Years | | At 65 Years | | At 70 Years | |
	Male	Female	Male	Female	Male	Female	Male	Female
1930–32	49.05	49.76	27.79	28.87	12.98	13.72	10.06	10.63
1940–42	49.57	51.76	27.60	29.67	12.81	14.08	9.94	10.93
1950–52	50.76	54.71	28.05	31.14	13.31	14.97	10.41	11.62
1955–57	51.19	55.80	28.28	32.09	13.36	15.60	10.51	12.17
1960–62	51.51	56.65	28.49	32.82	13.53	16.07	10.06	12.58
1965–67	51.50	57.37	28.55	33.51	13.63	16.71	10.83	13.14

Sources: DBS, *Life Expectancy Trends, 1930–32 to 1960–62* (Ottawa: Queen's Printer, 1967); idem, *Life Tables, Canada and Provinces, 1965–1967* (Ottawa: Information Canada, 1971).

Note: Newfoundland included 1950–52 to 1965–67.

these trends in stimulating a demand for public pensions. Most individuals do not anticipate early mortality in their own cases, regardless of what the averages might show. To the extent that people have been aware of the trend to increasing longevity, however, their interest in old age security has probably been heightened.

3. ALTERNATIVES TO PUBLIC PENSIONS

The traditional methods of providing income maintenance for the aged are through municipal relief, private charity, and institutional care. Quantitative data are not available on municipal relief or private charity before the adoption of Canada's first public pension plan. Splane found that in the latter part of the nineteenth century most Ontario municipalities were providing assistance to indigents, though there was no legal obligation on them to do so, and their total expenditures on this account were not inconsiderable.[19] In the western provinces with their less highly developed systems of municipal government, local assistance may not have been as widespread. This, however, was probably less true of the two older provinces, Manitoba and British Columbia, than of Saskatchewan and Alberta. In the poor law provinces, on the other hand, there was considerable local assistance for the poor, as well as private charity. In Quebec, the ideological emphasis was reversed between public relief and private charity, but the well-organized system of private charity existing there was probably as effective in relieving distress as the predominantly municipal systems of the other provinces. It is hard to believe that any of these methods was very effective. Then even more than now the financial resources of municipalities and charitable organizations were quite inadequate to provide income maintenance on anything but an emergency distress basis. The parsimonious approach which financial necessity dictated was reinforced by the prevailing belief that indigency in most cases was the result of moral turpitude. This had particularly severe consequences for the aged poor, since their indigency was irreversible. To accept relief or charity which was permanent of necessity was to proclaim oneself a pauper, the ultimate disgrace in a society where material success was highly esteemed.[20]

The alternative to local or private assistance which was preferred in theory if not always in practice was institutional care. If the aged poor could not fall back on their children, what better place for them than in an institution? Thus, in 1924 the mayor of Sault Ste. Marie enunciated the policy of his municipality as follows: "We have, where possible, compelled the son or daughter [of aged applicants for municipal relief] to render assistance and in other cases sent them to the Home, which in most cases is the most comfortable home they have ever had."[21] Partly as a result of the legislation of 1903 and 1912 referred to in section 1, Ontario developed a comprehensive network of county poor houses, which was supplemented by municipal homes in some cities and by private institutions. Nova Scotia and to a lesser extent New Brunswick also had a substantial number of homes, though they were not as ubiquitous as in Ontario. In the western provinces there were fewer homes, and none at all in Saskatchewan and Alberta. On the other hand, Quebec's encouragement of religious organizations to establish homes resulted in substantial availability of care. The pride with which many Quebec elites viewed these religious institutions is indicated by this statement of Senator C. P. Beaubien in 1926: "The biggest and perhaps the finest building in my province is now dedicated to poor people who cannot take care of themselves, most of whom are incurable. . . . There is an admirable system organized by charity, which an improvident hand, through political interference and nothing else [enactment of public pension legislation], wants to brush aside altogether."[22]

The plain fact, however, is that there have never been anything like enough institutions to accommodate all old people in need. The first comprehensive survey of institutions in Canada was undertaken as part of the 1931 census. Four main classes were distinguished: general hospitals, mental hospitals, charitable and benevolent institutions, and penal and reform institutions. The charitable and benevolent category covered both public and private institutions, as well as other subclassifications. Homes for the aged were not segregated because many institutions catering to old people accepted younger inmates as well. All were bulked together under "homes for adults." Table 8 shows the number of such homes in Canada in 1931 and the number of inmates over age 60. Institutions for specific disabilities with populations over 60 also existed. These are not directly relevant to my analysis because the older inmates were there primarily for reasons other than age. Nevertheless, to complete the picture, table 8 shows the over-60 population of all charitable and benevolent institutions (including homes for adults). By 1931 the Old Age Pensions Act of 1927 was in force in Ontario and the four western provinces. This made no difference in Saskatchewan and Alberta because there were no homes for adults there anyway. In Ontario and in Manitoba and British Columbia in smaller degrees, the operation of the act may have reduced the aged population of homes for adults. Even with allowance for that, the import of the table is clear. There were fewer than 10,000 inmates over 60 in all charitable and benevolent institutions and fewer than 6,500 in institutions which

TABLE 8

HOMES FOR ADULTS AND
ALL CHARITABLE AND BENEVOLENT INSTITUTIONS,
CANADA AND PROVINCES, 1931

	Homes for Adults			All Institutions		
	No. of Homes	No. of Inmates		No. of Insts.[b]	No. of Inmates	
		61–70	Over 70		61–70	Over 70
CANADA	118	1,817	4,505	456	2,492	6,216
Prince Edward Island	1	0	62	5	0	62
Nova Scotia	9	64	158	43	80	211
New Brunswick	8	26	115	30	124	298
Quebec	28	610	1,554	128	976	2,745
Ontario[a]	63	983	2,215	180	1,078	2,356
Manitoba[a]	4	38	189	28	132	314
Saskatchewan[a]	0	0	0	10	0	0
Alberta[a]	0	0	0	9	6	18
British Columbia[a]	5	96	212	23	96	212

SOURCE: 1931 Census of Canada, vol. 9, pt. 3, *Institutions*, tables 6, 9, 10.

[a]Old Age Pensions Act, 1927, in force.

[b]This column includes many institutions for children only, as well as institutions accepting adults and children, and adults only.

accepted them mainly because of their age—in a year when the 70-and-over population alone was 345,000.

Another method of providing income security in old age is through personal investment programs during earning years. Except in the case of annuities, no data are available on the number of Canadians whose long-term savings have been sufficient to provide even minimum comfort in old age. There is little doubt that such savings were negligible, especially before the middle of this century. The development of a diversified institutional structure to mobilize long-term savings of individuals is a recent phenomenon in Canada. Until World War II the field was left almost entirely to life insurance companies, a substantial and growing proportion of whose policies contained some savings features, though such savings were not necessarily for old age. Major growth of mutual funds and investment trusts did not get under way until the 1950s, and even now they are relatively unimportant competitors of the life companies for long-term savings.[23] The paucity of institutional outlets for long-term savings suggests that few Canadians considered it feasible to save significant amounts for their old age or other long-term purposes. Rising personal incomes after World War II have made possible a substantial increase in such saving, but this has been channelled mainly into private pensions plans—a separate category in this analysis. As late as 1961 investments were the major source of income of only 9.3 percent of males and 14.7 percent of females aged 65 and over.[24]

For many years annuities provided the principal means through which modest savings could be converted into old age security, but this device too was slow in developing. Not until 1911 was the annuities business of life insurance companies significant enough to be segregated even in the statements of individual companies published by the Superintendent of Insurance. Totalling the annuity items shown in those statements, one finds that at the end of 1910 fewer than 2,000 contracts for annuities proper were in force in the whole country, two-thirds of them underwritten by one company (Sun Life).[25] The federal government tried to fill the vacuum with its Government Annuities Act of 1908 under which it offered to sell small annuities to the public at rates which at the time were more favourable than those offered by private companies. There was hardly a stampede of applicants. Less than 12,000 contracts for government annuities were in force on March 31, 1931, nearly a quarter of a century after the act came into effect. The annuities business of private companies expanded during the 1920s, and by 1930 the Superintendent of Insurance began to publish tabular summaries of it. Table 9 shows the growth of this business for both the government and the life companies. From a very low level in 1930 it has grown steadily, but even by the 1960s the number of contracts in force was only about 300,000. The number of people covered was smaller by an amount which cannot be determined because some individuals held more than one contract. The figures include vested annuities (contracts which have matured so that benefits are being paid), which formed a substantial part of the total in the 1960s.

Participation in private pension plans provides a third alternative to public pensions. Almost all private pension plans in Canada have arisen out of the contract of employment. Plans sponsored by voluntary associations for their own members, mainly craft unions, have long existed and continue to exist, but their coverage constitutes a small proportion of the total. The first formal pension plan relating to employment was established by the federal government in 1870 for its civil servants. This was the beginning of what eventually became a ubiquitous network of plans—usually called superannuation plans—for employees of governments at all levels and their agencies. In the private sector, the Grand Trunk Railway established a plan for clerks and some other inside

TABLE 9

INDIVIDUAL ANNUITY CONTRACTS IN FORCE, CANADA, SELECTED YEARS, 1930–1965

	Government	Insurance Companies	Total
1930–31[a]	11,781[b]	3,589	15,370
1940–41	55,004	50,740	105,744
1950–51	137,514	96,159	233,673
1960–61	191,019	100,555	291,574
1965–66	174,915	125,438	300,353

SOURCES: Superintendent of Insurance, *Reports* (Ottawa: King's and Queen's Printer, 1931–66); Department of Labour, *Annual Reports* (Ottawa: King's and Queen's Printer, 1931–66).

NOTE: Because of minor variations in the information published over the years, the figures are not in all cases strictly comparable from period to period, but the resultant distortion is inconsequential.

[a]Dec. 31, 1930, in the case of life companies and Mar. 31, 1931, in the case of government annuities. Similarly with subsequent years.

[b]May include a small number of contracts purchased by private pension plans. Before 1940 the Department of Labour annual reports did not segregate contracts purchased in connection with private pensions plans. The number of such contracts in force in 1940 was 1,240, and it is assumed that it was smaller in 1931.

workers in 1874, and by the 1920s most employees of railways, banks, and some other financial institutions had been brought under plans. In private industry generally, however, significant expansion did not come until World War II and after. A fillip was given by the government's wartime wages policy. This severely restricted immediate wage increases but was indulgent to pension plans as a form of deferred wages which would help to offset the anticipated postwar decline of consumer spending without contributing to inflationary pressures. Employers competing for labour in a tight market sometimes turned to pension plans as an inducement. A Dominion Bureau of Statistics survey for 1947 found that more than two-thirds of the plans covered originated after 1939.[26] After the war, organized labour in the automobile industry made pensions one of its main contract demands, and other major unions soon followed suit. This kept the issue to the fore in employment policy, and plans were introduced in increasing numbers in both union and non-union employment units.

Late in 1936 the National Employment Commission attempted the first survey of private pension plans.[27] The survey indicated that 7.7 percent of the reporting firms, employing 34 percent of the employees in such firms, had formal pension plans. No information was obtained as to the proportion of employees actually covered by the plans. Later surveys suggest that if that information had been available, the figure of 34 percent would probably have been cut in half. The survey did not touch a great many people attached to the labour force (including the unemployed), while plans for public servants, members of the armed forces, and bank employees were not included. For these and other reasons, there is no way of estimating what proportion of the labour force was covered by pension plans. A reasonable guess is that it was in the neighbourhood of 10 or 15 percent, but even this figure probably overstates the case. An employee can be covered nominally by a plan and still accumulate no pension benefits if he separates from employment before contributions vest in him. Long vesting periods—twenty years and more—were commonplace thirty-five years ago in private industry.[28]

In 1950 the Dominion Bureau of Statistics published the survey for 1947 already mentioned, and in 1951 the federal Department of Labour began to include questions on pensions periodically in its annual surveys of working conditions in industry.[29] These surveys are open to most though not all of the objections raised against the Employment Commission survey of 1936. The most that can be said of them is that they strongly suggest a substantial increase in the coverage of pension plans in private industry after 1947.[30] The first comprehensive survey was for 1960.[31] It covered all types of plan, including those sponsored by governments and government agencies for their own employees and the armed services. The figures were updated in similarly comprehensive surveys relating to 1965 and 1970.[32] The number of plans in existence increased by over 80 percent between 1960 and 1970—from 8,920 to 16,137. The increase in the number of employees covered was somewhat less dramatic—from 1.8 million to 2.8 million, or by 55 percent. The explanation is that a considerable proportion of the new plans were of the "top hat" variety, as firms took advantage of relaxed interpretations of the Income Tax Act from 1959 on to provide what amounted to tax-free bonuses to executives and other highly paid personnel.[33] Even with allowance for this, a 55 percent increase in coverage in a decade is impressive, and lends support to the suggestion made above that substantial coverage of private pension plans is a recent phenomenon. It may be, however, that coverage is now reaching a plateau, since the rate of increase was substantially greater between 1960 and

1965 than between 1965 and 1970. The introduction of compulsory public contributory pensions in 1965 is probably an important factor in this slower growth.

The coverage of private pension plans is still far from universal, notwithstanding rapid growth in the two decades after World War II. In 1970 covered employees amounted to 39.2 percent of the paid labour force and a slightly smaller percentage of the total force. Many of the covered employees continued to be excluded in effect by vesting provisions. Comparison of the 1960, 1965, and 1970 reports discloses a noticeable trend towards reduction of the vesting period. Even in 1970, however, some plans, representing 2.4 percent of the total employee coverage, made no provision at all for vesting. Those providing immediate and full vesting represented only 6.7 percent of the employees covered. There were a variety of vesting arrangements between these extremes, but by far the most common was based on length of service or participation. For 57.3 percent of the employees covered by this type of arrangement, the vesting period was ten years or less, but it was twenty years or more for 13.9 percent. It is still quite possible for an employee spending his entire working life in employment units with pension plans to end up with little or no pension if he changes his employment three or four times in a forty- or forty-five-year period. The situation is only marginally affected by the Ontario Pension Benefits Act of 1965 and similar legislation enacted later by the federal government and three other provinces. These acts require employer contributions to be vested and employee contributions to be locked in whenever an employee has completed at least ten years of continuous service with an employer or of participation in a plan *and* has reached the age of 45.

4. Economic Hardship in Old Age

Quantitative data on income distribution did not become available until the 1950s. They point up the low levels of income accruing to most of the aged even in a period of growing affluence. In the 1961 census, income data were gathered from a 20 percent sample of the nonfarm population.[34] Before that the data were accumulated from smaller samples in the *Surveys of Consumer Finances*, the earliest of which was published in 1952 and related to 1951. Podoluk reworked the data for the information of the Senate Committee on Aging, and her main findings on income distribution among the nonfarm population of 65 and over are summarized in table 10 and in the discussion that follows.[35] As table 10 shows, the situation was worse for women than for men because of their lower earning capacity, but both sexes were

TABLE 10

PERCENTAGE DISTRIBUTION BY SIZE OF INCOME OF
NONFARM POPULATION 65 AND OVER,
CANADA, 1951 AND 1961

Annual Income	1951			1961		
	Male	Female	Total	Male	Female	Total
Under $1000	52.2	88.0	66.4	37.4	70.7	53.7
$1000–1999	23.9	8.0	17.6	25.0	17.7	21.4
$2000–2999	13.4	2.6	9.1	13.6	5.9	9.8
$3000–3999	5.9	0.3	3.7	9.1	2.5	5.9
$4000–4999	2.3	0.4	1.6	5.1	1.2	3.2
$5000 and over	2.3	0.7	1.7	9.5	2.1	5.8

SOURCE: J. R. Podoluk, "Income Characteristics of the Older Population," in Sen. Special Committee on Aging, *Proceedings* (Ottawa: Queen's Printer, 1964), pp. 1249–73.

heavily concentrated in the lowest income groups. In 1951, 84 percent and, in 1961, 75 percent had incomes of less than $2,000 a year. The median income was $643 in 1951 and $960 in 1961. Inclusion of farm population would probably have worsened the picture. The distribution curve shifted upward between 1951 and 1961, but this represented increased purchasing power only in part. The median income increased by 49 percent, but the consumer price index (1949 = 100) rose from 113.7 to 129.2. Median income in 1949 dollars rose by 33 percent, from $566 to $743. In a significant sense the 1951 figures are more relevant to this phase of my analysis than those for 1961 because they were less influenced by public pension payments. In 1951 a pension of up to $40 per month was payable at age 70 on the basis of a means test. In 1961 the amount was $55 and it was payable universally at 70 and on a means-test basis at 65. That this change accounted to a considerable extent for the improvement in the income position of the 65-and-over age group can hardly be questioned. Government transfers in 1961 were the major source of income of 48 percent of the males and 72 percent of the females in the group.

One can infer from this account the grinding poverty many of the aged must have suffered in the first quarter of the century when there were no public pensions and general income levels were much lower than they are now. This inference is supported by contemporary records. A report of the Toronto medical officer of health filed with a parliamentary committee in 1924 described the situation in his municipality as follows:

> Under existing industrial conditions many men and women, especially married couples who have reared a family, have found it impossible to provide for their old age. . . . the institutions for the aged are filled and have a long waiting list. These private organizations accommodate at any time only a limited number, who are absolutely destitute. It has been our experience that a large number of old people will practically starve in preference to entering an institution. High rents, overcrowding in houses, make it difficult for the poor to provide for their aged parents. It has been the experience of social agencies that many of the old men and women in their districts are suffering from the lack of the necessaries of life.[36]

That this was not a newly emerging situation in 1924 is indicated by testimony before a House of Commons committee appointed in the 1911–12 session and reconstituted in 1912–13.[37] Many witnesses professionally engaged in welfare and related work in provinces, municipalities, and private organizations appeared before the committee. Their testimony was unanimous on all material points.

Wages, they said, were too low and, in a climate where seasonal employment was common, too intermittent to permit working people to save for their old age. In the words of the officer in charge of Children's Aid and Associated Charities in Ottawa: "The wages that prevail generally for the working man . . . are such that unless a man has the propensities of a miser he cannot save anything, and if he has those propensities his family will suffer." By the same token, it was futile to expect adult children to support aged parents if they themselves had families. The result for the aged was "a hopeless, heartless life," in the words of a probationary officer from Montreal. The secretary of a charitable organization operating a home for the aged near Winnipeg said: "There are a large number in the city whom we cannot find and never do find until they are picked up starving. They will not ask for charity." The Salvation Army commissioner for Canada said, on the basis of reports from his officers across the country, that poverty among the aged was widespread not only in cities but in towns and villages as well. Private organizations could not cope with it. Of almost equal importance in the minds of the witnesses was the effect on those who were approaching the end of their working lives. The superintendent of Children's Aid Societies for Ontario reported: "There are thousands of worthy citizens who go through life, leading useful and respectable lives, who never get beyond the actual needs of the day, and they live under the constant shadow of having to spend their declining years in penury and abject dependence on others."

Officials responsible for provincial supervision of institutions stated that institutional care was not appropriate for mentally and physically competent old people. Married couples were sometimes separated, the mentally sound often had to live in close association with senile patients, and institutional life in general was so totally different from the previous living patterns of the aged that many of them could not adapt to it. The chief inspector of industrial establishments and public buildings in Quebec said: "As a Catholic I have visited nearly all the homes controlled by the nuns and religious orders of the province, and I have found so many objectionable features in connection with the keeping of poor people in these homes that I would be most happy to see anything in the shape of a pension fund established." The aged themselves frequently resisted going to institutions. As the officer in charge of Children's Aid and Associated Charities of Ottawa put it: "We have unfortunately a number of old people, quite a considerable number, who refuse to go into any home owing to their pride, and yet are living in a more miserable condition than if they were in a home."

To sum up, the aged have formed an increasing proportion of the total population. At the same time, urbanization and industrialization have reduced both the capacity of the family unit to provide for them and their own capacity to do so. On the other hand, private pension plans and personal investments have not offered much security until recently, and even now they cover only a minority of the population. Meanwhile, the voting power of the older age groups has increased. To all this should be added the further phenomenon of the increasing capacity of the community to provide for its economically unproductive members. In 1929 the per capita gross national product in 1961 constant dollars reached $1,220 per year. It dropped to $805 in 1933, but thereafter it increased almost continuously to $3,287 in 1972.[38] This combination of circumstances provided the basis for a continuing challenge to the market ethos.

Chapter Three

Early Pressures for Public Pensions and the Government Annuities Plan

PUBLIC CONTRIBUTORY PENSIONS for specific occupational groups date back to 1791 when France established invalidity pensions for seamen. Not until 1889, however, was the first plan with broad coverage adopted. In that year Germany instituted a contributory plan for all wage earners and lower paid salaried employees. It applied to both old age and disability and was financed by tripartite contributions. Denmark established a means-test plan for the aged in 1891, and New Zealand adopted this type of plan in 1898. The Australian states of New South Wales and Victoria followed New Zealand's example in 1901, and in 1908 the Commonwealth government superseded these state plans with a nationwide plan, which also provided benefits for the blind and other permanently disabled. In 1911 Newfoundland adopted a means-test plan for the aged only. France established such a plan for both old age and disability in 1905, and in 1910 it superimposed on this a contributory plan providing old age, disability, and survivor benefits. Other countries to establish plans with comprehensive occupational coverage before World War I were Austria (1907), Luxembourg (1911), Romania (1912), and Sweden (1913). All four of these plans were contributory, all applied to both old age and disability, and two provided survivor benefits.[1]

Meanwhile, a prolonged campaign for old age pensions had been under way in the United Kingdom since the 1870s, and following implementation of the German plan in 1889, pensions became a prominent political issue. Two of the leading protagonists were Joseph Chamberlain, who favoured contributory pensions, and Charles Booth, who advocated a universal plan. After the New Zealand plan was adopted in 1898, a large-scale campaign was launched under the organizing genius of Francis Herbert Stead, warden of Browning Hall settlement house, who enlisted Booth's patronage to give prestige to the movement, mobilized interested organizations and individuals, mediated disputes, and revived interest whenever it flagged. In the election of 1906, twenty-nine Labour M.P.'s and twenty-four labour men sitting officially as Liberals were returned. This result brought the issue forcefully to the attention of the new Liberal government. On March 14, 1906, a Labour member's resolution affirming the principle of non-contributory pensions was debated in a crowded House of Commons and approved with only one dissenting voice. In November a concession was wrung from the government that it would proceed with legislation, and in May, 1907, a Liberal backbencher introduced a bill on the subject. Though the launching pad had been New Zealand's adoption of a means-test plan, the demand was for universal pensions as proposed by Booth. The estimated cost appalled the government and it tried to back away, but a renewed campaign, reinforced by government defeats in two key by-elections in July, 1907, induced it to accept the New Zealand principle as a compromise. The necessary legislation was passed in 1908.[2]

1. AWAKENING INTEREST IN CANADA

These developments did not go unnoticed in Canada. To Anglophone Canadians, who drew much of their inspiration from the United Kingdom, events in that country were of particular interest. By 1906 both trade unions and private members of parliament were raising the question of old age pensions for Canada.

As far as can be determined, the first attempt to bring the matter formally before the House of Commons was made in 1906 when E. Guss Porter, the Conservative member for West Hastings (Ontario), gave notice of a resolution on the subject.[3] His resolution was not called for debate, but in the next session R. A. Pringle, a Conservative representing Stormont (Ontario), was more successful. He moved that the government give "early and careful attention" to "the subject of improving the condition of the aged, deserving poor, and providing for those of them who are helpless and infirm."[4] This motion was debated briefly and drew strong support from a few members, notably Alphonse Verville, president of the Trades and Labor Congress of Canada (TLC) who had been elected to Parliament as a Labour member in a by-election in the Montreal constituency of Maisonneuve. Prime Minister Laurier argued that extensive inquiry was needed before the government could commit itself to a specific program and, on his suggestion, Pringle withdrew the motion.[5] Pringle was back again the next year, however, with a resolution proposing an inquiry by a select committee of the House into "a scheme or schemes of state aid or otherwise for making provision for the aged and deserving poor."[6] In the debate on this resolution, a clear-cut demand for a universal plan was made for the first time in Canada by Ralph Smith of Nanaimo, B.C., a former TLC president and professional labour representative who had entered Parliament in 1900 as "a Liberal but elected to protect the interests of organized labour."[7] By now the government had decided in favour of a voluntary annuities plan, but it went through the motions of accepting Pringle's resolution. A committee was set up under the chairmanship of Rodolphe Lemieux, postmaster general and minister of labour. After three perfunctory meetings, the committee ceased to function.[8]

Pringle lost his seat in the general election held later in 1908, and it was not until after the election of 1911, won by the Conservatives, that the pension issue was again put before the House by formal motion. In the first session of the new Parliament, two notices of motion on the subject were placed on the order paper, one by J. H. Burnham, the Conservative member for Peterborough, and the other by E. M. Macdonald, a Liberal representing the Nova Scotia constituency of Pictou. The government called for debate the resolution of its own supporter, Burnham, which proposed a special committee to inquire into an old age pension system for Canada.[9] The government accepted the proposal and a committee was constituted with Burnham as chairman. After extensive hearings, it reported that it had accumulated considerable information and recommended that still further information be sought.[10] On Burnham's motion, the committee was reappointed in the 1912–13 session, and after further extensive inquiries it indicated that it could complete its work if reconstituted in the following session.[11] Before action could be taken at that session, however, the government persuaded Burnham to drop the matter. "I am advised," he said, "that this Government has all it can do in the way of financing without being burdened at the present time by any scheme no matter how desirable it may be. Therefore this is not the time I think to press home all our arguments and all our evidence with a view to the consummation of our scheme."[12]

It was left to G. W. Kyte, a Liberal from the Cape Breton constituency of Richmond, to move that an old age pension system should be inaugurated.[13] He and two of the members of the previous committees (E. M. Macdonald and W. F. Carroll, a Liberal representing Cape Breton South) argued energetically that the information accumulated by the committee had clearly established the need for public pensions.[14] Their pleas were to no avail. The government had evidently decided to call a halt to the inquiry before it was faced with an embarrassing recommendation. Finance Minister W. T. White stated its position: there was no public demand for pensions, social and economic conditions in Canada were readily distinguishable from those in countries where pension plans were in effect, and if the government was to discharge its developmental responsibilities adequately, it could not spare money for a scheme which was really in the area of provincial and local responsibility.[15] On his motion the debate was adjourned, never to be resumed. World War I broke out shortly afterwards, and there were scant references to old age pensions in the parliamentary debates during the war years.

The Trades and Labor Congress of Canada made its first formal pronouncement on public pensions in 1905 when its annual convention adopted a recommendation that "in our opinion the time is opportune to introduce legislation making provision for the maintenance of the deserving poor, old or disabled citizens, who are unable to maintain themselves."[16] The National Trades and Labour Congress (NTLC), a labour central formed by branches of the Knights of Labor and some small "national" unions which had been expelled from the TLC in 1902 for "dual unionism," also took up the cry. The NTLC convention of 1907 went on record as favouring old age and disability pensions for workers "who are no longer able to support themselves," and in April, 1908, its annual deputation to the Cabinet urged the case for pensions.[17] Since, however, the NTLC's views and activities on the issue were not significantly different from those of the much larger TLC, I will confine my attention to the latter.

The TLC convention of 1907 noted Pringle's resolution with satisfaction and instructed the executive to increase its efforts to secure enactment of pension legislation.[18] Affiliated unions were already memorializing members of parliament,[19] and the congress itself began to include a demand for pensions regularly in submissions to the Cabinet.[20] In relation to Pringle's motion of 1908, the executive reported to the convention that it was preparing a comprehensive brief in support of public pensions.[21] The failure of the parliamentary committee to come to grips with the problem precluded any opportunity for representations, and in subsequent executive reports to conventions one can detect growing exasperation at failure to make headway. The 1911 convention was told that "while a sickening silence in parliament follows every request for old age pensions," subsidies for railways, iron and steel, and other industrial interests were readily granted.[22] Hope revived with the appointment of parliamentary committees in the 1911–12 and 1912–13 sessions, and the executive busied itself with preparing submissions and sending material to its constituent bodies so that there

48

would be a common trade union policy across the country.[23] In 1913 the TLC reported that the information accumulated by and representations before the parliamentary committees were "overwhelmingly in favour of pensions on a non-contributory basis," but in 1914 it noted sadly that the government was apathetic to legislation of interest to labour, including pensions.[24] The standard objection encountered by congress delegations to both the Laurier and Borden governments was that there was not the same need for public pensions in Canada as in industrially mature countries. The objection was contemptuously dismissed. It was asserted at convention after convention that aged indigents were regularly picked up by the police for vagrancy: "Canada still permits her aged and deserving citizens to retire to the jail. It's a handsome advertisement. No country that continues such conditions and professes Christian charity can have a speck of it in its heart."[25]

The Trades and Labor Congress usually expressed its position in broad principles, and it is not entirely clear what kind of program it had in mind or even if it had given much consideration to specifics. It seemed to assume that pensions would be paid only to those who had little or no resources of their own, but there is no indication that it had a solution to the problem of distinguishing the needy. On one point, however, it made itself abundantly clear: it did not want a contributory plan. In 1907 the TLC suggested that a fund for the payment of pensions could be established by the sale of public lands,[26] but in general it took the position that the problem of finance was of secondary importance. If money could be found for "bounties, subsidies and payment of senators, whose appointment really makes them pensioners of the state," then it could also be found for the aged poor.[27] In particular, the voluntary contributory principle embodied in the Government Annuities Act of 1908, though unobjectionable in itself, was not accepted as a substitute for public pensions.[28]

This, however, is precisely how the government of the day regarded the annuities plan. In the view of Senator Sir Richard Cartwright, minister of trade and commerce in the Laurier administration and chief architect of the plan, public pensions were a necessary evil in "old and densely populated lands where a large proportion of the population are leading a life from hand to mouth," but in Canada any industrious, able-bodied man could provide for his old age if given an opportunity to do so. It behooved the government to exercise foresight, he said. Steps taken immediately to establish convenient facilities for workers to invest their savings for their old age would be a guarantee that the government would not be forced into "socialistic experiments" later.[29] The annuities plan failed to eliminate the demand for public pensions, but even after the need for a full-fledged public plan was recognized and acted upon, annuities continued in a kind of twilight existence with successive governments unwilling either to give them a meaningful role in the developing pension program or to dispense with them. Section 3 outlines the history of the annuities plan.

2. THE NOVA SCOTIA ACT OF 1908

An independent line of development in Nova Scotia culminated in the enactment of a statute (stillborn as it turned out) to provide public pensions for coal miners. Few occupational groups have as great a need for pensions as miners. Not only are working conditions too onerous for aged or disabled men, but mining is usually carried on in isolated communities where alternative opportunities are meagre. The very harshness and isolation of life in mining communities create in their inhabitants a sense of solidarity which leads readily to joint action. In 1879 a strike against a wage cut at Springhill, N.S., gave birth to an indigenous trade union, the Provincial Workmen's Association (PWA), which spread to every colliery in the province. Attempts to organize other industrial groups ended in failure, and the PWA was first and last an organization of coal miners. Its leadership was cautious to the point where critics branded it a company union. Strikes were regarded as a desperate last resort. The preferred method was to secure legislation to remedy abuses. No government could completely disregard the votes of coal miners, and the PWA's achievements in the legislative field were significant. Its influence was beneficial to another mutual aid movement which it encouraged. A miners' relief society was organized in Springhill in 1880 to provide sickness, accident, and death benefits, and the society persuaded the employer to contribute equally with the employees to the fund. The idea spread, and in 1889 the PWA was instrumental in securing legislation that gave the societies a statutory basis and provided for government contributions to their funds. They did not have enough resources, however, to deal with the long-term conditions of permanent disability and old age.

The PWA, in common with the main body of trade unionism in Canada, was aware of the trend in other countries to government action on pensions, and it set as one of its objectives the securing of pensions for coal miners by legislation. In 1907 the provincial government was persuaded to appoint a commission to inquire into the organization and administration of the relief societies and the feasibility of a pension plan.[30] Two of the four members were the PWA's grand master and past grand secretary. The commission concluded that pensions were a logical extension of the work of the relief societies. Its report, tabled in the Legislature on February 24, 1908, made two main recommendations: consolidation of the societies in a single, provincewide organization and establishment of a separately administered pension fund based on contributions by employers, employees, and the government. The commission estimated that, after an interval of ten years, contributions on the scale it proposed would make possible disability pensions of $5.00 a week and old age pensions of $4.00 a week at age sixty-five.[31]

Government legislation was brought in almost immediately and was passed on May 12, 1908. The act incorporated the commission's recommendations regarding relief societies, but in the case of pensions it merely provided for the creation of a board with authority to work out the details of a plan. The *Halifax Morning Chronicle* on March 26 hailed this as a great step forward: "The government has shown foresight and courage in dealing so rationally with what is probably the greatest and most perplexing sociological problem of the day." A counteroffensive was, however, under way. Notwithstanding the fact that the commission had held extensive public hearings throughout the mining areas of the province, Premier G. H. Murray advised the Legislature that the mine operators had had no opportunity to present their point of view. Therefore, the act would not come into force until it was proclaimed.[32] It was not in fact proclaimed, and it was dropped from the provincial statutes in the consolidation of 1923. There does not appear to have been any serious follow-up campaign to have the legislation implemented. A possible explanation is that the PWA was by then engaged in a life and death struggle, which absorbed most of its energy and resources, with the more militant United Mine Workers of America.

3. Government Annuities, 1908

In 1907 Sir Richard Cartwright tabled a draft annuities bill in the Senate for discussion. The next year an official government bill was brought in which altered some of the details of Cartwright's draft but not its basic principles. This bill was enacted as the Government Annuities Act, 1908, which came into effect on September 1 of that year. The most comprehensive discussion of the principles involved occurred in the Senate in 1907.[33] Cartwright himself and Senator Donald Ferguson, a Conservative from Prince Edward Island, contributed most to the discussion.

Cartwright conceded that few Canadians had taken advantage of the opportunity already open to them to buy annuities from private insurance companies, but he had a simple explanation. People of limited means were not willing to entrust their savings to private companies. They trusted the government implicitly, however, and the government could offer terms which were impossible for profit-making companies. Thus, the act provided not only that there would be no profit on government annuities but also that administrative costs would be defrayed out of the public treasury. Moreover, purchasers were given wide latitude in making contributions as and when their circumstances permitted. Since it was considered necessary to prevent the well-to-do from taking undue advantage of this largesse and to prevent the poor from dissipating their investment before they reached old age, a number of restrictions were imposed, of which two were particularly important. First, a limit of $600 (increased to $1,000 in 1913) was placed on the total amount of annuity or annuities which could be issued to any individual. Second, it was provided that, except in the case of death before maturity of a contract, contributions could be taken out only in the form of annuities which normally were not payable until age fifty-five. The plan was not funded, but the act required a separate account to be kept of annuity transactions in the consolidated revenue fund. The interest rate imputed to annuity contributions was set by regulation at 4 percent compounded annually,[34] which at the time was slightly in excess of the government's estimated long-term borrowing rate. In the event of death before maturity of a contract, however, the rate payable on refunded contributions was fixed by the statute itself at 3 percent, a practice continued until 1920.

Ferguson did not question the conventional wisdom regarding the demoralizing effect of noncontributory pensions. He argued that working people would not voluntarily buy annuities for the simple reason that they could not afford them no matter how favourable the terms. Contributions should be compulsory, he said, but there should be subsidization to lighten the burden. He favoured the tripartite principle of the German model. Millionaires and even multimillionaires were being made in Canada, but the position of the working man had improved little in twenty years. It was therefore legitimate to tax the rich to cover the state's share of the cost of a subsidized pension plan for the poor. He did not oppose the government's plan, but he predicted that little or no advantage would be taken of it by the people for whom it was mainly designed.

The sequel proved him to be right. A 1915 analysis of a random sample of annuity contracts revealed that purchasers were mainly people in the lower paid professions (notably teachers and clergy), clerks, skilled tradesmen, farmers, and small businessmen.[35] Labourers accounted for only 4 percent of sales. Occupational breakdowns, published in the annual reports of the Department of Labour during the 1920s, revealed much the same pattern. Moreover, as indicated in chapter 2, section 3, the volume of sales was negligible. It does not follow that the plan was of no value. The people of modest means who took advantage of it, few in number though they were, had a genuine need for old age security, and the act gave them a useful outlet for their small savings.

Administration was entrusted initially to Cartwright, who tried to promote sales by providing "lecturers" for small meetings. The number of contracts issued exceeded 1,000 in both the 1910–11 and 1911–12 fiscal years.[36] The Borden government, which did not share Cartwright's enthusiasm for the plan, transferred administration to the Post Office and dispensed with promotion. This, coupled with rising general interest rates, resulted in a much lower level of sales for the rest of the decade. An imputed interest rate of 4 percent may have made government annuities unattractive to prospective purchasers but not to the finance minister of 1920. In order to corral more of this cheap money, he had the act amended to increase the ceiling to $5,000.[37] He did not indicate how he arrived at the conclusion that the public would buy large annuities under conditions which were not inducing it to buy small ones in significant volume. At any rate, the increased ceiling had no appreciable effect on sales. A more important departure occurred in 1922 when the King government transferred administration to the Department of Labour. That department resumed modest promotional efforts and gradually built up a small staff of commission agents stationed at strategic points across the country. Sales were facilitated by the fact that rates were not being adjusted to the increasing longevity of the population because the 1893 Annuitants Table of Great Britain was still being used even though it was by then well out of date. It was estimated that continued use of this table had the same effect as an interest rate of 5 percent rather than 4.[38] In the 1927–28 fiscal year new contracts issued passed the 1,000 mark for the first time since 1911–12, and in 1930–31 they reached 1,772.

This development attracted the attention of the insurance industry. Life companies and their agents were by this time developing a profitable sideline in annuities, and they viewed government competition with disfavour. They felt that their own representations were suspect,[39] but they were not lacking in friends to state their case for them. The most enthusiastic were the *Financial Post*, the Canadian Chamber of Commerce, and some senators. The campaign was reinforced behind the scenes by top officers of the Department of Insurance. There is no evidence, nor is there any reason to believe, that there was collusion between the department and the industry it regulated. Officers of the department, however, had the same background and training as industry officers and they thought the same way.[40]

In its issue of January 8, 1931, the *Financial Post* published lengthy extracts from a letter received from a "leading" but unnamed Canadian actuary. A series of articles attacking the act followed.[41] These were hailed with enthusiasm by a host of insurance executives, who in turn provided additional ammunition. The essence of the criticism was that the Labour Department's Annuities Branch had departed far from the act's original purpose of providing the poor with a convenient and inexpensive method of saving for their old age. A "costly" sales organization had been built up which was making large commissions by selling annuities to people who could well afford to buy them from insurance companies. These costs were being charged to the taxpayer. Even worse, the outdated mortality basis was creating an undetermined but awesome liability for taxpayers of the future. The public was being forced to subsidize people who stood in no need of subsidization, and in the process the bread was being taken out of the mouths of insurance companies and their agents. The Bennett government responded with legislation to reduce the ceiling from $5,000 to $1,200. The *Financial Post* on May 7, 1931, hailed this as a victory. Apparently it had been misled by its own propaganda. The issue of annuity contracts to a value in excess of $1,200 had never been significant—Senator G. D. Robertson, minister of labour, said in 1931 that less than 5 percent of the contracts issued in the preceding decade had been for amounts in excess of $1,200, and Peter Heenan, Robertson's immediate predecessor, noted that only 47 of the 1,772 contracts issued in the 1930–31 fiscal year had been for such amounts.[42] The reduction in the ceiling did not at the time reduce the branch's modest business.

Indeed, the sharp decline in general interest rates occasioned by the economic depression was soon to have the opposite effect. Life insurance companies had no alternative but to increase their premiums for annuities. By the mid-1930s it was variously estimated that the Annuities Branch was undercutting their rates by anywhere from 15 to 25 percent. The number of new contracts issued by the branch rose to 2,412 in 1933–34, 3,930 in 1934–35, and 6,357 in 1935–36. A new campaign was called for and this time the Senate became the forum. On the motion of Senator F. B. Black, whose business connections included directorships in both an insurance company and a trust company, a committee was set up in 1936 to inquire into the operation of the plan.[43] Senator Black, who was chairman, surrounded himself with a comfortable majority of committee members with financial or Chamber of

Commerce connections.[44] The star witnesses were A. D. Watson, chief actuary of the Department of Insurance, and Professor M. A. Mac-Kenzie, an actuary from the University of Toronto who was also president of the Teachers' Insurance and Annuity Association of America. E. G. Blackadar, superintendent of annuities, also appeared but no attention was paid to what he said.[45] The report painted a picture of impending disaster which would be avoided only if the plan were put on a "sound" financial basis immediately. The committee recommended, among other things, that the mortality basis should be updated, the imputed interest rate should not exceed 3½ percent, and administrative costs should be charged against the plan. One member of the committee—Senator James Murdock, a onetime railroad worker who had been minister of labour in the King Cabinet of 1921–25—protested that the report had been rushed in without his even knowing it had been prepared and that it told only one side of the story.[46] His protest was to no avail. The Liberal government's leader in the Senate, Raoul Dandurand, himself president or director of several financial institutions including Sun Life, welcomed the report and said he would bring it to the attention of the government immediately.[47]

The government's first response was to increase rates for annuities by 15 percent across the board as an interim measure. Labour Minister Norman McLeod Rogers did not panic, however. He commissioned MacKenzie to make a further study of the mortality basis, and as a result of MacKenzie's report, the old table was abandoned in 1938 in favour of the "a(f) and a(m) tables" with a reduction in age of one year.[48] The imputed interest rate remained unchanged at 4 percent, and administrative costs continued to be charged to general revenues. In 1940 the regulations were changed to give the branch greater freedom of action in underwriting group contracts, a type of business which was then on the verge of rapid expansion.[49] The 4 percent interest rate continued to be favourable, and in addition the mortality basis adopted in 1938 was gradually becoming outdated. Sales increased to both individuals and groups. In the 1946–47 fiscal year, a total of 43,585 individual contracts and certificates under group contracts were issued.

The plan was again under mounting attack from outside and inside the government. On the outside, the Chamber of Commerce led off with a brief to the government in 1940. On the inside, the Department of Insurance continued to question the actuarial soundness of the plan, and the Department of Finance began to complain that it could raise money on the market at a lower rate than 4 percent.[50] In 1946 an actuary was added to the branch's staff to carry on a continuing analysis of the actuarial basis of the plan. Slavish acceptance by the government of his recommendations, without compensating adjustments in other directions, proved to be the beginning of the end. Orders in council of April, 1948, cut the imputed interest rate to 3 percent and rated the a(f) and a(m) tables down three years.[51] The decline in sales was dramatic: the combined total of new individual contracts and group certificates fell to 36,332 in 1948–49 (from 43,585 in 1946–47) and to 17,038 in 1951–52. The branch nevertheless believed that the plan would be viable if some of the restrictions were removed. On June 11, 1948, a bill was introduced to give greater flexibility in converting and altering contracts and to increase the ceiling from $1,200 to $1,500. Though it was a government measure, it was not proceeded with. Labour Minister Humphrey Mitchell announced that he proposed to have a special committee of the House inquire into the entire operation of the plan at the next session.[52] No such inquiry took place.

The Annuities Branch was presented with a new opportunity after the introduction of the Old Age Security Act of 1951 which provided for universal pensions at age seventy. Health and Welfare Minister Paul Martin announced that a new type of contract would be authorized under which the universal pension could be dovetailed into government annuities for those who retired before seventy.[53] A bill was introduced to permit this change and several others, of which the most important were an increase in the ceiling to $2,400 and cash surrender privileges under conditions to be determined by regulation. The bill was referred to a standing committee of the House of Commons, and the insurance industry, supported by the Chamber of Commerce, turned out in force to oppose it.[54] The committee first decided by a narrow margin to recommend limitation of cash surrender to $500 but later changed its mind and reported the bill without amendment.[55] The industry turned its attention to lobbying ministers and members, and the bill died on the order paper. Martin's pledge was subsequently honoured by order in council.

The plan was now on the road to extinction. Following the orders in council of April, 1948, it was subjected to the strict requirements of actuarial orthodoxy while continuing to be circumscribed by restrictions imposed in an earlier period.[56] The $1,200 ceiling of 1931 bore no relation to postwar earnings. It created complexities in the administration of private pension plans which the administrators of such plans were willing to tolerate only as long as rates were considerably more favourable than those offered by private companies. The lack of a cash surrender option and other inflexibilities created similar problems. Adjustments in the imputed interest rate were made from time to time, but always about a year after they were recommended, with the result

56

that they lagged behind the rates insurance companies could obtain on the market. Charging administrative costs to general revenues was simply not enough to overcome this combination of disadvantages. Sales declined and, in many group plans, premium payments under government annuity contracts already in effect were suspended and the money diverted elsewhere.

In 1962 the Glassco Commission, accepting uncritically the mythology which the insurance industry and its allies had been promoting for a generation, recommended that the sale of government annuities be discontinued.[57] The Porter Commission echoed the recommendation, though for different reasons. It argued that the Old Age Security Act and the growth of private pension plans had removed the need for government annuities.[58] The stage was set for what amounted to the destruction of the plan. On November 3, 1967, Labour Minister J. R. Nicholson announced a drastic reduction of field services in the Annuities Branch and cessation on November 30 of promotional activities.[59] Existing contracts are still being serviced, but new contracts are now issued only to those who seek out the branch, and it has little of benefit to offer them.

The main line of attack on the annuities plan over the years was expressed in terms of the broad public interest. The plan was actuarially unsound, its critics said in effect, and in time the public would have to pay. Much was made of lack of funding. This argument was sheer mystification. Funding is a device designed to ensure that as benefits become payable, there will be money on hand to pay them. Some such guarantee is necessary in a private plan, but it is superfluous in a plan backed by the source of all legal guarantees, the state. In the latter case, pay-as-you-go financing is not only legitimate but has the advantage of permitting a lower level of contributions than would otherwise be necessary. The only essential is that there should always be a substantial surplus of revenue from contributions over expenditure on benefits. The appropriate amount of the surplus is a matter of judgement, but, from the inception of the plan up to and including the 1965–66 fiscal year, there was invariably a surplus and usually a large one. It was undoubtedly necessary to adjust rates from time to time to take account of increasing longevity, but as long as this was done—and it was done with excessive zeal, if anything, from 1948 on—there was no burden, actual or potential, on the public treasury. The interest credited annually to the annuities account was purely a bookkeeping entry. So also were the "transfers" which were solemnly made "to maintain the reserve."[60] There was in fact no subsidization of administrative costs. Technically, these costs were charged elsewhere in the public accounts, but they were covered many times over by the annual surpluses of contributions. Indeed, those surpluses regularly provided the government with funds for other purposes on which it paid no interest whatever.

That situation could have been expected to continue for as long as revenue from the sale of annuities expanded more rapidly than expenditures on matured contracts. The large and growing interest in private pension plans after World War II, as well as population growth and the declining value of money, created a favourable climate for expansion, but restrictive government policies prevented it. Ironically, these restrictions, by limiting the sale of new contracts, have had the precise result which it was alleged they would avoid. In the 1966–67 fiscal year, benefit payments exceeded revenues from contributions for the first time. The plan has now become a deadweight burden on the public treasury and will continue to be so until it is finally wound up.[61]

Government spokesmen have repeatedly taken the position that Canada's successive public pension plans were designed only to provide a basic minimum of security in old age. Those with the means and inclination to do so were expected and urged to provide additional security for themselves either by individual action or through private pension plans. This was stated repeatedly even in relation to the Canada Pension Plan, which in itself is a form of supplementation of the basic old age security pension. With expansionist rather than restrictive policies, the Government Annuities Act could have become a companion piece to the public pension programs, providing both groups and individuals with the opportunity for supplementary protection at more favourable rates than private companies could offer. The government would thereby have made a major contribution to realizing an objective which it itself said was important, and in the process it would have been provided with a growing volume of interest-free money. Private carriers, however, would have found their opportunities in this field severely restricted, if not entirely eliminated. In the end their interest prevailed.

There were two main reasons for this. First, the insurance industry and its allies represented themselves as the defenders of private enterprise against "unfair" government competition, and this accorded well with the market ethos. Second, they constituted a small, well-organized group with a clear-cut, specific objective arrayed against diffuse interests. A strong minister of labour managed to resist them in the late 1930s, but weak ministers were unable or unwilling to do so in 1948 and 1951. Groups which would have benefited from an expansion of the plan lacked singleness of purpose. The trade union movement, for example, favoured expansion, but it was preoccupied with many other problems which ranked higher in its scale of priorities. It made no effort to organize a counterlobby.[62] Private members of parliament tended to be sympathetic to the plan, but they lacked the means to influence policy. Emasculation was accomplished by order in council, while bills designed to remove restrictions were quietly dropped. Such devices are largely beyond the reach of private members in the cabinet system. At the same time, the existence of widespread though diffuse support made outright abolition of the plan inexpedient. An overt move to end it might well have crystallized diffuse support into an organized campaign. Opponents occasionally called for abolition, but it suited their purposes equally well and was less dangerous merely to render the plan ineffective. It was only after most prospective purchasers had been induced to go elsewhere that the plan could be quietly left to die.

Chapter Four

Means-Test Pensions, 1927

IN 1915 AN OBSERVER STATED that public pensions were for all practical purposes dead as a political issue in Canada: "The agitation for old age pensions has persisted in spite of the establishment of the government annuity system; but it is an agitation kept up by a few enthusiasts, aided by partisans, and has no grip on the public mind."[1] This was not an unreasonable inference at the time. However, forces were already gathering that led to the establishment of Canada's first public plan twelve years later. Section 1 describes the design of that plan, and subsequent sections, the circumstances which brought the pension issue to the point of government commitment and led to the choice of one specific design in preference to others.

1. THE 1927 PLAN

The Old Age Pensions Act, 1927, authorized the federal government to enter into an agreement with any province to reimburse that province for half the cost of pensions paid under provincial legislation which met the requirements of the federal act and regulations. Administration was entirely a provincial responsibility, but an administrative scheme and any changes in it had to have federal approval in advance. The provinces were protected against being left high and dry after having once committed themselves to the plan by a provision requiring the federal government to give ten years' notice of termination of an agreement. A province for its part could terminate at any time simply by repealing its legislation.

The basic requirements the provinces had to meet were not subject to discretion on their part. Pensions were payable to those who (a) were seventy years of age or over, (b) were British subjects or widows of aliens who had been British subjects before marriage, (c) had resided in Canada for twenty years and in the province concerned for five years immediately preceding commencement of benefits, and (d) had not transferred property to qualify for pension. Indians as defined by the Indian Act were excluded. Actual payment of the pension was the responsibility of the province in which the pensioner resided at the time of qualification. That province, however, was entitled to reimbursement on a pro rata basis from any other province or provinces in which the pensioner had resided in the twenty qualifying years. The pension was reduced proportionately in respect of residence in a province or provinces which had not implemented the plan. It ceased if the pensioner left Canada, but was revived if he returned.

The amount of the pension was set at $240 a year subject to a means test, and a regulation provided for payment in regular monthly instalments. The pensioner was permitted a total annual income of $365 including the pension, a figure resulting from an empirically unverified assumption prevalent in government circles at the time that an old person required a minimum of $1.00 a day to live. The pension was reduced by any amount by which outside income exceeded $125 a year, and a person with an income of $365 a year or more was ineligible. Assets were not a disqualification in themselves, but income value was attributed to them in a manner prescribed by the regulations. Provincial pension authorities were empowered to recover from the estates of deceased pensioners the total amounts of the pensions paid to them, together with interest at 5 percent compounded annually. Recoveries were not made, however, from any part of an estate which went to another pensioner or to a person who had contributed to the pensioner's support during the three years preceding his death in an amount considered reasonable by the provincial pension authority. The pensioner's interest in the house he lived in was excluded from the calculation of the income value of his assets if he assigned that interest to the pension authority. If the pensioner died or moved, the authority could sell the assigned interest and retain the total amount by which the income value of the house would have reduced pension payments, plus 5 percent compound interest.

Administrative matters such as the method of making applications, determination of age, nationality, and residence, definition of income, recoveries for nondisclosure or misrepresentation, the mode of payment, and the settlement of intergovernmental accounts were dealt with in the regulations, the first of which were approved on June 25, 1927. Among other things, the regulations authorized the appointment of an interprovincial board to advise on the interpretation and amendment of the regulations, and the board was first constituted on October 3, 1928.[2] The early regulations were amended frequently until 1932 when a consolidation was approved incorporating previous changes.[3] To an important extent this consolidation reflected the recommendations of the Interprovincial Board. On the vital question of what constituted income, it provided for inclusion of these items: (a) annuities at their full amount; (b) 5 percent of the assessed or market value of real property, whichever was deemed to be more equitable, less encumbrances; (c) the amount of a government annuity which could be purchased by personal property, not including a reasonable allowance for clothing and furniture; (d) net profits, gains, or gratuities from any source; (e) salaries, wages, and other means of livelihood in cash or kind which pensioners "may reasonably be expected to receive." The regulations also provided that a married pensioner would be deemed to be in receipt of half the joint income of the couple. In effect, the maximum allowable income in such a case was $730 a year (twice $365), including either one or two pensions depending on whether one or both of the spouses qualified.

2. WORLD WAR I AND ITS AFTERMATH

Almost from the beginning of the war, trade unions, labour and socialist parties, and other organizations on both sides of the western front raised a persistent demand that peace should usher in a new era of social reform. Late in 1914 the American Federation of Labor called for a world labour congress to be held at the same time and place as the peace conference, an initiative supported strongly by the Confédération générale du Travail of France. As a result in substantial measure of the diplomatic efforts of the United Kingdom Home Office and Ministry of Labour and of George N. Barnes, Labour member of the War Cabinet, social reform became a subject of discussion, not at a separate labour conference, but at the peace conference itself. The Labour Convention, which became part XIII of the Treaty of Versailles, declared in its preamble that "conditions of labour exist involving such injustice, hardship and privation to large numbers of people that the peace of the world is imperilled; and an improvement of those conditions is urgently required." The convention listed a number of examples of the kind of ameliorative programs required, including "pensions for old age and injury." The International Labour Organization, representative of governments, employer organizations, and trade unions, was established to promote legislation implementing these recommendations throughout the world. A permanent secretariat, the International Labour Office, was established at Geneva.[4]

In Canada the Trades and Labor Congress continued to be the leading voice of social reform. In 1915 it decided that it should concentrate on a few specific measures, with old age pensions being given high priority,[5] but repeated representations to the government had no effect. National registration and conscription, seen by many affiliates especially in the West as weapons for the destruction of trade unions, served to crystallize the congress' long-simmering exasperation at its failure to achieve social reform into outright opposition to the government. The result was renewed interest in partisan political action. In 1906 the congress had called on its provincial executives to sponsor the formation of independent labour parties in their provinces.[6] A few such provincial parties had been formed, the most active of which was the one in Ontario established in 1907, but none of them had achieved significant success at the polls. In 1917 the congress went a step further and called for the formation in Canada of a United Kingdom style of labour party to unite the numerous factious labour and socialist parties then active.[7] A Canadian Labour party was in fact set up, independent of the congress but with its blessing. This party was unable to achieve the hoped-for unity of the Left, and it failed to sink roots in Canadian society. It nevertheless carried on in an ineffectual way until 1927 when it was wrecked by Communist infiltration.[8] The experiment in partisan political action failed, but vigorous if uncoordinated political participation in the context of postwar discontent resulted in the election of a number of federal and provincial Labour candidates at a critical period in the development of public opinion on the pension issue.

The dislocations of war and postwar readjustment brought into the open major tensions in Canadian society, which, among other things, shattered the two-party system. Prairie farmers were in revolt and the disaffection spread to Ontario and even, to an extent, to the Maritimes. Farmers became convinced more and more that they had to elect their own representatives who would not be smothered by what they saw as the business and largely central Canadian domination of the old party caucuses. Farmer parties, usually designated as United Farmers provincially and Progressives federally, sprang up almost overnight. In the Ontario election of 1919 an upset victory was scored by the United Farmers supported by the Independent Labor party, and a Farmer administration was formed with two ILP ministers. Farmer victories in provincial elections followed in Alberta in 1921 and in Manitoba in 1922. In Saskatchewan the powerful Liberal machine contained the Farmers provincially, but only by dint of much skilful political manoeuvring. In British Columbia, too, the Liberals retained office, partly because of the inability of the radicals to work together, but in 1924 37 percent of the vote went to candidates other than those of the traditional parties. In all these provinces, Labour members were elected to the legislatures in the immediate postwar years. In Nova Scotia and New Brunswick both Farmer and Labour candidates were successful in the provincial elections of 1920. The spirit of revolt was evident in the federal arena as well, with the election of sixty-five Progressives and two Labour members in the general election of December, 1921.[9]

Trade unionism in the West long had overtones of extreme radicalism. Early in the century syndicalism had gained a foothold in the western labour movement, especially in British Columbia. Moderated somewhat by the more pragmatic socialism of U.K. immigrants, it reached its zenith in a decision taken in March, 1919, to form the One Big Union. This development represented a break with the cautious approach of the Trades and Labor Congress in favour of a collision course with industrial capitalism. A crisis came quickly in the Winnipeg general strike of May and June, 1919, which reflected the same explosive discontent as that which gave rise to the emerging One Big Union, though the union had not actually been formed when the strike broke out. Comfortable burghers had horrendous visions of Bolshevik revolution and repressive measures were severe. At the same time some efforts were made to discover the causes of discontent. A commission headed by Chief Justice T. G. Mathers of Manitoba, which had been appointed by the federal government before the outbreak of the strike, speeded up its work and presented its report on June 28, 1919.[10] It recommended, among other things, "immediate inquiry by expert boards" into "state insurance against unemployment, sickness, invalidity and old age." This recommendation was supported by the National Industrial Conference, representative of the federal and some provincial governments, management, and labour, which was held in Ottawa in September, 1919, to consider the report.[11] The conference proposed that, as a first step, studies be undertaken immediately by the public service to provide at an early date the necessary information on which to base decisions regarding concrete programs. After a lapse of eighteen months and with the time for a federal election drawing nigh, it was announced in the 1921 Speech from the Throne that the Labour Department was investigating "systems of Unemployment Insurance and Old Age Pensions."[12]

The Liberals were the first political party to take a stand on old age pensions. After the electoral defeat of 1911, Laurier concluded that there was need for a national party convention to reconsider policy. Because of the war he postponed action, but late in 1915 he established the National Liberal Advisory Committee to provide background material for a postwar convention. Subcommittees were set up in major policy areas, and their reports were dealt with at a plenary session in July, 1916. Joseph E. Atkinson, publisher of the *Toronto Star*, chaired the subcommittee on social welfare and seems to have done most of its work, although he consulted W. L. Mackenzie King frequently. He concluded that it would be relatively simple to institute old age and widows' pensions but that much more study would have to be given to other social security measures. On his recommendation the advisory committee adopted a resolution setting a broad social security program as an ultimate objective and proposing early action on pensions. Laurier's long-projected convention was held in August, 1919. As it turned out, its main purpose was to select his successor, but a comprehensive program was adopted. King, who had published his own personal testament on social conditions a year earlier in a 529-page book,[13] was chairman of the convention committee on labour and industrial conditions. The committee's report, which was accepted by the convention without debate, proposed: "That insofar as may be practicable, having regard for Canada's financial position, an adequate system of insurance against unemployment, sickness and dependence in old age and other disability, which would include old age pensions, widows' pensions and maternity benefits, shall be instituted by the Federal Government in conjunction with the Governments of the several provinces."[14]

There is no doubt that King was personally convinced of the need for old age pensions. As he approached the responsibilities of power, however, his ardour cooled perceptibly. In 1921, as leader of the opposition, he expressed doubt about the willingness of the people to accept the expenditure required for a pension program in view of the high taxes and public debt resulting from the war.[15] The result of the general election held at the end of the year removed any inclination he still might have had to proceed with the alacrity suggested by the advisory committee in 1916. The Liberals won 116 of the 235 seats, but 65 of the government supporters were from Quebec, most of them highly conservative in their social outlook. King's main preoccupation was simply with staying in office. To do this he had to have the support of at least some of the 65 Progressives. Keeping their favour without creating intolerable tensions in his Quebec wing was a tactical enterprise that left little scope for new policy initiatives.[16]

The pension issue would not, however, go away. The Trades and Labor Congress continued its agitations,[17] and it was joined by provincial and federal legislators. In March and April, 1921, the Legislatures of Nova Scotia and Ontario adopted motions on old age pensions and related matters, and the New Brunswick Legislature did the same in April, 1922.[18] In December, 1921, the British Columbia House unanimously passed a government-sponsored resolution dealing exclusively with old age pensions in its operative section and asking specifically for federal legislation on the subject.[19] In the House of Commons a few private members from all parties took up the issue. Most prominent in this activity were the two Labour members, J. S. Woodsworth (Winnipeg North-Centre) and William Irvine (Calgary East), as well as an Independent, A. W. Neill (Comox-Alberni, B.C.), and a Conservative, T. L. Church (Toronto North). On the government side the Nova Scotian E. M. Macdonald, who had been prominent in the struggle for public pensions before the war, asked King's permission to introduce a resolution for a committee to investigate the subject.[20] Nothing came of this proposal, but another Liberal backbencher, J. E. Fontaine of Hull, succeeded in getting before the House a resolution asking the government to "consider the advisability of devising ways and means for the establishment of a system of old age pensions in Canada."[21] The resolution, though adopted unanimously, had no immediate effect, but it provided leverage for other members who were already asking questions as to the government's intentions and continued to do so throughout the life of the Parliament.[22] In 1924 King himself moved to set up a special committee of the House to inquire into the subject.[23] The work of this committee established a landmark in the development of pension policy in Canada. For the first time an attempt was made to work out a concrete plan, and the plan recommended by the committee in its final report was almost identical with that ultimately adopted in 1927.[24]

Since provincial participation was an essential ingredient of the proposed plan, a second special committee was set up in the 1925 session to consider the 1924 report in the light of provincial government responses solicited by the federal government.[25] These responses were not encouraging. The maritime provinces and Quebec all stated that they could not contemplate additional expenditures in view of their existing obligations. The premier of Ontario said he would be "glad to consider the matter," although the acting minister of health later stated that his government could express no opinion until it had completed what he called a thorough study then under way of the cost in relation to other welfare obligations.[26] Manitoba reported that it did not have time even to consider the plan. The three westernmost provinces were inclined to support public pensions in principle but argued that they were essentially a federal matter. This was especially true of British Columbia where the provincial Legislature had responded to the report of the

1924 committee by adopting unanimously a government-sponsored resolution asserting the principle of exclusive federal responsibility.[27] In view of the stand taken by these three provinces, the committee obtained an opinion from the deputy minister of justice on the constitutional position, which read in part:

> The subject matter of pensions has been entrusted to the provincial legislatures rather than Parliament. I do not mean to suggest that Parliament has not the power to legislate upon the subject so as to assist the provinces or to establish an independent voluntary scheme, provided that in either case the legislation does not trench upon the subject of property and civil rights in the provinces, as for example by obligating any province or person to contribute to the scheme. The enactment of such legislation would, however, involve the assumption by the Dominion of obligations involving heavy expenditures with regard to a matter which does not fall specifically within the Dominion field of legislation.[28]

When informed of this opinion, the British Columbia government moderated its stand,[29] and in the 1925 session the provincial Legislature unanimously adopted a resolution of two Labour members, advocating cooperation with the federal government in formulating a plan.[30] No other province, however, showed any disposition to do the same.

Faced with this lack of provincial interest, the 1925 committee recommended the calling of a federal-provincial conference. It rejected any notion that the federal government should undertake the pension plan alone. Its reasons were financial rather than constitutional: the estimated cost of $23 million a year.[31] Woodsworth and Irvine, however, could see no other way of salvaging the plan except through exclusive federal responsibility. Asserting that the consent of all the provinces could not be expected "this side of the next thousand years," Irvine moved to refer back the committee's report with instructions "to consider and report on a purely Federal scheme."[32] The motion was rejected by a vote of 17 to 139. Apart from the two Labour members, only thirteen Progressives and two Conservatives (one of whom was Church) voted for it.[33]

Public pensions dropped off the government's agenda altogether. In the general election campaign of October, 1925, no reference was made to them in the Liberal party's election propaganda.[34] The results of the election drove them even further from King's mind. It is difficult to interpret those results as anything but a defeat for the government. King lost his own seat, and his party obtained only 39.8 percent of the vote and 99 seats in the 245-member House, 59 of them in Quebec. Even the election of 4 sympathetic Independents (one of them Neill) left the Liberals well behind the Conservatives, who won 116 seats with 46.5 percent of the vote. Progressive representation was cut to 24 seats. Irvine was defeated, but Woodsworth won reelection and was joined by another Labour member, A. A. Heaps of Winnipeg North. King's sole motive now was to cling to power. More than ever he needed the support of the Progressives, several of whom could not be counted on. It was with this in mind that he set about preparing the Speech from the Throne for the first session of the new Parliament. Pensions were not mentioned in it, and there is no evidence they were considered.[35]

3. THE PRECIPITANTS

Suddenly and unexpectedly the two Labour members, Woodsworth and Heaps, brought the pension issue to the top of the agenda. On the opening day of the session (January 7, 1926), they jointly sent identical letters to King and Meighen, asking if it was their intention "to introduce at this session legislation with regard to (a) Provision for the unemployed; (b) Old Age Pensions."[36] Meighen's reply, which was dispatched almost immediately, was haughty and noncommittal. King's initial response was to invite the Labour members to discuss the matter with him privately. In the negotiations which followed,[37] King agreed to proceed with old age pensions and to offer assistance to the provinces and municipalities in providing emergency relief for the unemployed. He was not unhappy to have the issue forced on old age pensions. His problem was to convince some of his cabinet colleagues that it was necessary to make so large a concession to secure the support of only two members. Proof was provided on January 14 when the House divided on the first nonconfidence motion of the session. The motion was defeated by only 3 votes (120 to 123), with Woodsworth and Heaps supporting the government.[38] On January 26 Woodsworth and Heaps met the Cabinet informally, the result being recorded in King's diary:

> This morning at my office we accomplished a really important stroke of work. I had the members of the cabinet meet Woodsworth & Heaps & discuss old age pension legstn. tho some members of the Cabinet, Lapointe in conversat'n and Robb by memo from Finlayson opposed attempting anything, when they were confronted in discussion all agreed on a bill which would apply to the Dominion as a whole, letting each province come under, on a 50-50 basis, for a non-contributory scheme applicable to persons over 70 years of age. . . . It was agreed to have a bill immediately drafted.[39]

On January 28 King replied formally to the Woodsworth-Heaps letter, confirming the understanding previously arrived at.

The government's proposal, which was presented to the House in March, gave rise to no little confusion in Conservative ranks. R. S. White of Montreal attacked it as involving an unfair transfer of income which would discourage thrift, and R. B. Bennett argued strongly for the contributory principle,[40] but five other Conservatives announced that they would support the bill.[41] Party leaders managed to maintain a semblance of unity by couching their criticisms in tactical rather than substantive terms. Whether or not the bill was sound in itself, they argued in effect, it was mere window dressing: it would not become operative for lack of provincial cooperation and the government's first step ought to be to engage in meaningful consultation with the provinces.[42] This position appears to have satisfied most of the party backbenchers. No one was prepared to vote against the bill, and it passed all stages without division.

Senators were less inhibited. The Conservatives, still in the majority in the upper chamber, attacked the bill strongly, and several Liberals were also unhappy with it. The old arguments were revived: the bill would penalize thrift, it would militate against family responsibility and private charity, it did not differentiate between the deserving and undeserving, and there was no public demand for it. The main attack, however, centred on provincial rights. The bill, it was argued (often vituperatively), represented an unwarranted intrusion into the provincial field. The provinces did not want to participate and, indeed, many of them could not afford to do so. The federal government was already taxing the people heavily to discharge its proper responsibilities. Welfare matters should be left in the hands of local and private agencies which were better qualified to deal with them.[43] In vain did Senator G. D. Robertson, minister of labour in the former Borden and Meighen administrations, appeal to his fellow Conservatives to avoid giving the impression that they opposed old age pensions in principle.[44] The bill was defeated on second reading by a vote of twenty-one to forty-five.[45] Forty-three of the fifty-three Conservative senators were present and all but Robertson voted against it. So did three Liberals, while seventeen others (of a total of forty-one) were absent or abstained.

The Commons was by now too preoccupied with other matters to give further consideration to pensions. The government was rocked by the customs scandal, and King tried to avoid almost certain defeat on a censure motion by applying for dissolution. He resigned when this was refused, proclaiming that the Governor General had violated a fundamental principle of the constitution. Meighen undertook the responsibility of forming an administration, but it survived the Commons' wars for only three days. Dissolution was inevitable and a new election took place in September. It resulted in a clear majority for the Liberals, even though the Conservative share of the vote declined only fractionally (from 46.5 to 45.3 percent). Capitalizing on a falling off of Progressive support, the Liberals increased their percentage from 39.8 to 46.1. This was enough to elect 128 members in the 245-seat House.[46] Conservative strength was cut to 91 and Meighen was personally defeated. Twenty Progressive members were returned, 11 of whom had run as United Farmers of Alberta, along with 3 Labour members and 3 Independents.

King saw the election campaign as a struggle between the forces of darkness, represented by the Governor General and the Conservative-dominated Senate, and the forces of light, represented by himself and the Liberal party. Issues took their place within this framework. First came the so-called constitutional issue, followed by several of the government measures which the Senate had rejected or emasculated. Among these was the old age pensions bill, the defeat of which was seen by King primarily as demonstrating the need for Senate reform.[47] On the hustings, however, pensions proved to be an issue in their own right, especially in the West. The *Calgary Albertan* reported of a meeting in Calgary attended by more than 5,000 people: "Mr. King's references to Mr. Bennett, the Robb budget, income tax reduction, the return of penny postage, old age pensions, particularly Mr. King's declaration of the Liberal intention to re-introduce the last measure until it was forced past the Conservative opposition in the Senate, were the points . . . which aroused the greatest applause."[48] Two candidates in the 1926 election who were interviewed in the preparation of this study—of whom one was elected as a Liberal in Alberta and the other defeated as a Conservative in Saskatchewan—asserted that old age pensions were an important issue at the grass roots level in their constituencies. The successful Liberal said: "I mentioned it in every speech. . . . A great many of these people went in [to southern Alberta] as homesteaders, and years went by and they were able to make very little because of the dry weather . . . so that there were a great many people who were 70 years of age who had nothing to live on and whose children were unable to keep them."

It would be going too far to say that the pension issue won the closely contested 1926 election for the Liberals. Probably the most important single factor was the intensive work of Liberal lieutenants

71

who managed to produce cooperative electoral arrangements between Liberals and Progressives in many constituencies. Moreover, times were prosperous and the Liberal government had been able to bring in a sunshine budget before it left office. Many of the politicians themselves, however, attributed major significance to the pension issue. Senator H. W. Laird (Conservative) said that the issue was "discussed on every platform from one end of the province [Saskatchewan] to the other" and "was one of the most important factors which led to the decision at the polls."[49] In the House of Commons members on both sides expressed similar opinions.[50] Whether these politicians were entirely right, the fact that they held such views undoubtedly influenced their future conduct. In any case, they were not entirely wrong. In Neatby's assessment the two most important issues were the budget and pensions; the constitutional issue was useful to the Liberals mainly in offsetting the effect of the customs scandal.[51]

The 1926 pensions bill was reintroduced in the Commons in February, 1927, and was passed in March. In the Senate it was received by a chastened body of men. A few diehards remained, but the great majority were not prepared to contemplate the wrath which might descend on them if they once again rejected the bill.[52] C. E. Tanner argued that the Senate, having discharged its responsibility by rejecting a bill it considered defective, should now accept the judgement of a government which had recently been endorsed at the polls.[53] Most of his colleagues accepted defeat less rationally. Finding malicious satisfaction in the thought that failure of the provinces to cooperate would make the bill a nullity, they professed willingness to let the people see what a "delusion and hollow mockery" it was.[54] A last-ditch attempt to refer the bill to a committee for further study was unceremoniously rejected.[55]

King's troubles were not over. Almost from the moment when he resumed office in the fall of 1926 he was caught in a crossfire within his own Cabinet and party. On the one side were the Liberal government of Quebec and Raoul Dandurand, government leader in the Senate. On the other were the Liberal government of British Columbia and Peter Heenan, newly appointed minister of labour.

Acting as intermediary for Premier L. A. Taschereau of Quebec, Dandurand wrote repeatedly to both King and Finance Minister J. A. Robb, advocating at first that the 1926 bill should not be reintroduced until it had been fully discussed with the provinces, and then, after the bill had become law, that no agreement should be entered into with any province until the whole matter had been placed before a federal-provincial conference scheduled for the fall of 1927.[56] Taschereau himself intervened with a similar request:

> It has been figured out that our share would amount to perhaps three million dollars per annum, which would leave us with a huge deficit. . . . I know that a great pressure will be brought to bear on us by the Labour Associations . . . and this will probably be one of the most difficult situations that we will have to deal with in the near future. But we are determined to say no. . . . I know that you do not want to embarrass us, for every attack directed against us might also affect the Liberal Party.[57]

Heenan, a former railroad engineer who had run for Parliament as a Liberal-Labour candidate, was equally convinced that the future success of the party depended on early implementation of the plan.[58] By himself he probably could not have offset the Quebec pressure, since King had a low opinion of him,[59] but he had a powerful ally in the gove nment of British Columbia. Notwithstanding that government's earlier contention that pensions were a federal responsibility, it was now eager to proceed with a joint plan. On September 15, 1926, the day after the federal election, Premier John Oliver informed King that he had "stated repeatedly" during the election campaign his government's intention to implement the 1926 bill if Parliament passed it.[60] He demonstrated that he meant business by getting an enabling act through the provincial Legislature a month before the federal act became law.[61] King procrastinated, but in August, 1927, the Gordian knot was cut. On a trip to British Columbia, which appears to have been undertaken for other purposes, Heenan signed an agreement, dated August 17, to implement the plan in that province. In a laboured explanation to King, he claimed that the pressure on him had been irresistible.[62] When it appeared that the federal government might delay approval of the provincial administrative scheme—a statutory prerequisite for making the August 17 agreement operative—J. D. MacLean, premier after the death of Oliver, wrote to King: "Should your government now hesitate in putting the Act into full force . . . we would as a party lose all the benefit that has undoubtedly accrued."[63] The plan went into effect in British Columbia in September. Not until two months later—at the federal-provincial conference of November 3 to 10, 1927—was it discussed formally with the provinces for the first time, and then only as one of the last items on a long and controversial agenda.

Such difficulties as the Conservatives may have had in defining a position on public pensions were resolved by the results of the 1926 election. They decided to outbid the Liberals. In 1925 they had voted almost to a man against Irvine's proposal for a purely federal plan, but in 1927 Hugh Guthrie, acting leader after the personal defeat of Meighen, took this stand: "Shall we make two bites of the cherry, I ask? Why not pay the whole amount out of the federal treasury in order that we may have a uniform scheme throughout Canada."[64] This position was confirmed at the party convention, held later in the year, at which R. B. Bennett was chosen national leader. Senators were present who had fought to the last ditch for provincial rights in 1926 and even in 1927, but they remained silent.[65]

The tables were now turned on the Liberals. A. D. McRae, Conservative whip in the Commons and *de facto* director of party organization, reported after an extensive organizational tour of the Maritimes in 1929: "The Conservative proposal for a federal bill which will ensure equal treatment of all old people alike from the Atlantic to the Pacific and which will be paid in full by the federal government, will in my judgment be the best vote getting plank in our platform in the Maritimes and perhaps in Quebec and elsewhere."[66] Opening the 1930 election campaign with a speech in Winnipeg, Bennett made the proposal one of the items in an eight-point program.[67] Special efforts were made to exploit the issue in the Maritimes and Quebec where provincial action had still not been taken to implement the 1927 act. Bennett and other Conservative speakers stressed their proposal in speech after speech in these areas. Local Conservative associations in Nova Scotia placed large newspaper advertisements stating that old age pensions would become a reality with the election of a Bennett government. King was on the defensive. He argued that it was constitutionally impossible for the federal government to assume the full cost of old age pensions. To which Bennett replied: "We say that if the federal government could provide one half of the cost it could provide the other half without wrecking the constitution."[68]

With the economic depression already under way, the defeat of the King government in 1930 could hardly be attributed to the Conservative pledge on pensions. Indeed, it is by no means clear that it was decisive even in the Maritimes.[69] Nevertheless, a firm commitment had been made from which it was difficult to escape. The western provinces and Ontario had implemented the 1927 plan, but they were not averse to unloading their obligation in a period of declining revenues.[70] In 1931 Bennett honoured his pledge to the extent of assuming 75 percent of the cost of pensions. He explained that the change "is but temporary in character and contemplates a contributory system."[71]

4. CHOICE OF DESIGN

By 1926, when Canada's first public pension bill was before Parliament, there were numerous examples of public plans in operation throughout the world. As noted at the beginning of chapter 3, both means-test and contributory plans were instituted before World War I, and the number increased after the war. Uruguay adopted a means-test plan providing old age and disability benefits in 1919, and plans for the aged only were attempted in Alaska in 1915 and some of the U.S. states from 1923 on. An approach to the universal principle was made in Holland (by legislation passed in 1913 but not implemented until 1919) and in Spain (1919) in plans which established pension benefits for all employed persons out of funds established by contributions solely from employers and the state. The Dutch plan applied to both old age and disability, while in Spain only old age benefits were provided. In general there was a tendency to favour the contributory principle. Five of the ten plans in effect before the war were of this type, and a sixth country, France, had moved from a means-test plan to a combination of the means-test and contributory principles. Contributory plans applying to all employed persons were established in the Swiss canton of Glarus in 1916, in Italy in 1919, in Bulgaria, Czechoslovakia, Belgium, and Chile in 1924, and in the canton of Appenzell in 1925. Most of these plans provided disability or survivor benefits or both, in addition to old age benefits. In 1925 the United Kingdom superimposed a contributory plan, providing old age and survivor benefits, on its means-test plan of 1908.[72] From this variety of working models Canada chose a means-test plan, notwithstanding the trend towards contributory plans. It is necessary to explain this choice.

The International Labour Charter, the reports of the Mathers Commission and the National Industrial Conference, and the Liberal convention resolution of 1919 had all envisaged wide-ranging social security programs without priority necessarily being given to old age pensions. Some action was taken in Canada in other welfare areas. By 1920 six provinces, Nova Scotia, New Brunswick, Ontario, Manitoba, Alberta, and British Columbia, had replaced the old employer liability approach to workmen's compensation with plans providing for collective liability through accident funds. Five, Ontario, Manitoba, Saskatchewan, Alberta, and British Columbia, had established mothers' allowances (pensions) on a means-test basis. Unemployment insurance and health insurance were often discussed, but they did not enter the realm of practical politics until much later. Old age pensions were unquestionably *the* social security issue of the 1920s. There were two reasons for this. First, as indicated in chapter 2, section 4, poverty among the aged was acute, widespread, and chronic: upturns in the business cycle did little to alleviate it. Second, old age pensions, at least those of the noncontributory variety, were thought to be relatively simple to institute. Atkinson had marked them out as early as 1916 as the logical first step to comprehensive social security.

Why, however, did the leading advocates of pensions—the trade union movement and the M.P.'s from Pringle's day on who tried to keep the issue before Parliament—look to the federal government for action? The traditional view was that the federal area of responsibility related to development. Welfare was a local matter of no significance in nation-building. This view was expressed with full vigour in the Senate in 1926. Most of the senators, however, were opposed to public pensions as such. They championed provincial rights not so much out of a desire to protect the freedom of the provinces to act in this field as in the belief that the provinces would in fact do nothing. The provinces for their part showed no desire to assert their jurisdiction. Even though several of them had adopted mothers' allowances and the new type of workmen's compensation, the first plan required only small expenditures and the second was financed entirely by employer contributions. Old age pensions involved a financial burden of a different magnitude. Reluctance to accept even half of the expenditure came out clearly at the conference of November, 1927: "The discussion showed an inclination on the part of most of the provinces to have the Federal Government make its contribution without involving the provinces in a similar obligation."[73]

The views of the champions of pensions were the obverse of those of most senators. The fact that the provinces were not likely to act was a reason why the federal government should step in. The difficulty of getting all provinces to proceed with workmen's compensation and mothers' allowances may well have lent strength to this opinion. To those who saw an expanding role for the state, involvement of the central government was a necessary corollary. That government alone had the financial resources to undertake a major plan and it alone could guarantee that the plan would be countrywide in its operation.

The federal authorities, however, were reluctant to get involved. They had financial problems of their own, and the policy departure they were being asked to make represented a major break with the past. King favoured federal involvement, but his parliamentary group, with its strong Quebec orientation, was by no means fully in agreement with him. Action would probably have been delayed indefinitely had not the

Woodsworth-Heaps coup, which was made possible only by an electoral fluke, forced the issue to the top of the agenda. The adoption of a concrete plan by the House and its rejection by the Senate dramatized the issue for the public and provided a focal point for what had previously been only a diffuse awareness of need. Even then it required another coup, by the British Columbia government and Heenan, to bring the measure to fruition. The report of the 1924 committee provided a ready-made design which could be whipped into legislative form quickly, once the government was committed. The committee hit on an ingenious compromise between provincial responsibility and federal initiative, in that in form at least its proposal was merely for a federal offer of financial assistance to the provinces in implementing provincially enacted and administered plans. This compromise not only limited the financial obligations of the federal government, but it also made it possible to argue that that government was not invading provincial jurisdiction.[74] The argument had no validity, since in fact Ottawa unilaterally established public pensions as a priority item for the provinces and dictated how they were to be dealt with. Nevertheless, this argument was a useful rationalization for easing federal entry into a large new field.

The 1924 committee obtained information on pension plans in a number of countries, but both its report and proceedings suggest that it looked mainly to the experience of the United Kingdom, New Zealand, and Australia for guidance.[75] This undoubtedly predisposed it to the means-test type of plan, since that was the only type in effect in any of those countries in 1924. In any case, the committee's own basic approach led almost inevitably to the same conclusion. It was breaking new ground in Canada and it proceeded with caution. It was careful to keep the estimated costs within limits which it hoped would be acceptable. That automatically ruled out a universal plan financed out of general revenues. Charles Booth had argued the case for such an approach over a period of many years and had written two books on the subject,[76] but his proposal had not commended itself to governments elsewhere and it was not seriously discussed here. Trades and Labor Congress President Tom Moore conceded at the committee hearings that "those who have assured incomes of a reasonable amount should not be eligible to participate."[77] A contributory plan appeared to be almost equally impractical. The administrative problems, which were complicated enough in a unified plan, appeared in the 1920s to be insuperable in a joint plan.

R. B. Bennett argued vigorously for the contributory principle in the 1926 debate in the House of Commons.[78] In his view, pensions not earned by previous contributions would destroy the moral fibre of the nation. "There is nothing more serious in a new country," he said, "than that men should grow up with the idea or thought that they are to rely upon what is now called in England the dole. . . . habits of thrift and economy should be encouraged and developed among the people if we are to take our place among the great nations of the world." Bennett concurred in the opinion of the deputy minister of justice that the federal government could not impose contributions. Bennett suggested federal subsidization of provincial contributory plans as one way of avoiding the difficulty. Recognizing that it would not be easy to get agreement on such plans, he proposed the expansion of government annuities as a possible alternative. His idea was that federal subsidies should be offered to reduce the purchase price of annuities by 20 or 25 percent. King agreed that a contributory plan was preferable in principle,[79] but he noted that it would be of no benefit to those already at or near pensionable age. Claiming (erroneously) that most countries with contributory plans had started with means-test plans, he argued that Canada would be well advised to follow their example. He expressed confidence that the proposal then before Parliament would ultimately be developed into a comprehensive social insurance program —a conviction he reaffirmed on numerous occasions in subsequent years. Dandurand stated in 1927 that the Department of Labour was then studying a contributory plan.[80]

There were numerous criticisms, in the 1924 committee sessions and at the committee stage of the 1926 and 1927 bills, of the details of what became the 1927 plan. These focused mainly on the amount of the pension and the qualifying age. They were not, however, pressed to the point of jeopardizing the plan itself. Woodsworth's attitude was that the plan as it stood was better than nothing and he would take what he could get, even though he hoped for improvements in the near future.[81] The Trades and Labor Congress decided that criticism of specific provisions could wait until later; the need of the moment was to persuade the provinces to implement the plan.[82] The *Labour Gazette* and the daily press from 1926 on contain many references to deputations from trade unions, including the Catholic unions in Quebec, pressing the provincial governments to act.

5. RELATED PENSION PLANS

No account of Canada's first pension plan is complete without a passing reference to measures which, though not an integral part of old age pension policy in Canada, nevertheless complemented it to an extent. These were pensions for the blind and other disabled not covered by provincial workmen's compensation, and war veterans' allowances.

After the passage of the 1927 Old Age Pensions Act, there was a persistent campaign, sparked by the Canadian National Institute for the Blind, to have the pension plan extended to cover the blind.[83] The campaign bore some fruit in 1937 when the Old Age Pensions Act was amended to reduce the qualifying age for the blind to forty. In addition, the limit of allowable income was set at a higher level for the blind than for the aged. All provinces quickly entered into agreements with the federal government to implement this new plan. In 1947 the age of eligibility was reduced to twenty-one. Pensions for the blind continued to be paid under the 1927 act until 1951 when the entire pension program was restructured. The lower level of the new program provided means-test pensions for the sixty-five to sixty-nine age group in a joint plan based on equal sharing of costs by the federal and provincial governments. Under the 1927 act as amended in 1931, however, the federal government's contribution had been 75 percent, and this basis of sharing had applied to pensions for the blind from their inception in 1937. It was continued by a new Blind Persons Act passed in 1951, which also continued preferential treatment of the blind in regard to the means test. In 1955 the age of eligibility was reduced to eighteen. The Disabled Persons Act of 1954 inaugurated a joint means-test plan for persons totally and permanently disabled for causes not covered by the Blind Persons Act or provincial workmen's compensation. It provided for a fifty-fifty basis of sharing and the same means test as applied to old age assistance.

During and after World War I, the federal government established a variety of social security plans for the benefit of veterans and their dependants. These did not, however, deal adequately with the problem of the prematurely old ("burnt out") veteran, and in 1930, under considerable pressure from veterans' organizations, Parliament passed the War Veterans Allowance Act. The federal government assumed full responsibility for paying means-test pensions to veterans who were at least sixty or were adjudged to be permanently unemployable, provided that they had served in actual theatres of war or were in receipt of war pensions. The basic benefit and means test were the same as under the Old Age Pensions Act of 1927, so that in effect old age pensions became available to certain veterans at a lower age than for the general population. The veterans had an additional advantage: a higher pension was paid to a married man regardless of his wife's age and to a widower with one or more dependent children. During World War II benefits were extended by order in council to widows and orphans of qualifying veterans. A reenactment of 1946 incorporated these changes, made additional classes of veterans eligible for benefits, and increased the maximum pension and allowable income above the levels applicable to old age pensions. This differential was increased subsequently. The benefits of the plan are available to veterans of the Korean War, and in 1962 they were extended to certain classes of civilians (merchant seamen, auxiliary services personnel, and others) who had been directly exposed to enemy action in World War II.

Chapter Five

Implementation of the 1927 Plan

THE 1927 OLD AGE PENSIONS ACT remained on the statute books for twenty-four years until 1951. Three main problem areas arose during that period. First, it was nearly a decade before all provinces accepted the plan. Second, rising living costs immediately before and after the outbreak of World War II gave rise to a politically significant demand for increased benefits. Third, since administration was exclusively in provincial hands, discrepancies arose among provinces.

1. COMPLEMENTARY PROVINCIAL ACTION

In terms of the adoption of the plan, the nine provinces of the time divide neatly into two groups on the basis of both geography and chronology. In the four western provinces and Ontario, the plan was in full operation before the end of 1929. In the maritime provinces and Quebec, it did not come into effect until 1933 or later. As a result, it was quickly removed from the area of political controversy in the former group, while it became a chronic political issue in the latter.[1]

As noted in chapter 4, British Columbia implemented the plan as quickly as possible after it was approved by Parliament. Saskatchewan and Manitoba were only slightly less prompt. The question first came formally before the Saskatchewan Legislature in February, 1927, when a Labour member moved a resolution supporting the principle of public pensions.[2] All parties supported this resolution. In a letter of November 19, 1924, Premier J. G. Gardiner, then minister of labour and industry, had responded to the federal government's request for the province's reaction to the proposal of the 1924 committee by saying that the federal government should accept full responsibility.[3] He now explained that he had been concerned purely about the provinces with large aged populations. Saskatchewan, he said, would have no difficulty implementing the plan and was merely waiting until the details were finalized. The necessary provincial legislation was passed at the 1928 session, and the plan went into operation on June 1 of that year. In Manitoba, the Labour M.L.A.'s brought the question before the Legislature in 1926, while the first federal bill was still under discussion in the House of Commons, by moving a resolution urging the provincial government to cooperate in the proposed new plan. The Liberals brought in a similar resolution in 1927.[4] The provincial government's response was cautious but not hostile, and after the 1927 act became law, it evidently decided to participate. Its position at the 1927 federal-provincial conference is recorded as follows: "The province of Manitoba, while taking the view that the Dominion Government might well bear all the cost, and that if it did not it should pay at least half the cost of administering the Act, declared the readiness of the province to introduce a bill later and seek a source for securing the necessary revenue."[5] On his return from the conference, Premier John Bracken announced publicly that Manitoba would proceed, and the plan became effective on September 1, 1928.[6]

Alberta held out for a year mainly because its government, formed by the United Farmers of Alberta (UFA), hoped to get better terms. The government argued that if Ottawa would not assume full responsibility for the pension plan, it should at least take over 75 percent of the cost. This position became untenable, however, because of weakness at the home base. The issue led to a split with the Labour members who had consistently supported the UFA government since it was first elected in 1921. As in Manitoba, a Labour resolution was introduced in 1926, urging the government to cooperate in the plan then being considered by Parliament. On that occasion the Labour members were persuaded to withdraw their resolution and substitute one asking for an immediate federal-provincial conference to work out satisfactory financial terms.[7] In 1927 the issue was again brought to the floor of the House by a Liberal resolution. A complicated series of amendments and counter-amendments followed in which the government mobilized its supporters to make its view prevail. The Labour members voted with the opposition consistently.[8] The government could get along without their support, but in time it was faced with division in its own ranks. Before the opening of the 1928 session, a UFA delegation urged the government to accept the federal plan. Premier J. E. Brownlee attempted to forestall opposition resolutions in the House by giving notice on the opening day of a motion proposing that legislation should be deferred in favour of further negotiations with the federal government. The motion was called on February 20 and the debate raged all afternoon and evening.[9] Far from burying the issue, it brought the division in government ranks into the open. When the Labour members offered an amendment urging immediate acceptance of the federal plan pending completion of negotiations, three UFA members joined the combined opposition to vote for it. The *Edmonton Bulletin* reported that only an emergency caucus held during the supper adjournment prevented further defections. The government brought in enabling legislation in the 1929 session, and the plan went into effect on August 1 of that year.

The Conservative government of Ontario was basically unsympathetic to the pension plan. Premier G. H. Ferguson clung to the view that the relief of poverty was inherently a matter for private charity or for municipal action, if private action failed. Alternatively, he said, the federal government should accept full responsibility, it being inexpedient for a province to act alone since there would be an influx of old people into its territory. This negative attitude was hard to maintain in Canada's most urbanized and industrialized province. Apart from the almost continuous agitation of trade unions, an Old Age Pension Association had been formed in Toronto in 1924 to develop a climate of opinion favourable to pensions,[10] and in May, 1927, it claimed that it had secured 35,000 signatures in Toronto and environs on a petition asking the province to implement the 1927 act.[11] In addition, the municipalities were pressing the province to proceed.[12] The government temporized by announcing in 1928 that the civil service was making a thorough study of the subject, even though it had professed three years earlier that such a study was being made then.[13] The Liberal opposition attempted to capitalize on the issue by making it the subject of its Throne Speech amendment in the 1928 session,[14] and Peter Heenan, federal minister of labour, intervened with attacks on the government for its procrastination. Ferguson took the wind out of the opposition's sails by announcing in October that the necessary legislation would be brought down at the 1929 session. The plan came into effect in Ontario on November 1, 1929.

Manitoba, Alberta, and Ontario charged some of the cost of the pension plan to their municipal governments. The original Manitoba statute permitted the provincial government to raise the whole of its share, exclusive of administration, from local sources. In 1930, however, the province itself accepted responsibility for half of its share, thereby cutting the municipal obligation in half. In other words, the municipalities had to pay 25 percent of the total cost of pensions as long as the federal share was 50 percent, and 12½ percent after the federal share was increased to 75 percent in 1931. Under the original Alberta statute,

10 percent of the total cost excluding administration was charged back to the municipalities and improvement districts, and this was unaffected by the increase in the federal share. In Ontario, Premier Ferguson's original intention had been to make the local governments responsible for 25 percent (half of the province's share), but faced with strong opposition from the municipalities, he cut this to 20 percent. It was reduced to 10 percent by the federal government's increase in its share.

The municipalities in Alberta and Manitoba were involved in administration to the extent that applications were filed with them and they inquired into the means of the applicants. Apart, however, from the Winnipeg Social Welfare Commission, local authorities exercised little discretion in awarding or determining the amount of pensions. Ontario, in line with Ferguson's belief in the primacy of local responsibility in the welfare field, aimed at a substantial degree of local discretion by establishing an elaborate network of local boards. The result was an administrative nightmare. Competence in welfare administration was generally of a low order at the local level, and decisions were often based more on the prejudices of local administrators than on any attempt at objective application of the regulations to individual cases. At the extremes, some boards demonstrated their devotion to the market ethos by taking an extremely hard line with applicants and pensioners, while others exhibited generosity which left federal officials shaking their heads, especially after the local share of the cost was cut to 10 percent.[15] The province tried to ensure some semblance of uniformity by inspection. This became increasingly strict until little local discretion remained, and in 1935 the local boards were abolished except in the five largest cities. In 1937 the province relieved the municipalities of financial responsibility. Simultaneously, local boards were reestablished on a county basis, but their role was confined to the initial processing of applications. Local financial responsibility was eliminated in Alberta in 1949, but it continued for the life of the plan in Manitoba.

The three maritime governments were placed in a common dilemma by the 1927 act. Their ratio of people of pensionable age to total population was substantially higher than the national average, while the independent resources of these people were probably substantially lower on average.[16] Thus, the need for public pensions was greater in those provinces than in the others. At the same time, the very circumstances which created that greater need also resulted in lower government revenue capacity. Implementation of the 1927 act posed an extremely difficult problem, but failure to implement had the anomalous effect of diverting federal tax revenue collected from maritime people to subsidize pensions in other provinces.

In the Nova Scotia election of 1925, the Conservatives ended a long Liberal reign with a smashing victory, winning forty of the forty-three seats. The three members of the Liberal opposition put on a dispirited performance until the pension issue instilled new life in them. They made it the main subject of discussion in the Throne Speech debate in the 1928 session and devoted their nonconfidence amendment to it.[17] Premier E. N. Rhodes declared his support of pensions in principle but argued that his government needed full information before it could define its policy. In August, 1928, he appointed H. E. Mahon of Halifax as a one-man royal commission of inquiry, and shortly afterwards called a snap election for October 1. The Liberals tried to make old age pensions a major issue in the election campaign. To the government's claims that it was taking the necessary first step, they replied that it was merely stalling. The government was returned, but four of its ministers lost their seats and its margin in the House was reduced to three (twenty-three Conservatives against twenty Liberals). Meanwhile, Mahon had embarked on an exhaustive inquiry which included field surveys in six counties of differing characteristics and Halifax. He was able to produce only an interim report for the 1929 session since by then his field survey was incomplete except in Hants county, but his tentative findings were not materially altered in the final report, which was tabled in 1930.[18] These were predictable: implementation of the plan would involve the province in heavy additional expenditures which would require a substantial increase either in taxation or in federal subsidies.

The death of a cabinet minister made it necessary to call a by-election in Halifax for January, 1930. This was crucial to the government in view of its narrow margin in the House. At his opening meeting in the campaign, Rhodes roused his audience to a high pitch of enthusiasm with a three-point pledge: the government would immediately initiate mothers' allowances, minimum wages for women, and old age pensions.[19] This pledge became the main theme of an extensive advertising campaign and of speeches by government supporters. The Conservative candidate was elected by what was reported to be the largest majority in the constituency's history. Rhodes honoured his pledge on mothers' allowances and minimum wages, but old age pensions continued to be a perplexing problem. A welcome diversion was found in the federal election campaign of 1930 in which the Conservatives could direct their fire against the Liberal federal government for its alleged discrimination against the maritime provinces on pensions and other matters. After the successful conclusion of that campaign, Rhodes went to Ottawa to join Bennett's Cabinet. His successor as premier, G. S. Harrington, got off to a good start on the pension issue by piloting an enabling act through the 1931 session. Perhaps he hoped that Bennett would make it unnecessary ever to bring this act into force. If so, he was doomed to disappointment. The increase in the federal share to 75 percent in 1931 did not move him. He now argued that only renegotiation of the overall financial arrangements with Ottawa would make pensions feasible in Nova Scotia. In the provincial election of 1933, Liberal leader Angus L. Macdonald concentrated his attack on the government on three main points: economic stagnation, alleged administrative waste, and old age pensions. In a House which was reduced to thirty seats, the Liberals won twenty-two. On the very day on which the new government was sworn into office (September 5, 1933), it proclaimed the enabling act of 1931 in force. Pensions became payable in Nova Scotia on March 1, 1934.

A Conservative government was also in office in New Brunswick after 1925, and it adopted much the same approach to old age pensions as its counterpart in Nova Scotia. In 1929 it appointed a royal commission to inquire into the subject and, at the request of organized labour, extended the terms of reference to include mothers' allowances. The life of the Legislature being due to expire in 1930, an interim report of the commission dealing with old age pensions only was hurried in late in the 1930 session. It gave evidence of being strongly influenced by the more thorough Mahon study in Nova Scotia, and it painted a similarly discouraging financial picture. The government nevertheless proceeded to enact legislation on old age pensions, mothers' allowances, minimum wages for women, and child protection. All four acts were to come into force only by proclamation, but they served to get the government through the election. After the government was confirmed in office, it did not proclaim any of them. The final reports of the royal commission (one on old age pensions and the other on mothers' allowances) were tabled in the 1931 session, and the government used the financial problems these reports depicted as a reason for delay. The federal government's decision to take over 75 percent of the cost did not alter the provincial position.[20] As the depression advanced, pensions declined as a political issue. Trade unions complained that New Brunswick was the most backward province in Canada in social legislation, but the Liberal opposition failed to raise the issue in the 1932, 1933, and 1934 sessions. As the election of 1935 approached, however, its interest revived. While the government held to the position that it would implement old age pensions as soon as it was financially able to do so, the Liberals made a firm commitment to proceed immediately regardless of financial difficulties. Shortly after the election, which they won in a landslide, the 1930 enabling act was proclaimed, and the plan went into operation in the province on July 1, 1936.

In Prince Edward Island, which had the largest percentage of population aged seventy and over of all the Canadian provinces, pensions became a subject of controversy in the late 1920s. The government in office was Liberal, and it could not blame Ottawa for its own failure to act. On the other hand, both before and during the federal election campaign of 1930, the Conservative opposition made much of their national party's promise to take over the whole cost of pensions. At the 1931 session of the provincial Legislature, the Liberal government enacted enabling legislation (to come into effect by proclamation), in anticipation of a general election to be held later in the year. The legislation raising the federal share to 75 percent was passed in the interval between the session and the election, and much bickering resulted during the campaign as to which party had done most to forward the cause of old age pensions. In view of the advanced state of the economic depression, this controversy was probably a minor factor in the decision of the electorate. At any rate, the Liberal government was defeated. After making a survey of the number eligible for pension, the new Conservative administration announced in the Speech from the Throne of the 1933 session that it would bring the plan into operation effective June 1 of that year.[21] To limit costs, it instituted an administrative policy which cut the maximum pension to $15 a month.[22]

While pensions were clearly an issue in all of the maritime provinces in the early 1930s, it could hardly be said that, in those depression years, they constituted the decisive issue which overturned governments. Indeed, the Conservative government of Prince Edward Island, which implemented the 1927 plan, suffered the same ignominious defeat in the province's 1935 election as befell the Nova Scotia and New Brunswick governments in 1933 and 1935. Even so, the politicians clearly acted on the assumption that there was a public demand for pensions. Governments delayed, but as they did so they repeatedly averred their firm intention to implement the plan, while their oppositions condemned them for their delays. It is significant that two of the provincial enabling acts were passed immediately before elections. Moreover, failure to proclaim the legislation became an election issue in both Nova Scotia and New Brunswick. Even in Prince Edward Island the parties were still vying in 1935 for the credit for having brought pensions to the province.

Quebec had been governed continuously by Liberal administrations since 1897, with L. A. Taschereau as premier since 1920. Public pensions became a not inconsequential element in a complex combination of circumstances which brought this long reign to an end in 1936.

The Quebec Liberals had abandoned their nineteenth-century anti-clericalism but had firmly embraced economic liberalism. They saw the future well-being of the province not in the self-sufficient rural community idealized by the clergy and other elites, but in industrial development undertaken by private enterprise on the basis of the province's natural resources. Taschereau brought this policy to fruition in the 1920s. Concession after concession was made to American and English-Canadian corporate enterprises, which grew and flourished uninhibited by any attempt at regulation for the protection of either workers or the public. Cabinet ministers themselves got into the swim, accepting corporate directorships and other favours, and the large prizes to be awarded led to corruption in the public service. The clerical and intellectual nationalists declaimed against the alienation of the province's resources, the destruction of the rural life, and the reduction of French Canadians to the status of hewers of wood and drawers of water for "foreign" corporations. Industrialization meant higher standards of living, however, and as long as times remained prosperous, the Taschereau policy was not seriously threatened. Nevertheless, urbanization was producing profound social changes. Industrial workers in Quebec were subject to the same insecurity as their counterparts everywhere, and even the family farm had lost much of its self-sufficiency as it was drawn into the market economy.[23]

Taschereau's economic liberalism, which eschewed all forms of state intervention, harmonized neatly with the traditional Quebec approach to social welfare as outlined in chapter 2, section 1. The difficulty was that religious and other charitable organizations could not raise enough money to meet the growing volume of demands upon them. Taschereau's solution was the Public Charities Act of 1921, under which the provincial government provided financial assistance to approved private organizations and municipalities. Though this act was viewed at first with suspicion by some clerical and other elites, it soon came to be regarded as the definitive expression of the state's welfare role.[24] Taschereau's standard response to those who advocated implementation of the 1927 plan was to point to the large expenditures, amounting to about a third of the provincial budget, which were made annually under that act.[25] He adopted a tactic of passive resistance to the pension plan. In 1929 he secured opinions from three leading Quebec lawyers, one of whom was Louis St. Laurent, that it was *ultra vires* Parliament, but he did not challenge it in the courts. Instead he took the position that though it might well serve the needs of other provinces, it was foreign to Quebec's social philosophy. He and his ministers called repeatedly for a federal-provincial conference to work out an arrangement that would meet the needs of all provinces. J. N. Francoeur, formerly Speaker of the House and later a minister, proposed in 1929 that Ottawa pay Quebec $1 million a year as a substitute for the 1927 plan, on condition that the province use the money for the care of the aged in a manner compatible with its own philosophy.

The Conservative opposition, led by Arthur Sauvé, was restrained by the fact that its attitude to social welfare did not differ materially from Taschereau's, but one Conservative member, Aimé Guertin of Hull, who had entered the House in the 1927 election, was not similarly inhibited. He was the earliest and through the years by far the most persistent advocate of provincial adoption of the federal pension plan and other social welfare measures. At first he was a voice crying in the wilderness, but in the 1929 session he gained a powerful ally in Camillien Houde, mayor of Montreal, who had been a Conservative member before the 1927 election and had returned in a by-election in October, 1928. Houde was proud of his working class origins and saw himself as the champion of the poor. Guertin, who operated an insurance and real estate agency, was essentially petty bourgeois in his outlook, and he could harangue against "the trusts" with the best of the nationalists.[26] At the same time, he had once worked for wages and he retained his membership in the Order of Railway Telegraphers. Perhaps because of this background, he held more advanced views than most of his associates on the policies required to meet the social problems created by urbanization and industrialization. His first success in precipitating a debate in the Legislature on the pension issue was in February, 1929, when he moved for the production of all correspondence between Quebec and Ottawa on the subject.[27] He argued, with strong support from Houde, that the federal plan was a realistic approach to the problem of old age security in the modern age. The official Conservative position was set forth a month later in a resolution, moved by Sauvé and seconded by Maurice Duplessis, asking for an expert study "to seek out and find what method could best be followed to protect our indigent old people, without any injustice and without affecting the economic system of the Province."[28]

Later in the year Houde was elected Conservative leader to succeed Sauvé who retired after the session. There was a marked change of emphasis in party policy, epitomized in the Throne Speech amendment of 1930 regretting the government's failure to "acknowledge the pressing need for social legislation adapted to present requirements."[29] The government itself apparently began to recognize that the Public Charities Act might fall short of perfection, for it appointed a Social Insurance

Commission to review the whole gamut of welfare policy in the province. In the 1931 election Houde attacked the government on all fronts, and in most speeches he made an emotionally charged appeal that old folks should be enabled to live out their lives in their own homes instead of being herded into institutions. His flamboyant style did not appeal to the electorate, however, or perhaps his social policies were still premature. The Liberals won another lopsided victory and Houde lost his own seat. Duplessis took over as acting leader (confirmed at a convention in 1933), and the party returned for a time to its more conservative stance on welfare.

The basic assumptions of the traditional philosophy regarding social welfare were, however, being challenged. It was only to be expected that trade unions affiliated to the Trades and Labor Congress should press for implementation of the federal pension plan. Less predictable was the fact that the Confédération des Travailleurs Catholiques du Canada, which had been formed under clerical auspices in 1921 to protect French-Canadian workers from "godless" international unionism, was equally insistent in this demand, its first resolution on the subject being adopted in 1926. Early in 1929 the Montreal Labour Council, embracing the Catholic unions in the area, issued a bulletin asserting that social measures such as the pension plan gave true expression to Catholic social doctrine as declared authoritatively by the papal encyclical *De Rerum Novarum*. This assertion came as a shock to Liberals, nationalists, and clerical elites alike, most of whom had been inhibited by their antistatist predilections from comprehending the encyclical. The position was strikingly confirmed by *Quadragesimo Anno* issued in 1931, which prompted the Jesuits of Montreal to sponsor a study by leading laymen of social problems in the contemporary setting. The pamphlet they produced in 1933, *Le Programme de restauration sociale*, devoted one of its four main sections to an extensive program of labour and social legislation. The Social Insurance Commission arrived at a similar position. In its second report dated January, 1932, it declared:

> The population of Quebec has led, for centuries, a simple life, founded on the family and the community. . . . The family was self-sufficient and could always rely upon the aid of neighbours. . . . Furthermore, religious institutions and communities came to its assistance for the care of children or the aged. This administrative regime has worked with success for centuries but today it is powerless before the complications and dangers of modern life.[30]

On the specific question of public pensions, the commission argued strongly for the contributory principle. The majority, however, took the pragmatic position that since Quebec residents were being taxed for a plan from which no benefits were being received, the province should accept the 1927 act, pending federal action on a contributory plan.[31]

With all this eminent authority to appeal to, Guertin was now irrepressible in his demands for action on the 1927 plan, as well as mothers' allowances and other social and labour measures.[32] More and more members, including some Liberals, were speaking up in support of his position and heated debates ensued in the Legislature. Duplessis, who was nothing if not an astute politician, added pensions and mothers' allowances to his repertoire of anti-Taschereau philippics. The government itself was losing confidence in its position. Whereas it had previously dismissed resolutions advocating implementation of the federal pension plan with amendments lauding the "admirable system" of religious charity, it was more circumspect in its treatment of a Conservative resolution on the subject in 1935. It merely proposed that action be deferred until "the new legislation regarding the Federal Old Age Pensions Act, as announced by the Prime Minister of Canada, is submitted to the Canadian House of Commons."[33] Moreover, the government was in difficulty in its own party. Under the leadership of Paul Gouin, son and grandson of former premiers, a group of young dissidents with nationalist leanings formed l'Action Liberale Nationale (ALN) to reform the party on the basis of *Le Programme de restauration sociale*. Both inside and outside the party, attacks on the government were mounting in intensity for its subservience to foreign capital, its corruption, and its inadequate social policy.

Taschereau took courage in the Liberal victory in the federal election of October 14, 1935, in which the party amassed nearly 55 percent of the vote in Quebec. Hoping to capitalize on this favourable result, he called a Quebec election for November 25. In speeches made during the year he had veered steadily away from his previous position on pensions. He now announced that the federal plan would be implemented at the next session of the Legislature, prompting Gouin and Duplessis to charge that they had forced a death-bed repentance on him. Gouin had despaired of reforming the Liberal party from within and had established the ALN as a separate party. Shortly after the election was called, he and Duplessis announced that their parties would campaign cooperatively under the label of Union Nationale, with Duplessis as the acknowledged leader. The Taschereau government was returned, but with only forty-eight of the ninety seats (compared with seventy-nine in the previous election), including one Independent Liberal. The ALN elected twenty-six members and the Conservatives sixteen, for a combined opposition of forty-two.

Taschereau tried to refurbish the government's image by introducing new blood into his Cabinet and by announcing a reform program in the 1936 Speech from the Throne, including old age pensions and an amendment to the Sunday Observance Act which had long been demanded by nationalist groups.[34] Duplessis soon reduced these efforts to a shambles. With his greatly enlarged support in the House he was able to force the government to reactivate the long dormant Public Accounts Committee. For more than a month in May and June, 1936, he used the investigatory powers of the committee to bring to light case after case of corruption in high places, involving even Taschereau's brother. Simultaneously, he led a filibuster on the budget which brought the business of the House to a standstill. Unable to get supply, Taschereau saw no option but to apply for dissolution. Before doing so, he appealed to Duplessis to let certain uncontroversial private bills go through. Duplessis countered with the proposal that the old age pension and Sunday observance bills should also pass, and when Taschereau agreed, he trumpeted that he had forced the government to deal with these measures. The House was not only dissolved but Taschereau resigned as premier and Liberal leader. Adélard Godbout was called upon to take over. He speeded up negotiations with the federal government on pensions, with the result that the plan came into operation on August 1, 1936, even though it was quite impossible in the short time available to organize the administrative machinery needed to process the flood of applications that poured in. The election, which took place on August 17, was no contest. The Union Nationale, now an integrated party, obtained 57 percent of the vote and seventy-six of the ninety seats. Duplessis immediately called a special session of the Legislature to deal with certain legislation which he declared to be urgent, including amendments to Taschereau's enabling act on pensions.

2. REVISION OF THE PLAN

During the depression of the 1930s old age pensioners could be said to have been well off compared to the thousands of people on relief. Not only were their benefits paid regularly and in cash but the purchasing power of the pension increased. The old cost of living index (1935–39 = 100) declined from 120.5 in 1928 and 121.7 in 1929 (the pre-depression peak) to 94.4 in 1933. This trend was reversed by the minor economic revival towards the end of the decade and especially by wartime inflation. By 1941 the index stood at 111.7. As Finance Minister J. L. Ilsley was quick to point out,[35] this was lower than in the late 1920s when the pension plan first came into operation, but pensioners remembered only the rising prices of more recent years. In any case, living costs continued to rise. Cost of living bonuses were being paid to other groups under wartime wages policy, but the income of pensioners remained frozen.

A growing agitation for either an increase in the pension or a cost of living bonus resulted. Since the provinces were the administrators of the plan, much of the agitation was directed at them. The heat was felt first in British Columbia, where active pensioners' associations existed with ready access to the press. Communications sent by the provincial government to Ottawa during 1941 contained the following:

> Every day I [Premier T. D. Pattullo] am subjected to innumerable importunities, and continuously through the press representations are made, that the Old Age Pensions should be increased. (July 12)

> This question has been the subject of a great deal of discussion in this Province and everyone is in sympathy with the Old Age Pensioners. (August 14)

> Matter of pensions very acute. (telegram, October 6)[36]

Ilsley, however, set his mind against any increase on the part of the federal government. In a prepared statement delivered on November 14, 1941, he conceded that he had received many representations to increase the pension, but he argued that federal resources were already strained to the limit in financing the war. By contrast, he said, the provinces were enjoying increased revenues without corresponding increases in expenditure. In any case, pensions were fundamentally a provincial responsibility. Therefore, he would do no more than exempt from the calculation of means supplementary benefits which any of the provinces might decide to pay.[37]

British Columbia and Alberta, while not conceding that the federal government should absolve itself of responsibility, accepted this offer in the first half of 1942, and both instituted flat supplements of $5 a month for all pensioners. Ontario followed with a supplement of 15 percent of the actual pension paid, that is, $3 a month for those receiving the maximum pension of $20 a month and correspondingly less for those on partial pension. Effective January 1, 1943, Manitoba paid a supplement of $1.25 a month, which it represented as its share of a $5 increase.[38] Saskatchewan adopted a similar policy in mid-1943, and Nova Scotia authorized a means-test supplement of up to $10 a month. The purpose of the latter was to fill the gap between the maximum pension of $240 a year and the maximum allowable income of $365 for those with little or no outside income. The limit on total income, including pension and supplement, remained at $365 so that where outside income exceeded $5 a *year*, the supplement was reduced accordingly.

The only provinces not paying supplements of some kind were Quebec, New Brunswick, and Prince Edward Island. Nevertheless, the fact that two-thirds of the provinces were paying them did not reduce the pressure on the federal government to increase the basic pension. Trade unions, churches, and other organizations, as well as newspaper editorials and letters to the editor, were clamouring for such a step.[39] So also were members of parliament, including many Liberal back-benchers.[40] On top of this, several provinces were intent on deflecting the pressure on themselves to Ottawa. Manitoba tried to organize what amounted to a lobby of provincial governments. Acting on a resolution adopted by the Legislature in February, 1943,[41] Attorney General James McLenaghan wrote to all the provinces, proposing that they should join in a campaign to persuade the federal government to increase the maximum pension to $25 a month.[42] The joint campaign did not get off the ground, partly because Quebec wanted to include a proposal to reduce the age of eligibility to sixty-five, but ultimately all provinces made their own individual representations. Ilsley finally relented. On July 24, 1943, just before Parliament adjourned for the year, he advised the House that the pension would be increased to $25 a month by order in council under the War Measures Act.[43] The ceiling on allowable income ($365 a year) was left unchanged until 1944 when a further order in council increased it to $425, thus restoring the previous margin between the maxima of pension and allowable income.[44] All provinces quickly accepted both changes. Manitoba, however, cancelled its supplement of $1.25 a month, except in the few cases where cancellation would have resulted in reduction of total benefits. Ontario continued to pay its maximum supplement on the basis of 15 percent of $20, and Nova Scotia did not increase the ceiling on allowable income for its means-test supplement, thus in effect reducing the maximum supplement to $65 a year. On the other hand, the Saskatchewan supplement was increased to $3 a month in 1945, while British Columbia and Alberta continued their $5 supplements.

Notwithstanding Ilsley's revision of 1943–44, demands for improvement of the plan increased in intensity as the years passed, both in Parliament and throughout the country. Opinion polls conducted during the period, which are summarized in table 11, indicate strong public support for both an increased pension and a reduced qualifying age. The case for increasing the pension was particularly strong, since both the cost of living and standard of living were rising in the country: the

TABLE 11
PERCENTAGES OF SURVEY SAMPLES IN FAVOUR OF
SPECIFIED PENSION AMOUNTS AND QUALIFYING AGES

	Nov. 1946	Jan. 1949	Apr. 1950	Feb. 1951
AMOUNT:				
$30 or less	13	5	1	1
$31–40	21	11	11	10
$41–50	27	29	29	27
Over $50	34	47	52	53
No opinion	5	8	7	9
AGE:				
60 or less	45		39	
65	41		45	
70	6		6	
No opinion	8		10	

SOURCES: Canadian Institute of Public Opinion, releases dated Nov. 20, 23, 1946; Jan. 22, 1949; Apr. 15, 1950; Feb. 24, 1951.

cost of living index (1935–39 = 100) rose from 119.5 in 1945 to 166.5 in 1950; per capita personal income (in 1949 constant dollars) from $755 to $1,130. Statutory action would in any case be necessary sooner or later to prevent the maximum pension from reverting to $20, since the increase to $25 had been authorized under the War Measures Act. An amending act of 1947 increased the maximum to $30 a month, and in 1949, on the eve of a federal election, a further amendment increased it to $40.

The 1947 act also modified some of the restrictive features of the plan. The following were dropped altogether: the exclusion of aliens; the provision relating to the transfer to the pension authority of the pensioner's interest in his home; and the requirement of residence in the province where application was made for at least five years immediately preceding commencement of benefits. The requirement of residence in Canada for twenty years immediately preceding commencement of benefits was relaxed to permit the applicant to offset nonresidence during those years by prior residence equal to at least twice the period of nonresidence.[45] In addition, the maximum allowable income, including pension, was increased to $600 a year for a pensioner who was single or widowed, $1,080 for one who was married, and $1,200 for

95

one whose spouse was blind.[46] These maxima were not changed when the pension was increased in 1949.

The provinces were not consulted about the amendments of 1947 and 1949. Nor were they bound to accept them since they had valid agreements with the federal government under the old set-up. Indeed, they were ostensibly given a freedom of action in relation to benefits which they had not previously enjoyed. As the amending statutes were worded, the federal government undertook reimbursement for 75 percent of the cost of pensions up to $30 or, in 1949, $40 a month, subject to the designated limits on allowable income. The provinces were free to set the pension at whatever level they wished, though they would not be reimbursed beyond the prescribed maximum.[47] In practice, however, it was politically inexpedient for them to provide anything less than that maximum. All provinces except Nova Scotia accepted the 1947 act from the moment it became effective (May 1), and Nova Scotia got into line on August 1. In 1949 the only province which delayed was Newfoundland, where the $30 pension had come into force only on April 1, 1949 (the date of the province's entry into Confederation), but the $40 rate became effective there on April 1, 1950.[48]

A revealing political byplay took place between the Quebec and federal governments over the 1947 and 1949 increases. In 1947 the province's Social Welfare and Youth Minister Paul Sauvé sent a circular to all old age and blind pensioners, advising them that because of the generosity of the Union Nationale government, their pensions were being increased by $5 a month. National Health and Welfare Minister Paul Martin wanted to reply calling attention to the more significant federal role in the increase. Under the practice current at the time, however, pension pay lists submitted by the provinces to the federal government did not include addresses. Steps were taken to get this information, but the Quebec department delayed until a reply by Martin would have been pointless. In 1949 Sauvé again circularized the pensioners, claiming full credit for the Union Nationale for the $10 increase of that year. This time Martin was ready. He sent out his own circular pointing out that the increase had resulted from federal legislation and that the federal government was contributing 75 percent of the cost. Sauvé replied in a further circular dismissing Martin's claim as political propaganda and asserting that old age pensions had come to Quebec in 1936 solely because of the Union Nationale.[49]

In 1947 Nova Scotia increased the maximum income permitted for its means-test supplement from $365 to $425 a year, thus bringing it belatedly into line with the maximum established in 1944 for the basic pension. When, however, the maximum benefit of $30 was accepted by

96

the province a few months later, the supplement was again limited *ipso facto* to $65 a year, while the further benefit increase to $40 in 1949 wiped it out. In 1947 Ontario replaced its 15 percent supplement with a formula under which up to $10 a month could be paid in exceptional circumstances (the main such circumstance being the high rents paid by many pensioners in urban areas), and abandoned supplements altogether when it accepted the increase in the basic pension to $40 in 1949. About four months before Ontario abandoned supplements, it revised its formula to provide a supplement of 8.33 percent of the actual pension paid, plus an amount of up to $7.50 a month for exceptional circumstances. Legislation passed in the spring of 1949 in Manitoba authorized the province to pay half the difference between the pensioner's annual income (including the basic pension which was then $30 a month) and $480. After the basic pension was raised to $40, this provision became meaningless and it was repealed in 1950. After the increase to $30 in 1947, Saskatchewan suspended its supplement. In 1948 it instituted a new means-test supplement of up to $5 a month subject to essentially the same income limits as applied under the federal statute, but reduced this to $2.50 after the 1949 increase. On the other hand, the flat $5 supplement in British Columbia was increased to $10 in 1947, and in Alberta it was increased to $7 in 1948, $7.50 in 1949, and $10 in 1950. It remained at $10 in both provinces for the life of the 1949 plan. A $10 supplement was instituted in the Yukon in 1949, shortly after the federal plan came into effect there.

3. ADMINISTRATION OF THE PLAN

When the 1927 act was passed, there had been no accumulated experience in welfare administration at the federal level except in regard to veterans' programs. This was advanced as a reason for involving the provinces in the pension plan. For example, a leading cabinet minister, C. A. Dunning, said:

> The administration of a completely effective scheme, supported one hundred per cent by the federal government, would mean the setting up of a complete new piece of federal machinery. . . . On the other hand there is scarcely a province in the Dominion which is not at the present time administering, directly or through the municipality, some analagous undertaking . . . such as the mothers' allowance scheme, or . . . the various child protection acts.[50]

As it turned out, this confidence in the ability of the provinces to take the administration of the plan in their stride was unduly optimistic.

Welfare administration was underdeveloped at the provincial level too. The sketchiness of the early regulations and the need to amend and amplify them frequently indicated how little both federal and provincial officials appreciated the problems they were about to face. Even such apparently straightforward matters as the determination of age, nationality, and residence posed many difficulties in practice.[51]

British Columbia, the first province to adopt the pension plan, entrusted administration to its Workmen's Compensation Board, and both Manitoba and Alberta followed that example. The previous experience of these boards, however, was not particularly relevant to a means-test pension plan. Their role was to adjudicate claims on the basis of a relatively well-developed body of rules and precedents. The administration of means-test pensions required a welfare, rather than a judicial, orientation. As befitted their quasi-judicial function, the boards were independent of the governments of the day, but this was practical in the case of workmen's compensation only because the substantial funds disbursed came from assessments on employers levied by the boards themselves. The funds required for old age pensions were a charge on the regular budgets of the provincial and federal governments. It was thus impossible to avoid the inherently political problems involved in cabinet responsibility for spending and in financial relations between levels of government. The attempt to do so created conflicts which in turn gave rise to caution and rigidity in administration.

Ontario, when it entered the plan in 1929, adopted the device of a commission which was solely concerned with old age pensions, and this became the standard pattern of provincial administration in time. Quebec and the maritime provinces established these specialized commissions or boards when they entered the plan, and Alberta, British Columbia, and Manitoba shifted administration to such bodies in 1940, 1943, and 1945, respectively. Saskatchewan was unique in that it accepted the principle of departmental responsibility in pension administration. A separate commission had the advantage of permitting the administrators to specialize, but it also perpetuated the illusion that pension administration could be independent of the political framework in which it operated. As provincial involvement in welfare programs increased and the services required to administer them grew in size and professionalization, there was a tendency to integrate pension administration into general welfare administration. The commissions were not formally abolished, but more and more they became part of the larger structure. Complementing this process was the transfer of federal administration in 1945 to the then recently established Department of National Health and Welfare. The emerging welfare orientation in administration was reflected in a thorough-going revision of the regulations in 1947,[52] following a meeting of the Interprovincial Board (only the fourth meeting in nearly twenty years) in November, 1946.

That, however, was a late development. Throughout most of the history of the plan, the federal side of administration was essentially negative in its influence. Initially the task was entrusted to the Department of Labour, mainly because the notion persisted that pensions were basically a labour measure. Since substantial sums of federal money were being spent, the federal financial control officers necessarily became involved. It was not long before the auditor general noted lack of uniformity in the determination of income and questioned the legality of some of the payments he had come across.[53] The onset of the depression, which resulted in a decline in both government revenues and opportunities for the aged to earn outside income, gave rise to growing concern that expenditures might get out of control. This was intensified by the government's decision of 1931 to increase its share of the cost from 50 to 75 percent.[54] Since the auditor general's function was confined to postaudit, the most he could do was to call attention to doubtful practices and expenditures long after they had occurred. Moreover, his staff was inadequate for anything but limited spot-checking.

Therefore, the amending act of 1931, which increased the federal share of the pension, also made payment conditional on a province's conceding the right of the federal authorities "to order an examination, inspection and audit of all expenditures of such moneys in the province." Pressed by the comptroller of the Treasury, the Department of Labour gradually built up a field staff to examine provincial accounts before federal reimbursement was made. The departmental files of the period consist in large measure of inspection reports on administrative inconsistencies and questionable payments. The difficulties were partly due to genuine differences of interpretation of the regulations, but they arose even more out of the fact that financial control procedures at the time were less adequate provincially than federally. In the event of disputes which could not be resolved by discussion, the federal authorities had the last word, because refusal by them to approve an account eliminated federal reimbursement. Occasionally a provincial government would accept responsibility for such an account, but usually its administrators were at pains to ensure that their errors were on the side of safety.

The preoccupation with financial control was formalized in 1935 when administration was transferred to the Department of Finance. In an effort to produce some order out of the chaos in which it felt itself engulfed, that department called the third meeting of the Interprovincial Board in 1937.[55] All aspects of the administration of the plan were reviewed under the careful guidance of federal officials. The result was a series of unanimous recommendations for revision of the regulations. These were implemented federally by an order in council which took effect early in 1938.[56] To an extent, the new regulations aimed at greater uniformity and consistency in administration, but the basic motivation was economy.

Three decisions taken at the conference were particularly significant in their long-run effect in undermining public confidence in the plan. First, a previous regulation, which had merely left it to provincial authorities to take all steps necessary to ensure that pensions were paid only to those entitled to them, was replaced by one specifically requiring a thorough investigation before grant of a pension and annual investigations thereafter. This undoubtedly resulted in more effective sifting out of unwarranted and fraudulent claims, but it also meant that legitimate claimants were made to feel the full indignity of the means test. Second, there was a renewed attempt to make adult children accept what were regarded as their proper filial obligations. Early in the 1930s much resentment had been caused by vigorous efforts to enforce provincial parents' maintenance legislation. Some provincial authorities had become disillusioned with this policy,[57] and a new tack was now taken. The regulations were amended to provide explicitly what had only been implicit before, that contributions which children could be reasonably expected to make were to be included as income whether or not they were actually made. Third, the Finance Department pressed the provinces to take more effective control of the property of pensioners so that full advantage could be taken of the power to make recoveries from estates. Actually, recoveries were negligible over the years,[58] but the mere existence of the power and the exercise of it from time to time were a constant source of grievance to the aged, even to the point where some who could qualify for pension did not apply.

The Finance Department averred that it was interested in promoting equality of treatment of pensioners and applicants. That, however, depended largely on how the means test was administered, and here the department was handicapped by the stress placed from the beginning on provincial responsibility for administration. The department was ready to advise but it did not believe that it could interfere beyond insisting on proper accounting for the expenditure of federal funds. It could not even advise its government to amend the regulations without provincial consent, since once an agreement had been entered into and an administrative plan worked out, they could be altered only by renegotiation. In any case, every detail could not be covered by regulation, and the provinces varied substantially in such matters as the evaluation of free board and lodging and income from property.[59] Even on points specifically covered by the regulations, considerable scope for administrative discretion remained.

There is reason to believe that the means test was more rigorously applied in some provinces than in others. For example, figures prepared by the Department of National Health and Welfare for the joint committee of 1950 show that in September, 1949, the proportion of pensioners receiving the maximum pension was well below 50 percent in all three of the traditional maritime provinces. It ranged from 70 to 80 percent in the other provinces, except in Newfoundland where it was 92.4 percent. The department's memorandum commented: "It seems difficult to escape the conclusion that the reason for the small proportion of full pensioners in these [maritime] provinces is attributable to the differences in the manner in which pension authorities . . . apply the general means-testing procedures."[60] There are also some indications that the means test was severely applied in Ontario. Throughout the 1940s the proportion of the seventy-and-over age group in that province receiving pensions (full or partial) averaged about one-third, a substantially lower figure than in any other province. No doubt the difference arose in part from the relatively high level of nonpension income enjoyed by Ontario's aged. That this is not the whole story, however, is suggested by the fact that year by year Ontario's percentage of pensioners to total population in the age group was from four to eight points lower than British Columbia's.[61] On the other hand, Newfoundland, after its entry into the plan, seems to have followed the most liberal interpretation of the means test of all the provinces.

Chapter Six

Universal Pensions, 1951

MANY OF THE TRADE UNIONS, private members of parliament, and others who had been pressing for public pensions did not regard the 1927 plan as satisfactory, and it was not long before they were advocating changes in it. Reduction of the age of eligibility was a leading objective of reformers in the 1930s. Such reduction was seen both as providing some security for the many workers who were being forced into retirement before seventy and as an inducement to older workers to retire voluntarily and make jobs available for younger people. Other features of the plan which came in for attack were: attachment of pensioners' property, recoveries from estates, pursuit of children to support their parents when they could hardly support themselves, residence requirements, discrimination against aliens of long residence, the narrow limits on outside income, and the amount of the pension. The attacks, however, were sporadic and uncoordinated. It could fairly be said, in the words of a writer of an earlier period,[1] that they were the work of "enthusiasts" and "partisans." The pension plan was not a leading political issue in the 1930s, except in provinces where its very adoption was at stake. The depression brought other matters more forcefully to governmental notice.

It was the economic expansion of the 1940s which gradually lifted pensions back up the scale of priorities. As we saw in chapter 5, section 2, the main government action in that decade related to the amount of the pension. It would be wrong to conclude that this was the only matter on which action was demanded. Almost everyone who advocated a higher pension proposed a lower qualifying age. Sixty-five was often suggested, but there were advocates of sixty, as well as sixty-five for men and sixty for women. The means test also came under growing attack, in terms of specific grievances and in principle. This test had, in fact, two consequences which were hard to justify. First, close and re- curring scrutiny of a pensioner's personal affairs was humiliating, and to humiliation was added fear that such limited property as he might have would be attached—a bitter blow to a person schooled in the market ethos. Second, individual provision for old age, unless it was substantial, was largely self-defeating because its main effect was to reduce or eliminate the public pension. Belief in the efficacy of the spirit of thrift and self-reliance was central to the market ethos and had been reinforced by pioneer experience. The means test was seen as dis- couraging that spirit.

Increases in the amount of the pension did not involve any real change in the 1927 plan, but merely adjusted it in some measure to the rising prices, living standards, and government revenues of the period. A reduction in the qualifying age posed a more serious problem for it would bring in a whole new group, while abolition of the means test required a complete restructuring of the plan. The solution finally adopted was a hybrid program which eliminated the means test for the seventy-and-over group and introduced a new means-test plan for the sixty-five to sixty-nine group. Section 1 describes the program, and the succeeding sections consider the circumstances which led to its adoption.

1. THE 1951 PROGRAM

The Old Age Security and Old Age Assistance Acts of 1951 provided the statutory basis of the new program. There were two sessions of Parliament in that year, the Old Age Assistance Act being passed at the first and the Old Age Security Act at the second. Priority was given to the former because it involved participation by the provinces, and the federal government wanted to give them as much time as possible to adjust to it. The two acts, however, were regarded as constituting a single program, and both came into force on January 1, 1952. Two important features were taken over from the old 1927 plan as it had been revised in 1947 and 1949: the basic pension remained at $40 a month, and the residence requirement continued to be the twenty years immediately preceding commencement of benefits for the means-test pension (approval of the application for the universal pension). As in the old plan after the 1947 amendment, absences during the twenty years could be offset by prior residence of at least twice the total length of absence, except that for the universal pension residence in Canada for at least one year immediately preceding approval of the application became an absolute requirement. The exclusion of Indians, which had been a feature of the 1927 plan from beginning to end, was dropped. In the case of the universal pension only, the provision for suspending benefits during absences from Canada was relaxed to permit payment of back benefits of up to three months if the pensioner returned to the country within six months.

The Old Age Security Act established a universal pension at age seventy subject only to the residence requirement. The federal government accepted full responsibility for finance and administration. A special levy, called the "old age security tax," was imposed to cover costs. Actually, it was a composite of three taxes: on the manufacturer's selling price or duty paid value of all items covered by the federal sales tax, and on the taxable incomes of corporations and individuals. The rate was initially set at 2 percent for all three components—which led the finance minister to call the combined levy the "2-2-2 formula"—but there was a ceiling of $60 a year on the tax on personal income, that is, it applied to only the first $3,000 of taxable income. Receipts were paid into an "old age security fund," which was kept as a separate account in the consolidated revenue fund, and benefits were paid out of this special fund. The minister of finance was authorized to make "temporary loans" to the fund if necessary.

The Old Age Assistance Act authorized the federal government to contribute to provincially administered means-test pensions for those who were at least sixty-five but less than seventy years of age. The basic principle of the 1927 plan was continued, but the limits on allowable income were raised to $720 a year for single and widowed pensioners, $1,200 for those who were married, and $1,320 for those whose spouses were blind. Thus the margin between maximum pension and maximum allowable income was restored to the level which had been established in 1947 but had been reduced by the failure to raise the income limits when the pension was increased to $40 in 1949. The discretion given to the provinces in 1947 with regard to the amount of the pension, referred to in chapter 5, section 2, was extended to the income limits and qualifying age. In other words, the provinces were free to make their own determinations, but federal contributions were not available beyond $40 a month and the specified income limits nor for pensions paid at an earlier age than sixty-five. The federal share of the cost was cut from 75 to 50 percent, but this reduction imposed no hardship on the provinces. Rather, their financial obligations were lessened, because the sixty-five to sixty-nine age group was smaller than the seventy-and-over group and contained within it a considerably smaller percentage of people who could qualify for means-test pensions even under higher income limits.[2] Regulations based essentially on those in effect in the final years of the 1927 plan covered administrative details. An advisory board representative of the provinces was established to perform the role of the old Interprovincial Board. Costs were defrayed out of general revenues, federal and provincial.

2. EARLY DISCUSSIONS OF ALTERNATIVE DESIGNS

Basically, there are two possible alternatives to a means-test plan: contributory and universal pensions. As noted in chapter 4, section 4, the contributory principle was rejected in the 1920s for both administrative and constitutional reasons. Nevertheless, Mackenzie King himself believed the 1927 act was essentially an interim measure which would have to be replaced by a contributory plan leading to comprehensive social insurance. In ensuing years a growing body of opinion favoured the contributory principle.

R. B. Bennett never lost his faith in the superiority of that principle. In 1926 he suggested subsidization of government annuities as a way of avoiding the constitutional problem (see chapter 4, section 4), and he pursued the idea after he became prime minister. A confidential memorandum prepared for him on November 9, 1934, outlined in detail a scheme for replacing the 1927 plan over a period of twenty or twenty-five years.[3] It proposed both a carrot and a stick to induce people to buy annuities. On the one hand, what was called a "bonus annuity" would be given to every purchaser of a deferred annuity, while on the other hand, the maximum pension under the 1927 act would be gradually reduced until no pension was left. This proposal involved a formula which was eventually rejected as too complex.[4] Instead, Bennett reverted to his position of 1926. A bill was prepared to provide a flat bonus of 25 percent for both government annuities and private pension plans. Though set in type,[5] the bill was not introduced. In a period of mass unemployment, revision of the pension plan was of low priority. The main social security measure in Bennett's "new deal" legislation of 1935 was the Employment and Social Insurance Act which, in spite of the comprehensive sound of its title, was primarily designed to establish an unemployment insurance plan and a national employment service. The act was declared *ultra vires*,[6] but the King government secured a constitutional amendment which made possible the Unemployment Insurance Act of 1940.

Permanent government officials were uncertain about the effectiveness of subsidized annuities,[7] but they were in no doubt at all that the existing means-test pension was unsatisfactory. This position came out clearly in a confidential brief prepared by the Finance Department for the Rowell-Sirois Commission and presented on December 23, 1938.[8] The lack of uniformity in administration and the difficulty of securing an acceptable degree of control over costs were outlined in detail. In addition, the brief reflected growing concern within the department over the long-term implications of the plan. On the basis of projections regarding the aging of the population only, and without allowance for possible liberalization of the plan, it was estimated that the annual cost of benefits (federal and provincial) would reach $62 million in 1951, $82 million in 1961, and $93 million in 1971. In the 1930s these appeared to be stupendous sums, and the brief raised the possibility that "any non-contributory scheme . . . eventually may reach the point where it may actually endanger the finances of the nation." Departmental officers were convinced that the cost factor created an urgent need to overcome the constitutional barrier to a contributory plan.[9]

Outside government circles, the Canadian Manufacturers' Association (CMA) was an early and consistent advocate of the contributory principle. It manifested only an academic interest in the work of the 1924 committee and even in the 1926 and 1927 bills, but when the 1927 bill became law, the association examined it more closely. An article of February, 1928, in its official journal, *Industrial Canada*, raised the spectre of rising costs,[10] and a report of its Industrial Relations Committee to the 1929 annual meeting condemned the 1927 plan as an example of "the non-contributory, deserving poor type of legislation" which had been a "comparative failure" wherever it had been tried because it put "a premium on thriftlessness and fraud." The proper alternative was "the contributory system which should serve the triple purpose of keeping down the expense, eliminating the incentive to thrift-lessness and stimulating, instead of sapping, self-reliance and independence."[11] In addition, the committee raised a specific objection to the 1927 plan which was of particular interest to the CMA: employers providing private pension plans were being discriminated against, since benefits under their plans merely served to offset entitlement to public pensions.[12] Few private plans were in operation at the time, but it was a leading objective of the CMA to encourage them as a means of improving employer-employee relations.

It has been noted in chapter 5, section 1, that in 1932 the Quebec Social Insurance Commission expressed a strong preference in principle for contributory pensions. Its views on the subject were both forthright and conventional:

[The 1927 plan] in many cases puts a premium on lack of foresight, negligence and laziness, accustoms the individual to count on the state alone, prevents the development of a spirit of thrift and is in danger by its method of leading to abuses and frauds which are not

107

always easy to detect. On the other hand, the insurance system which is contributory and obligatory stimulates, from an early age, the person who will later benefit thereby, to economize and to take thought for his old age.[13]

The Rowell-Sirois Commission was sufficiently impressed by the information presented to it by the Finance Department that it too was convinced of the need for a contributory plan. Both commissions were satisfied that such a plan was feasible only at the federal level. The Quebec commission urged its provincial government to take the initiative in stimulating the other provinces to make a joint request for federal action.[14] The Rowell-Sirois Commission was more circumspect. It argued that a contributory plan should be contingent on adoption of its recommendations for "a general reorganization of the tax structure to shift the emphasis from taxes on costs to taxes on income." The plan could then "be fitted into the general tax structure more equitably to workers and employers alike and with less danger of adversely affecting the national income." The report noted, however, that means-test pensions would have to be continued for an indefinite period even if a contributory plan were adopted, and it expressed "no strong objection to continuance of provincial administration" of those pensions.[15]

In contrast to the diversified body of influential opinion supporting contributory pensions, the voices tending in the direction of the universal principle were tentative and weak. The Trades and Labor Congress opposed contributions on the ground that most wage earners could not afford them.[16] It did not, however, go the whole way to universal pensions. Instead, it proposed a large increase in the amount of outside income permitted under the means test—its most frequent suggestion being $1,000 a year compared with the existing figure of $125.[17] The Cooperative Commonwealth Federation (CCF) alone explicitly advocated universal pensions, but it was a fledgling party which obtained less than 10 percent of the vote and elected only seven members in the general election of 1935. Considerable internal debate characterized the development of the CCF's position on pensions. Its first major policy declaration, popularly called the Regina Manifesto of 1933, spoke in general terms of "insurance covering illness, accident, old age and unemployment." The 1934 convention tried to give greater content to the social security plank. It was unable to come to a firm decision as between the contributory and universal principles, but in February, 1935, the National Council resolved the issue in favour of the latter.[18] At the 1936 and 1937 conventions attention was focused on the specific question of old age pensions, and the decision was in favour of a universal pension of an "adequate" amount at age sixty. A. A. Heaps, by then a CCF M.P., had already put a similar idea before the House of Commons in a resolution moved in February, 1936, calling for "retirement allowances" which would have involved an unspecified retirement test.[19] Finance Minister C. A. Dunning heaped scorn on it. Seizing upon a suggestion by Heaps that $50 a month was "adequate," Dunning claimed that the proposal would cost $500 million a year, although Heaps had argued that costs would be reduced substantially by the fact that many people would not retire at sixty. He admitted that the number would still be high, but he argued that a massive injection of purchasing power was precisely what the economy needed.[20] Even the stalwart champions of pensions in the old parties refused to support the resolution. T. L. Church dubbed it "state socialism" which would impose an intolerable burden on industry, and A. W. Neill charged that its only purpose was to embarrass members.[21] In an effort to broaden support for his resolution, Heaps watered it down in subsequent sessions to ask merely that the age of eligibility be reduced under the existing plan.[22]

3. REEMERGENCE OF PENSIONS AS A PRIORITY ISSUE

The greatest war in history, following hard after the greatest depression in history, created a strong sentiment in the western world—evidenced by the Atlantic Charter of August, 1941, and the Declaration of the United Nations of January, 1942—that there could be no return to the conditions of the 1930s. At the intellectual and policy-making level, the Keynesian revolution in economics promised the means whereby popular aspirations for a better world could be realized. The economist's image of the economic world was basically altered, including traditional assumptions regarding the efficacy of political intervention in socioeconomic life. Governments were now seen to have a major potentiality and responsibility for promoting economic growth and full employment and for providing wide-ranging social security. New methods to achieve these ends included income maintenance plans as a means, among other things, of maintaining purchasing power in the down-phase of the cycle. Thus, Keynesianism served as a critical mediating agent between the antagonistic impulses of the market ethos and the needs of the urban-industrial society.

In the social security field, the stress was on the integration of existing measures into comprehensive, coordinated programs covering all the vicissitudes of industrial society. A trend in that direction had already started in some countries before the war. New Zealand's Social Security Act of 1938 was of special interest in Canada, where it was often cited by reformers as worthy of imitation.[23] In 1942 the principle of comprehensiveness received worldwide publicity upon the publication of the

Beveridge Report in the United Kingdom.[24] Canada received its own study in the Marsh Report published early in 1943.[25] Marsh differentiated between what he called "universal risks," the category into which old age pensions fell, and "employment risks." Flat-rate benefits were proposed for the former, the purpose being to establish a basic minimum which individuals could supplement as their circumstances permitted and their preferences decreed. The report was not in the main stream of government policy-making, but it was a well-researched and reasoned study which propounded in specifically Canadian terms the rising doctrine of overarching social security. Canadians in increasing numbers were ready to make that doctrine the subject of serious public debate.

I attempt in what follows to disentangle the main threads of the voluminous discussions of social security which took place in the conventions, publications, and briefs of organized groups, in Parliament, and in the press, particularly as those discussions related to the narrower question of old age pensions. The inherent difficulty of this task is compounded by the fact that the discussions were characterized by substantial confusion of terms. For example, "social insurance" (widely used at the time) meant different things to different people. At the extremes, it conveyed the idea of (a) benefits which were directly related to ("purchased by") premiums, and (b) a guarantee to the entire population of a basic income in (insurance against) adversity. A related confusion arose in regard to "contributory." Some used it in the sense in which it was defined in chapter 1, as designating a plan in which receipt of benefits is conditional on prior contributions. Others merely had in mind the financing of benefits by taxes earmarked for the purpose. My taxonomy distinguishes between these two uses by classifying as "universal" any non-means-test plan in which contributions are not a condition of benefits, regardless of the particular method chosen to finance it. That distinction was not clearly drawn in the discussions of the 1940s, but in my summary I will designate as "universal" any proposals which fit my definition even though the advocates themselves may have described them as "contributory." Not unexpectedly, there was some inconsistency in the positions of the leading protagonists of differing points of view. For the sake of brevity, I have on the whole confined myself to their basic positions, at the cost of some oversimplification.

Vertical redistribution of income effected by a pension plan is determined in significant measure by the method chosen to finance it. It is not possible to relate these effects entirely to the broad distinction between contributory and universal plans. For example, a contributory plan with flat-rate benefits financed by earnings-related contributions will result in substantial downward redistribution, while a universal plan financed by regressive taxes can conceivably have the opposite effect. In most cases, however, actual proposals in Canada for contributory plans would have severely restricted downward distribution. Usually these proposals envisaged both benefits and contributions as being earnings related or, to put it another way, they were based in some measure on "insurance" principles in the first of the uses of that term mentioned above. On the other hand, the advocates of universal pensions usually had in mind, in varying degrees, redistribution favouring the lower income groups. They proposed flat-rate benefits financed by proportional or progressive taxes. Where they considered it expedient to talk of "insurance" to justify the payment of benefits "as of right," their use of the term approximated the second of the above meanings.

By the 1940s the Trades and Labor Congress was still the largest labour central in Canada, but it was no longer in the same dominant position. After the split in the trade union movement in the United States, it reluctantly expelled the CIO unions in Canada. In 1940 these joined with a small labour central called the All-Canadian Congress of Labour to form the Canadian Congress of Labour (CCL). The Confédération des Travailleurs Catholiques du Canada (CTCC) had a growing membership in Quebec. In 1945 the membership of unions affiliated to or chartered by the three centrals was: TLC, 312,391; CCL, 244,750; and CTCC, 68,205.[26]

The CCL was the most radical of the three centrals. Its social philosophy was similar to that of the CCF, which it endorsed in 1943 as "the political arm of labour." At its founding convention in 1940, it called for "social security in all its forms, in sickness, at work and in old age," a proposal it repeated and elaborated on throughout the 1940s.[27] The TLC moved in the same direction in 1942, asking that "old age, sickness and incapacity security legislation be enacted by the Dominion government."[28] By 1948 it had broadened this to a proposal for a national social security plan to provide "health, accident, hospitalization benefits, old age pensions, mothers' allowances, widows' allowances and such other social security measures which [sic] are necessary" including "cash benefits to maintain income during illness."[29] The CTCC, however, viewed with trepidation the idea of implementing comprehensive social security on a national basis. "How can this central power respect all that is distinctive with us: family, traditions, civil laws, etc.?" its president asked at its 1943 convention. He argued for concurrent provincial legislation as a condition of making federal social security legislation effective in any province.[30]

The TLC abandoned its earlier opposition to the contributory principle as it began to visualize old age pensions within the framework of comprehensive social security. In 1941 it suggested that "a contributory retirement scheme be incorporated in the Old Age Pensions Act,"[31] and in subsequent years its numerous resolutions and representations on social security in general and old age pensions in particular usually proposed tripartite contributions. The CTCC took a similar position.[32] The CCL, on the other hand, favoured universality. In the specific case of pensions it proposed that "the means test of eligibility be abolished and that pensions be paid by virtue of right."[33] Its official journal argued that the government should provide a basic pension without a means test and that this "should be supplemented by an industrial pension."[34]

To the political parties, too, social security and old age pensions were of growing interest in the 1940s. The Conservative party fell on evil days after the decisive defeat of the Bennett government in 1935.[35] The low point was reached in the York South by-election of February, 1942, when Arthur Meighen, who had been resurrected from the Senate to lead the party again, was defeated by a CCF candidate in his bid for a seat in the House of Commons. Even before that debacle, new men had been trying to revivify the party, and such efforts were now intensified. A "thinkers' conference" was held in Port Hope, Ontario, in September, 1942, to map out new policy approaches. A leadership convention followed in December, at which Premier John Bracken of Manitoba was brought into the fold as the new leader and the party's name was changed on his insistence to Progressive Conservative. The party continued to be an outspoken champion of private enterprise, but it also conceded that government has a significant role in stimulating the economy and providing a floor of social security. In the latter field the Port Hope conference proposed a "unified system" embracing a wide range of specific measures. Included in these was contributory "retirement insurance," with the further proposal that the existing old age pensions be increased and paid at a lower age "until such time as the retirement insurance scheme becomes fully operative."[36] Resolutions embodying this idea were adopted by both the leadership convention of 1942 and that of 1948 (at which Premier George Drew of Ontario succeeded Bracken as leader), and formed part of the election programs of 1945 and 1949.[37]

The CCF, which had enjoyed only minimal success in the 1935 and 1940 elections, began to gain strength in the more radical climate of opinion of the war period: a Canadian Institute of Public Opinion release of September 30, 1943, showed that, excluding the uncommitted, 29 percent of the respondents supported the CCF compared with 28 percent for each of the Liberals and Conservatives and 14 percent for others. The CCF responded by adopting a comprehensive new policy statement, Victory and Reconstruction, at its convention of 1942, followed by a CCF Federal Election Manifesto in 1944, revisions of those statements in 1946, and a First Term Program in 1948.[38] Though there were changes in emphasis in these successive declarations, and between them and the earlier Regina Manifesto, the basic theme continued to be the building of a new society in which there would be more nearly equal sharing of the fruits of production. Stress was laid on economic planning to achieve maximum production and on redistribution of income. A major instrument in achieving the latter objective was to be "a comprehensive, integrated social security system," which was seen as essentially a responsibility of the federal government since it alone had the necessary "resources and taxing powers." Universality was to be the essence of the program. Benefits were to be paid "as a fundamental human right and free from humiliating means tests." A social security levy proportional to income was proposed to finance the program in part, with the balance being charged against general revenues.[39] In the specific matter of old age pension benefits, party policy crystallized in the late 1940s in favour of a universal pension of $50 a month at age sixty-five.

Within the government the leading advocate of comprehensive social security was Mackenzie King himself, who was satisfied that he had anticipated most of the Beveridge Report in *Industry and Humanity*, his own book of more than two decades earlier.[40] The 1943 Speech from the Throne expressed the belief that "a comprehensive national scheme of social insurance should be worked out at once, which will constitute a charter of social security for the whole of Canada," and in both the 1943 and 1944 sessions King personally moved for the establishment of House of Commons committees to examine and report on such a plan.[41] The committees confined their attention almost exclusively to physical fitness and health insurance, but behind the scenes intensive study of all aspects of postwar reconstruction, including social security, was being undertaken by a small, informal group of key ministers and civil servants.[42]

King was the dominant figure, but he relied heavily on four colleagues —Justice Minister Louis St. Laurent, Munitions and Supply (later Reconstruction) Minister C. D. Howe, Finance Minister J. L. Ilsley, and Brooke Claxton, King's parliamentary secretary who later became the first minister of national health and welfare. They in turn relied on a few senior civil servants—W. C. Clark (deputy minister of finance), W. A. Mackintosh (on loan from Queen's University), and D. A. "Sandy" Skelton (research adviser in the Bank of Canada) merit special mention in this regard—and on a somewhat changing but always small

113

aggregation of younger civil servants mainly in the Finance Department and Bank of Canada. Together these men constituted a cohesive though unstructured group in which channels of communication across hierarchical lines were open and informal, and well-qualified and highly motivated civil servants had a unique opportunity to have their views on long-term policy considered by the most influential men in the Cabinet.[43] As a group they were a major channel through which Keynesian economics was brought to bear on public policy-making in Canada.

The fruits of the group's work first emerged to public view in a comprehensive way in the fall of 1943 under circumstances to which I will now turn. After a smashing victory in the election of 1940, King unilaterally declared a political truce for the duration of the war. The Liberal party's national headquarters were closed and its organization disintegrated.[44] The consequences were strikingly revealed in August, 1943, when the Liberals lost four by-elections in one day. King promptly called a meeting of the Liberal Advisory Council to revitalize the party in terms of both organization and policy. Brooke Claxton and J. W. Pickersgill, then King's personal secretary, condensed the work already done within the government into fourteen policy resolutions, which were accepted by the council with little modification and became the basis for the Speech from the Throne and a substantial legislative program in the 1944 session.[45] The unifying principle of the new approaches was made explicit a year later in the essentially Keynesian White Paper on Employment and Income.[46] The only social security measure actually enacted in this period was the Family Allowances Act of 1944,[47] but the 1944 Speech from the Throne also held out hope "for federal assistance in a nation-wide system of health insurance, and for a national scheme of contributory old age pensions on a more generous basis than at present in operation."[48] The old conundrum continued in the case of pensions. Substantial improvement of benefits and broadening of coverage were considered to be financially feasible only in a contributory plan, but such a plan could not be undertaken by the federal government without a constitutional amendment. Nevertheless, the Liberal platform in the June, 1945, election focused exclusively on a contributory plan.[49]

The government was returned in that election, albeit with a bare majority of seats and only 41 percent of the vote. It was faced almost immediately with a federal-provincial conference scheduled for August. Federal authorities regarded this conference as of critical importance to postwar reconstruction, and extensive preparations were under way before the election was called. These preparations were entrusted to two parallel committees—one consisting of key ministers headed by St. Laurent, the other of key civil servants chaired by W. C. Clark at first and by W. A. Mackintosh after Clark became ill. The committees worked together as a single task force along the lines of the informal procedures of the past. Several months of hard work produced the so-called Green Books, consisting of the federal government's formal proposals to the provinces and several volumes of supporting material called Reference Books.[50] The key to the proposals, which had already been enunciated in the White Paper, was that the federal government "should take the initiative in the maintenance of employment and income."[51] This involved, among other things, continuance in a new form of the control over the major direct taxes which Ottawa had exercised as a wartime expedient under the tax rental agreements, federal assistance to the provinces through conditional grants in a wide variety of fields deemed to be important in the development of human and material resources, and increased federal involvement in social security. The last was justified as "maintaining and stabilizing . . . incomes which are largely spent on consumption and . . . contributing thereby to the health, welfare and productive capacity of the Canadian people and to their employment."[52]

Comprehensive social security was almost impossible to achieve on a unified nationwide basis because of constitutional obstacles and provincial occupancy of some important fields. The authors of the Green Books necessarily had to think in terms of specific areas in which federal involvement was considered to be particularly important. The Unemployment Insurance and Family Allowances Acts being now on the books, it was decided that the greatest remaining needs were to provide income maintenance for the employable unemployed not covered by unemployment insurance, to institute health insurance, and to remedy the admitted defects of the existing old age pension plan.[53] The Green Book social security proposals were confined to these three areas. Pensions posed the difficult problem of eliminating the objectionable features of the 1927 plan without imposing a financial burden which the government would not accept. The government's preference, strongly supported by the Finance Department, had always been for the contributory principle. It was considered inadvisable, however, to inject a constitutional issue directly into negotiations with the provinces, which would be delicate enough without it. The task force's solution was a two-level program which in principle was identical with that enacted into law six years later, the only difference being in the amount of the pension.[54] This was set at $40 in 1951—the figure then in effect under the 1927 plan. The Green Book proposal was for $30 compared with $25 then in effect under the 1927 plan. The program was a compromise which attempted to deal with both the means test and the high qualifying age, while limiting the burden on the federal treasury. It was estimated that the proposed universal pension for the seventy-and-over age group would cost about $200 million a year. Extension of that plan to the sixty-five to sixty-nine age group would increase the cost by about two-thirds. A shared cost means-test plan for that group would cost $34–$40 million of which the federal share would be $17–$20 million.[55] The differing treatment of the seventy-and-over and sixty-five to sixty-nine age groups was justified on the ground that most of the latter were still capable of supporting themselves by remunerative work.

A significant difference of opinion developed within the task force over the financing of the proposed pension and health insurance programs. Some members, especially in the junior ranks, argued that administrative complexity could be avoided and flexibility of fiscal policy enhanced if the necessary funds were simply provided out of general revenues. To others, such a method had the serious practical defect of offering no defence against endless political demands for increased benefits. In their view, costs could be controlled only if benefits were related to specific contributions which the public would recognize as necessarily increasing whenever benefits increased. This was the approach the ministers favoured, but they were reluctant to put it bluntly before the conference because of their desire to avoid constitutional disputes. The issue was finally resolved when Mackintosh simply drafted a form of words which appeared in print as follows:

> It is within the power of the Dominion to finance its share of the combined cost of health insurance and of old age pensions out of the Consolidated Revenue Fund.

> There are, however, some definite advantages, in terms of administrative efficiency, compliance and popular understanding of the plans, in introducing features more specifically contributory in nature.[56]

The Green Book proposals were presented to the provinces as a single package and, as such, failed to gain sufficient provincial acceptance to make it feasible to pursue them. The federal government now changed direction. It entered into agreements with most individual provinces in regard to both taxation and specific conditional grants, while the three social security proposals of the Green Books fell into the discard. Opposition M.P.'s and trade unions urged that they be revived, and T. C. Douglas, CCF premier of Saskatchewan, pressed repeatedly for a new conference on social security.[57] The government argued that it was not legitimate to separate these particular proposals from the larger framework in which they had been placed.[58] Whatever the validity of this argument, it did not still the demand for a better pension plan. The demographic processes referred to in chapter 2, section 2, were now well advanced, while private provision for old age security was still in its infancy. The 1927 plan offered no more than protection against complete destitution at an advanced age. Private members of all parties were clamouring for abolition of the means test, not to speak of a reduced age and increased benefits. They more than anyone bore the brunt of complaints both of pensioners and of those excluded from benefits. Many M.P.'s were not particular as to the method used to eliminate the means test as long as it was eliminated.

4. CHOICE OF DESIGN

The alternatives to the means test were becoming more clearly delineated. The Green Book pension proposal gave the CCF and CCL what they interpreted as the support of an official government document for their case for the universal principle, and they cited it frequently. In 1947 the CCF tried to build up public support for its position by circulating a petition asking for a universal pension of $50 a month at sixty-five, together with a cost of living supplement and a full range of medical and related services, all to be financed by the federal treasury. In tabling the petition in the House of Commons, party leader M. J. Coldwell claimed that it bore more than 250,000 signatures.[59] The government for its part reverted to its long-term position in support of the contributory principle. The resolution on social security adopted at the Liberal leadership convention of August, 1948, at which St. Laurent was elected to succeed Mackenzie King, was proposed by no less an authoritative government spokesman than Health and Welfare Minister Paul Martin. It affirmed the party's commitment to "a national program of social security," which would "include a steady extension of insurance on a contributory basis to protect all citizens from a temporary loss of income and to provide for their old age."[60] In December, 1948, shortly after his accession to the prime ministership, St. Laurent said: "The Liberal aim is a contributory scheme in which everyone can pay in something during his working years to help provide security for his old age." He later quoted this to the House of Commons as a definitive statement of government policy.[61] In 1949 Martin stated that "until such time as we have a contributory pension . . . it is irresponsible to talk about elimination of the means test."[62]

Business was becoming alarmed at the cost implications of the pension proposals then in the air. "The potential threat to corporation profits," said *Canadian Business*, the official journal of the Canadian Chamber of Commerce, "is particularly serious here, where the need for capital for future expansion is still great."[63] *Industry*, a CMA publication, referred to the pension issue from time to time in 1949 and 1950. It conceded that there was a strong public demand for improved old age security which no political party could afford to ignore. It argued that the government should at least make the public aware of the costs involved. This harmonized fully with the thinking of Prime Minister St. Laurent, whose pregovernmental experience had been as a corporation lawyer in Quebec. In April, 1951, he told the Reform Club of Montreal that "the State can only pay out what it receives in taxes paid by the citizens themselves."[64] In February, 1950, he said to the House of Commons: "When we have a direct contributory system, we will get what we pay for and pay for what we get. When suggestions are made that the old age pension be increased by 50 per cent, it will be something for consideration. It will mean, however, that the contributions will also have to be increased by 50 per cent."[65] Opinion polls of the period suggest that the public accepted the government's preference for a contributory plan. A release of the Canadian Institute of Public Opinion of April 19, 1950, showed 67 percent favouring and 20 percent opposing "a government sponsored, contributory old age pension plan, to which all wage and salary earners would contribute."

In the immediate situation, however, the differences between the advocates of the contributory and universal principles were less important than their agreement on one fundamental point, namely, that the means test was no longer tolerable. In the 1949 election all parties made its abolition an important point in their campaign propaganda. Capitalizing on the avuncular image of their new prime minister and on a high level of economic activity, the Liberals scored a landslide victory, winning just under 50 percent of the vote and 193 of the 262 seats. George Drew, the new Conservative leader, was so disheartened by this result that he failed to move the traditional nonconfidence amendment to the motion to adopt the Throne Speech in the first session of the new Parliament, which was held in the fall of 1949. The CCF filled the vacuum with a motion which focused attention exclusively on the means test.[66] The motion caused considerable embarrassment to many government supporters, especially in urban areas, who had stressed removal of the means test in their personal election campaigns. Some of them deliberately abstained from voting.[67] The government did not have to be convinced that it had to act soon on the issue. Its difficulty was that it did not have a concrete proposal to place before Parliament. To deal adequately with the complexities of a contributory plan required extensive study which had not been done. The government resorted to

118

Mackenzie King's device of 1924—a parliamentary committee, this time a joint committee of the Senate and House of Commons—which was established early in the 1950 session.[68]

Meanwhile, the Canadian Congress of Labour had launched a massive postcard campaign in an all-out effort to pressure the government into eliminating the means test.[69] The records of this campaign have been lost, but those who were active in it report that it was supported not only by CCL affiliates but by individuals and local unions in the TLC, CCF associations, church groups, and others. More than a million printed postcards asking for removal of the means test were distributed with instructions that they be signed and mailed to the signatories' local M.P.'s. In addition, advertisements were placed in leading newspapers with coupons bearing the same message. There is no way of estimating the number of cards and coupons mailed in, but it may well have been in the hundreds of thousands. M.P.'s of the time who were interviewed about the campaign differed in their opinions of its effect, but it is probably fair to say, as one Liberal M.P. put it, that "it at least reminded members that the means test had to go." This reminder came in the weeks immediately preceding the deliberations of the joint committee.

The committee—or rather several of its members—embarked on the task with both energy and seriousness of purpose. Since it was a joint committee, the chairmanship was nominally shared, but in fact the function was performed by Jean Lesage from the Commons, a rising young politician who was to become a federal minister and later premier of Quebec. The most active members were David Croll (Liberal), Stanley Knowles (CCF), and Donald Fleming (Conservative). The co-chairman from the Senate was J. H. King who, as acting minister of labour in 1926, had piloted the first old age pension bill through the House of Commons. Between April 3 and June 23, 1950, there were thirty-eight public hearings at which submissions filling 1,334 pages were heard, and fourteen private sessions in which a 112-page report was arrived at.[70] The Department of National Health and Welfare presented studies of the 1927 plan and of eight leading programs in other countries, while other departments provided information in their particular fields. Briefs, supplemented in most cases by oral presentations, were offered by the principal business, labour, and welfare organizations, as well as by four provincial governments, several individual welfare experts, and others. Only the agricultural interest was inadequately represented, the sole presentation coming from the Union Catholique des Cultivateurs of Quebec (UCC). All major submissions but two—from the UCC and from Charlotte Whitton, an independent welfare specialist at the time—attacked the means test and proposed

119

that it be either eliminated or reduced to a subsidiary role. The UCC and the Confédération des Travailleurs Catholiques du Canada, both Quebec-based organizations, favoured continuance of joint federal-provincial participation. The rest regarded pensions as primarily a federal responsibility.

As noted in section 2, most of those who had given more than passing thought to the pension issue in the 1930s favoured the contributory principle. An analysis of the submissions to the joint committee indicates a shift of informed opinion by 1950, reflecting a growing belief that relating benefits to contributions would pose unnecessarily complex administrative problems and would defer the abolition of the means test for too long. The Canadian Manufacturers' Association continued its long campaign for a contributory plan, proposing equal contributions by employers and employees, with optional coverage for the self-employed. Of the other major briefs, however, only that of the Canadian Association of Social Workers suggested that the basic pension should be contributory in nature, and what it proposed would have had redistributional effects not contemplated by the CMA. Specifically, it advocated flat-rate benefits with contributions based at least in part on ability to pay. The CMA wanted both contributions and benefits to be earnings related, with a "reasonable maximum" on both, arguing that such a plan would have a restraining influence on future pension demands. The two other peak business organizations which presented briefs considered the objective laudable but argued that there were easier ways of achieving it. In particular, the insurance industry, which at the time was successfully resisting expansion of the government annuities plan, as discussed in chapter 3, section 3, was not willing to have its efforts defeated by a compulsory contributory plan. If both contributory and means-test pensions were to be rejected, the only alternative was a universal plan, and most of the briefs advocated such a plan in principle. Important differences arose, however, over the major cost factors (amount of the pension and age of eligibility) and methods of finance. In general, the business organizations were on one side, the labour centrals on the other, and the Canadian Welfare Council in between.

Both the Canadian Chamber of Commerce and the Canadian Life Insurance Officers Association started from the assumption that there was a demand which could not be ignored for the state to provide a basic income in old age. They argued that the income to be provided should not be such as to undermine individual responsibility or overburden the economy. Therefore, the pension should be minimal—the CCC suggested $30 a month, while the life officers favoured a figure of that magnitude but indicated that they would not oppose $40—and it should not be paid before seventy. The labour centrals had a more expansive view of what constituted basic need. The Trades and Labor Congress proposed $65 a month at sixty-five, the Canadian Congress of Labour $50 at sixty-five, and the Confédération des Travailleurs Catholiques du Canada $50 at sixty-five for men and sixty for women. In the CCL proposal, however, the universal pension was only the first level of a two-level program. A contributory earnings-related pension, based on tripartite contributions, was to be pyramided on it—the first proposal for the kind of program which was eventually adopted in 1965. The Canadian Welfare Council argued that the amount of the pension should be determined and adjusted on the basis of periodic empirical studies of the actual needs of the aged, and that it should not be less than the current figure of $40 a month, pending completion of the first such study. The council believed that the pension should not be paid universally before seventy so that younger people would not be discouraged from staying in productive employment where they were able, but that it should be available to unemployables of between sixty-five and seventy.

The Chamber of Commerce and life officers stressed the importance of making taxpayers conscious of the cost of pensions. To accomplish this required levies openly identified as being for pensions and the payment of such levies into a special fund. The chamber made no proposals as to specific levies, but the life officers suggested that any or all of the following would be appropriate: a proportional levy on personal income up to a specified maximum, a flat-rate head tax on adults below pensionable age, and a sales tax "on a broad group of items in more or less universal use." The labour centrals were not seized of a desire to create public consciousness of the cost of old age security any more than of other public policies. The CTCC proposed that benefits be a charge on general revenues, arguing that a country as wealthy as Canada ought to be able to provide for the minimum needs of its aged as long as its economy operated at full capacity. The other labour centrals, however, considered it necessary to answer the question of where the money would come from. The TLC and CCL both considered it legitimate to continue payments out of general revenues of the same magnitude as the means-test plan involved. Beyond that, the TLC proposed a proportional personal income tax with no maximum, while the CCL advocated a combination of increased corporation income taxes and graduated increases in the personal income tax. The Canadian Welfare Council noted the possibility of charging benefits to general revenues but was inclined to favour a specific social security tax, based on ability to pay, as the major source of revenue.

Behind the scenes there were conflicting influences from the committee's two principal advisers—George Davidson and Mitchell F. Sharp who at the time were, respectively, deputy minister of welfare and director of the Finance Department's Economic Policy Division—and these differences finally led to a full-scale debate at a private session.[71] Davidson was satisfied, on the basis of his department's studies of programs in other countries, that the contributory principle was a cumbersome and ineffective way of overcoming the evils of the means test.[72] His was a continuous influence for a universal plan. Sharp put forward the position of the Department of Finance that a contributory plan provided the only adequate control over costs, though the department was now prepared to include a small minimum pension (smaller than the $40 a month being paid under the means-test plan) which would be payable to anyone who had made any contributions. Sharp's case was bound to fail. The dominant motive of most committee members was to get rid of the means test as soon as possible. Even with provision for a minimum pension, a contributory plan would not accomplish that objective completely because noncontributors would still be uncovered. In any case, a minimum of less than $40 a month was regarded as politically unacceptable.

In relation, however, to the other important objective of reducing the age of eligibility, the committee faced the same problem as the group which had prepared the Green Books. Its solution was the same in principle, and so also was the underlying reasoning outlined in its report.[73] M.P.'s from different parties approached the committee's work with different preconceptions. CCF members wanted a $50 pension at sixty-five and Conservatives at least wanted an increase over the prevailing figure, while Liberals were anxious to avoid a recommendation which would be financially unacceptable to the government. A universal pension at seventy and a means-test pension at sixty-five, both based on the prevailing figure of $40 a month, constituted a compromise which all accepted. Specific proposals as to the financing of the program would probably have been more divisive, as indeed they were in the debates in the House of Commons (see chapter 9, section 1). That issue was evaded on the ground that "the raising of revenues is a technical problem which has a close relation to fiscal policy in general" and on which, therefore, a parliamentary committee could not appropriately make recommendations.[74]

The government appears to have been caught by surprise by the committee's report. Notwithstanding the fact that it had itself proposed essentially the same program five years earlier, it was now thinking primarily in terms of contributory pensions. The issue was regarded as urgent, however, and the committee had unanimously recommended a program that could at least be implemented. Under the circumstances, it could hardly be ignored. St. Laurent believed that something of the contributory principle could be salvaged by an earmarked levy which would to some extent represent the actuarial cost of a $40 pension at seventy. The Department of Finance was instructed to work out such a formula and to recommend such additional taxes as it considered appropriate to cover the balance of the anticipated cost of $343 million a year of the universal plan.[75] (It was taken for granted that the federal share of the means-test plan, $32 million, would be financed out of general revenues.) The department was further instructed to ensure that the revenues to be raised would, if anything, be somewhat less than estimated expenditures in order to avoid an accumulation of surpluses which might give rise to new demands. Departmental officers calculated that an annual contribution of $60 over forty years would purchase a monthly annuity of approximately $40 for a male at age seventy.[76] A 2 percent income tax with a $60 ceiling would raise the required amount from all those whose taxable income was $3,000 a year or more, while imposing a proportionately smaller but still identifiable burden on those with lower incomes who were subject to income tax. The tax would thereby serve as a symbol of the cost of the pension and create an immediate awareness of that cost in the minds of all those who paid income tax. There were a variety of reasons for selecting sales and corporation income taxes for the balance of the needed revenues, not the least of which, apparently, was the coincidence that 2 percent rates had the desired yield, thus creating a neat symmetry with the 2 percent income tax.[77]

The old age security tax as it was now projected raised substantial doubt as to Parliament's constitutional competence to impose it. The opinion of the deputy minister of justice, as expressed before the joint committee, was that pensions financed out of general revenues clearly were *intra vires* and contributory pensions clearly were not, while earmarked taxes constituted a grey area in which judicial determination would probably turn on the nature of the tax. As a guiding principle, the deputy minister suggested that there would have to be "complete disjunction" between tax and benefit. This, however, was precisely what the government wanted to avoid since the whole point of the income tax component was to create public awareness of a relationship between tax and benefit. The only example the deputy minister gave of an earmarked tax which he felt would escape judicial disapproval was a customs duty. An earmarked income tax, he believed, would almost certainly be objectionable.[78] St. Laurent, himself a constitutional expert, shared the deputy minister's doubts. The only safe course was a constitutional amendment.

The program envisaged in the committee's report was placed before a federal-provincial conference in December, 1950. The government there broached the question of a constitutional amendment in a preliminary way,[79] and pursued it in correspondence with the provinces in the early part of 1951.[80] The joint committee had recommended that if an amendment was considered necessary, it should provide for concurrent jurisdiction since the provinces were still to be involved at the lower level. The federal government now offered three alternative drafts to implement this proposal. The only major objection came from Premier Duplessis of Quebec. He was ready, even anxious, for the proposed new program to proceed, but he wanted the new power conferred on the federal government to be restricted to the absolute minimum necessary for the purpose. His concurrence was finally secured when a form of words was arrived at which assured provincial paramountcy in the field to his satisfaction.[81]

5. Implementation and Revision of the Program

In contrast to that of the 1927 plan, implementation of the 1951 program was hardly more than a formality in political terms. The federal government started in June to set up administrative machinery for the universal plan, even though the necessary legislation was not introduced until the fall. Requisite information was obtained from the provinces regarding pensioners already on the rolls, and registration machinery was established for the rest of the seventy-and-over age group.[82] As a result, the plan went into full operation on the target date of January 1, 1952. The means-test plan required provincial participation, but the federal government took the precaution of placing its total proposal before the federal-provincial conference of December, 1950. The provinces did not welcome their own involvement, and those paying supplementary benefits were somewhat concerned about the cost implications of the universal pension for those supplements. It was politically impossible, however, to reject a program which greatly expanded pension eligibility while reducing the provinces' basic financial obligations. All provinces except Newfoundland entered into agreements and passed enabling legislation which brought the full means-test pension of $40 a month into effect in their jurisdictions on January 1. In Newfoundland the effective date was delayed until April 1, and the maximum pension was at first limited to $30 a month, although it was raised to $40 in 1956.

With the coming into effect of the new program, Alberta, British Columbia, and the Yukon put their $10 monthly supplements on a means-test basis, thus preventing a sharp increase in the number of beneficiaries. Alberta and British Columbia paid the supplement to those in the sixty-five to sixty-nine age group who could qualify under the means test. Saskatchewan continued to pay its flat supplement of $2.50 a month on a means-test basis to the seventy-and-over age group only. The Yukon soon abandoned its special supplement and instead provided general welfare assistance in cases of need. On the other hand, Alberta and British Columbia increased the maximum of their supplements to $15 a month in the mid-1950s, and Saskatchewan changed its basis of payment to provide a minimum of $2.50 and a maximum of $10. In 1956 Ontario initiated a plan under which it offered to reimburse any municipality which undertook to pay a supplement of up to $20 a month for 60 percent (later raised to 80 percent) of the cost. Toronto was the only municipality to rise to the bait. Some other provinces supplemented the incomes of needy pensioners under general welfare legislation, and this practice spread after the coming into operation of the Unemployment Assistance Act of 1956 (replaced and liberalized in 1966 by the Canada Assistance Plan), under which the federal government undertook to reimburse the provinces for half the cost of welfare benefits. By the early 1960s all provinces were taking advantage of this federal reimbursement, with the result that on the whole old age supplements have been merged into general welfare programs.

There have been instances, however, of special treatment of pensioners by provinces within the general welfare framework. The most notable example has been British Columbia, which was a leader in the payment of supplements to pensioners from the inception of provincial supplementation in 1942. Even after the adoption of the federal Unemployment Assistance Act and Canada Assistance Plan, British Columbia continued to provide a specially designated supplement for pensioners who could qualify under a needs test. The maximum of this supplement was increased periodically until it reached $41.10 a month in 1972. For those who qualified, this was additional to both the universal pension and guaranteed income supplement (GIS) described in chapter 7, section 1. As a result of changes outlined in chapter 8, section 4, the combined universal pension and GIS reached $150 a month in 1972. Thus a B.C. pensioner who qualified for the full provincial supplement received a total of $191.10 a month. The effect of the needs test was such, however, that only about 18,000 received any supplement, and only 1,200 the maximum, out of more than 200,000 pensioners in the province.

The highly active pensioners' organizations of the province were far from satisfied with the plan, even though treatment of pensioners in

British Columbia was more favourable than in other provinces. Partly as a result of the efforts of these organizations, pensions became an important issue in the provincial election campaign of August, 1972, and the newly elected NDP government proceeded almost immediately after the election to liberalize greatly the conditions governing the provincial supplement in a restructured plan which has come to be known as Mincome. Beginning in December, 1972, the province guaranteed a minimum income of $200 a month to people sixty-five and over by legislation providing for a supplement equal to the difference between $200 and the recipient's income from all sources (including the universal pension and GIS) where that income was less than $200. In addition to the significant increase in the maximum provincial supplement produced by this change, the number eligible for full or partial supplementation increased from about 18,000 to over 100,000. In line with an increase in the combined universal pension and maximum GIS that came into effect on October 1, 1973 (see chapter 8, section 4), the Mincome guarantee was increased to $209.14 effective on the same date. Further, it was extended to those between sixty and sixty-five.

A much more modest attempt to provide a special supplement for pensioners was undertaken by Prince Edward Island in 1967. The enactment of that year was applied to GIS recipients of at least sixty-eight years of age who had resided in the province for at least five years and who continued in residence for at least ten months a year. The province undertook to bring the income of such recipients up to $100 a month wherever it would otherwise fall below that figure. The guarantee was made meaningless by increases in federal payments and was abandoned in December, 1970. At the end of 1973, Ontario paid a single, lump-sum grant of $50 to all GIS recipients in the province.

Under the federal legislation, those who had qualified for maximum benefit under the 1927 act as amended continued to receive the same $40 pension after 1951. This meant that these pensioners were substantially worse off than in 1949 (when the maximum was first set at $40) because living costs had risen by no less than 16.5 percent between that year and 1952. On the other hand, many more people received substantial benefit from the new program, namely, those in the seventy-and-over age group who had previously received no pension or only partial pension and those in the sixty-five to sixty-nine age group who could now qualify for the first time. On December 31, 1951, 308,825 were receiving pensions under the 1927 plan, some of them less than the maximum amount. On March 31, 1953, 686,127 were receiving the universal pension and an additional 87,675 the means-test pension.[83] Expenditures of an entirely new magnitude were involved, not to mention new taxes to cover them. The 1951 program was a large new venture which effectively eliminated pensions as a political issue for the time being. To the extent that it was a factor in the 1953 election, which the Liberals won handily, it undoubtedly redounded to the credit of the government.

Living costs stabilized for a time after 1952, but in 1956 they began to rise again and now the large new group which had gained under the 1951 program was affected. The consumer price index (1949 = 100) reached 116.5 in 1952, remained more or less stationary through 1955, but rose to 118.1 in 1956 and 121.9 in 1957. The case for increased benefits began to gain acceptance which it had lacked only two or three years earlier.[84] The government ignored the issue through most of the preelection session of 1956–57, but at the last minute it had an apparent change of heart when Finance Minister Walter Harris, in his budget speech, announced an increase of $6 a month (15 percent) in both the universal and maximum means-test pensions.[85] Harris' budget of the previous year had been directed mainly to curbing inflation. He now claimed that that objective had been realized sufficiently well to permit some increase in benefits in both the old age and most other federal income maintenance programs.[86] At the same time, he argued, inflationary pressures were still strong and it was imperative for the government to hold them in check. In his view, the increased benefits he proposed (which would still leave a small budgetary surplus) represented a sensible compromise between the needs of beneficiaries and the requirements of economic policy.

Though this could be represented as fiscal responsibility, it was nevertheless a political blunder in the climate of opinion of the time. The odd figure of $46 in itself created an impression of cheese-paring. An opinion poll indicated that 78 percent of the respondents considered the increase to be too small.[87] Liberal backbenchers from the cities were up in arms, but Prime Minister St. Laurent refused to countenance any change in what he considered to be a rational decision.[88] In the election campaign which followed all opposition parties tried to capitalize on the issue, but it was the prairie populist John Diefenbaker (chosen Conservative leader only a few months earlier) who was able to exploit it most tellingly. He used it as one of a number of weapons in a campaign whose cumulative effect was to overthrow the government.[89] The Conservative percentage of the vote, which had hovered around 30 since 1935, shot up to 38.9. This was two points below the Liberal percentage, but it elected 112 members compared with 105 Liberals to the 265-member House. St. Laurent resigned as prime minister and shortly afterwards as Liberal leader.

127

Among the first items of business presented by the minority Diefenbaker government to the new Parliament in the fall of 1957 were bills to amend the 1951 pension acts. These increased both the universal pension and the maximum means-test pension by a further $9, to $55 a month. In addition, the residence requirement was cut in half—to the immediately preceding ten years, with the same provision as before to permit offsetting of absences in all but the last year of the ten-year period by prior residence equal to at least twice the total of the absences. The reduction to ten years was a concession to the growing body of immigrants whose support Diefenbaker made special efforts to cultivate. A concession was made to long-term residents in 1960 in an amending act which permitted universal (but not means-test) pensioners to be absent from Canada indefinitely and still draw their pensions if they had lived here for at least twenty-five years after attaining the age of twenty-one. Other universal pensioners were enabled to receive benefits during absences of not more than six months.

Notwithstanding the rapid-fire increase in benefits in the politically unsettled year of 1957, no changes were made in the old age security tax, with the result that the fund was soon showing a large deficit.[90] In 1959, with the Conservative government now firmly in office after a landslide victory in the 1958 election, the 2-2-2 formula was changed to a 3-3-3 formula, with the maximum for the personal income tax component being increased correspondingly to $90 a year. On the eve of the 1962 election, both pensions were increased by $10 a month (to $65) without change in the old age security tax.

The increases in the means-test pension were accompanied by increases in maximum allowable income, which in 1962 became $1,140 a year (single), $1,980 (married), and $2,340 (blind spouse) compared with $720, $1,200, and $1,320 under the original act of 1951. There was no advance consultation with the provinces regarding any of the increases in maximum pension or allowable income, but all provinces accepted them without delay.

Major changes were made in the 1951 program after 1962, but these were so intimately connected with developments regarding the Canada Pension Plan that it is well to defer consideration of them.

Chapter Seven

Contributory Pensions, 1965

THE 1951 DECISION TO INSTITUTE a universal plan, though made with some reluctance by the government of the day, proved to be irreversible. Proposals were made occasionally in subsequent years to substitute contributory pensions, but they did not arouse noticeable public interest. It was not practical politics to abandon a plan which guaranteed to everyone a basic measure of income security in old age in favour of a quite different kind of plan of which Canadians had had no experience. On the other hand, the idea of relating pension benefits to earnings (which almost necessarily involved a contributory plan) began to gain favour in the late 1950s and early 1960s as a method of supplementing, rather than as a substitute for, the universal pension. There were three main reasons for this. First, there was the old consideration of controlling costs, which was prominent in the thinking not only of business organizations but of the government too and especially the Department of Finance. In addition, welfare specialists and others expressed some concern that undue emphasis on old age pensions would lead to an imbalance in the allocation of funds for total welfare needs.[1] In 1951 St. Laurent had hoped that the combination of earmarked taxes and a special fund whose income would barely cover obligations would put a damper on demands for increased benefits. The events of 1957 shattered that illusion. Second, those whose incomes during their working years were above subsistence but not high enough to permit them to acquire supplementary pensions (and their number was legion) usually suffered a sharp reduction in living standards on retirement. Private pension plans alleviated the problem to only a limited degree. As shown in chapter 2, section 3, even though such plans were growing in scope and coverage during the 1950s, they still benefited only a relatively small percentage of the population. At the same time, their very growth was a third factor contributing to increased interest in government action in the field. Many employees ostensibly covered by plans were deprived of benefits because their employment terminated before they acquired vested rights. There was a growing demand for "portable pensions," that is, plans in which workers would accumulate and retain benefit rights even though they changed employment. Some saw a public contributory plan as a way of ensuring a degree of portability.

In short, just as differing interests in opposition to the means test had converged in the late 1940s, so now those primarily concerned with controlling costs and those whose main motive was to improve benefits began to find common ground in advocating a contributory plan. It is worth noting that similar pressures were operating in other countries where the pension was on a flat-rate basis. Both the United Kingdom and Sweden, for example, superimposed contributory earnings-related pensions on their plans in 1959. In Canada, the old two-level program of 1951 was completely restructured in the mid-1960s. This chapter is devoted to an examination of the nature of the program then established and of the factors which brought pensions to the top of the government agenda again. Chapter 8 considers the interactions which determined the shape of the new program, as well as modifications in it which have taken place in the 1970s.

1. The Restructured Two-Level Program

The universal plan under which a flat-rate pension is paid was continued as the base of the restructured program. The qualifying age was seventy until 1965, but starting with the 1966 calendar year, it was reduced by one year every year until it became sixty-five in 1970. Moreover, since 1967 the universal pension has been supplemented in some cases by a guaranteed income supplement (GIS). A new contributory earnings-related plan was (or, more accurately, two geographically complementary plans were) superimposed on the universal pension in 1965 to form the second level of the restructured program. The contributory plan provides old age pensions (additional to the universal pension) and survivor, death, and disability benefits. The statutory authority for the universal plan, including the GIS, is the Old Age Security Act of 1951 as amended over the years. For the contributory plan, it is the Canada Pension Plan[2] in nine of the provinces and the territories, and the Quebec Pension Plan (*Régime des rentes du Québec*) in the remaining province. The Canada and Quebec plans were identical until the beginning of 1973, and divergences which took effect then were largely eliminated from the beginning of 1974. The summary presented here deals with the plans as they were until the end of 1972, with changes made after that being summarized in chapter 8, section 4. The means-test pension established by the Old Age Assistance Act of 1951 was phased out by progressive reduction of the qualifying age for the universal pension.[3]

Universal Pension and GIS. The first level of the program consists of two components: the universal pension and guaranteed income supplement. Initially, the terms of these two components were established by a series of amendments to the Old Age Security Act passed in 1963, 1965, and 1966. By further amending acts passed in 1970, 1972, and 1973, the terms were altered significantly. I will describe them here as they had taken shape by 1966. The nature of and reasons for the later amendments will be considered in chapter 8, section 4.

A basic universal pension of $75 a month was established in 1963 and was made subject after 1967 to upward adjustment in accordance with the behaviour of a specially constructed "pension index" (described in the next paragraph). The guaranteed income supplement was provided for in 1966 and first became payable for the 1967 calendar year. At the time, it was deliberately designed as a transitional measure which would ultimately phase itself out. Its purpose was to provide supplementary benefits based on an income test for recipients of the universal pension who had already qualified for that pension or would do so before 1976—the year when full benefits would become payable under the contributory plan. Since those earnings-related benefits were deemed at the time to constitute adequate supplementation by themselves, no one who had been born after 1910 and thus would reach sixty-five after 1975 was to be eligible for the GIS. This limitation was removed by the amending act of 1970. The maximum supplement payable in any year was set at 40 percent of the universal pension. This meant that the maximum was $30 a month in 1967 and that subsequently it moved upward proportionately to increases in the universal pension. The maximum was and continues to be payable only to pensioners whose income consists exclusively of the universal pension and supplement. Income is so defined, however, that the supplement is not reduced because of benefits under social assistance or workmen's compensation legislation, war pensions, disability awards under commercial insurance, proceeds from the liquidation of capital, or gifts. Other income is averaged on a monthly basis, and the supplement is reduced by $1 a month for each full $2 of such income. The effect of this flexible ceiling is to scale the benefit down for any amount of outside income. At the same time, a pensioner is not entirely disqualified unless his outside income is at least

131

double the maximum supplement. A married pensioner is deemed to be in receipt of half the couple's total income. Eligibility for benefit is determined on the basis of statements of outside income furnished annually by beneficiaries. A beneficiary's financial resources are not normally investigated in detail as under the old means test.

The pension index was an integral part of the earnings-related plan and its modus operandi was set forth in the Canada Pension Plan. In addition, it was incorporated by reference in the Old Age Security Act in 1965. The original legislation established a base, called the "pension index for the year 1967," which was the average of the consumer price index for the twelve months between July 1, 1965, and June 30, 1966. It was provided that the pension index for each subsequent calendar year would be the consumer price index average for the corresponding July 1 to June 30, whenever that average was between 1 and 2 percent above the average for the preceding July 1 to June 30. If it was more than 2 percent above, the increase in the pension index would be restricted to 2 percent. If, on the other hand, it was less than 1 percent above, the pension index would remain unchanged. The latter stipulation was designed not only to prevent small increases in the index but also to act as a ratchet to prevent decreases. The overall effect of the operation of the pension index in practice was that adjustments governed by it automatically reflected increases in the consumer price index to an extent. There was a time lag, however, and this was not inconsequential in a period of rapidly rising prices. Moreover, since the index could not increase by more than 2 percent for any year, the adjustments were bound to fall behind even the lagged consumer price index if the latter increased by more than 2 percent per year. The pension index served as the formula for adjusting both the universal pension and GIS for 1968, 1969, and 1970.[4] The procedure for determining the universal pension for each of those calendar years was to multiply the basic pension of $75 a month by the ratio of the pension index for the year concerned to the index for 1967. The GIS was automatically increased proportionately since it was set at 40 percent of the universal pension. The actual experience during this period was that the consumer price index was increasing much more rapidly than the pension index. As a result, though the pension and GIS increased by 2 percent per year, they fell further and further behind the cost of living.

The residence requirements for the universal pension as revised in 1957 were carried forward in the new program, and an additional option became available in 1965. As before, a person who had reached pensionable age was eligible if (a) he had lived in Canada for the immediately preceding ten years, or (b) his immediately preceding residence had covered at least one year and absences in the previous nine years had been offset by earlier residence equal to at least twice the total length of the absences. Under the additional option, residence in Canada for an aggregate of forty years after age eighteen became a sufficient qualification. A further amendment of 1965 permitted commencement of a pension to be dated back to any time up to a year before receipt of an application if the applicant was then eligible. Previously a pension could not under any circumstances take effect before the application was received. Both the pension and GIS are cut off if the pensioner is absent from Canada for more than six months, but they can be restored if he returns. However, the 1965 amending act continued a provision, first adopted in 1960, permitting a pensioner who had lived in Canada for at least twenty-five years after reaching the age of twenty-one to draw the universal pension outside the country indefinitely, and in 1972 the necessary residence was reduced to twenty years after the eighteenth birthday. This concession did not and does not apply to the GIS.

The universal pension continued to be financed out of the old age security fund and the GIS was also charged against that fund. The income tax component of the old age security tax was increased to cover the additional demand on the fund. Machinery was established in 1967 for hearing appeals from administrative decisions affecting either the universal pension or GIS.

Earnings-Related Pension. The Canada and Quebec Pension Plans impose contributions and provide old age, survivor, and disability pensions which are identifiably though not precisely related to income earned in employment. Both employees and the self-employed are covered. Contributions were first levied on income earned during the 1966 calendar year. Old age benefits (called retirement pensions in the legislation) first became payable in 1967, survivor benefits (including a lump-sum death benefit) in 1968, and disability benefits in May, 1970. There is, however, a ten-year transition or build-up period dating from the start of contributions, so that full benefits will not be payable until January, 1976.

Contributions are levied on earned income between a specified earnings ceiling and a related basic exemption. The ceiling was fixed at $5,000 of annual income for the 1966 and 1967 calendar years, but provision was made for adjusting it upward on the basis of the pension index for the period from 1968 to 1975 (the last year of the ten-year transition period). The governing conditions were such, however, that any adjustment occurring in that period would be in the amount of precisely $100 a year and this only if the pension index increased by the full 2 percent. The reason was that the ceiling had to be a multiple of $100. If an odd figure resulted from the application of the pension index, the ceiling was reduced to the next lower multiple. Since a 2 percent increase in the pension index in fact occurred annually from the inception of the plan, the ceiling reached $5,600 in 1973. Commencing with the calendar year 1976, the pension index was to have been replaced by an "earnings index" for the adjustment of the ceiling, so that the adjustment would have been related to changes in average earnings rather than in the cost of living. As will be seen in chapter 8, section 4, however, a revised formula for adjusting the ceiling came into effect on January 1, 1974.

The basic exemption was declared by the legislation to be 12 percent of the ceiling, but it too could be adjusted upward only in even amounts of $100 a year. Thus it continued at its original level of $600 a year through 1973 (12 percent of the original ceiling of $5,000), notwithstanding annual increases in the ceiling. In the case of the self-employed, only those earning at least 1⅓ times the basic exemption ($800 a year for as long as the basic exemption was $600) are covered, but the basic exemption in their case is still the same as that for employees.

Contributions are compulsory for most Canadian income earners who have reached the age of eighteen until they reach seventy, or until they draw benefits at an earlier age because of retirement before seventy or disability. The principal groups excluded are those whose earnings are below the minima just referred to, those who earn their living by odd jobs, and transient and casual employees in agriculture, horticulture, fishing, hunting, trapping, forestry, logging, and lumbering.[5] An individual may, of course, move in and out of pensionable employment, but his benefits will be adversely affected by too long a time in an excluded category. The rate of contribution is 3.6 percent of earned income between the basic exemption and the ceiling. This percentage is divided equally between employers and employees, but the self-employed pay the entire amount themselves. The maximum employee contribution in 1966 and 1967 was $79.20 a year, with the employer paying a like amount. As a result of adjustment of the ceiling, this maximum had increased to $90 by 1973. Contributions are deductible for income tax purposes.

The qualifying age for the earnings-related pension was subject to the same progressive reduction as for the universal pension. Thus it was sixty-eight in 1967, the first year in which the earnings-related pension was payable, and became sixty-five in 1970. A retirement test has been applied, however, where the pension has been claimed before seventy. The test was based on a complex formula which, for simplicity, I will describe in terms of the specific figures applicable in 1973. The pension was reduced by fifty cents for every dollar of annual earnings from employment of more than $960 but not more than $1,600, and dollar for dollar beyond $1,600. It was not affected by earnings of up to $960 a year, nor was it reduced in any month in which the pensioner did not earn more than $80. There has never been a retirement test for pensioners of seventy and over and that for the sixty-five to sixty-nine group was, at the time of writing, slated for elimination some time in 1974.

The monthly amount of the earnings-related pension is 25 percent of what are called "average monthly pensionable earnings," which are arrived at by a series of calculations. First, the contributor's earnings in each year in which he made contributions (up to the ceiling for that year) are adjusted: an average is taken of the ceiling for the year in which the pension is claimed and the ceiling for the two preceding years, and the contributor's pensionable earnings in each of his earning years are then multiplied by the ratio of this average to the ceiling for the year in which they were earned. Second, the adjusted earnings are aggregated into the contributor's "total pensionable earnings." Third, the latter are divided by the total number of months (other than months in which a disability pension was paid under the plan) in the period commencing when contributions were first levied (January 1, 1966) or when the contributor reached eighteen, whichever was later, and ending when he reached sixty-five or ceased making contributions if these continued after sixty-five. The resulting quotient constitutes the contributor's average monthly pensionable earnings, and the pension is 25 percent of these. The legislation stipulates, however, that the number of months used for the divisor may not be less than 120. As a result, a retirement pension based on less than ten years' contributions will be reduced proportionately. The principal effect of this is to reduce pensions awarded during the ten-year transition.[6] Where a disability pension has been received, the number of months during which it was received are deducted from the minimum divisor and therefore do not affect the retirement pension. Where a pension is awarded after the transition, some scope will be permitted for eliminating months of low or no earnings from the calculation, thereby increasing the pension. First, pensionable earnings after sixty-five may be either substituted for earlier earnings of an equal number of months or disregarded, depending on whether they were greater or less than earlier earnings. Second, up to 15 percent of the months before sixty-five may be disregarded. The overriding condition will prevail, however, that the divisor may not be less than 120. The original legislation provided for annual adjustment of the pension, after the initial award, on the basis of the pension index with its 2 percent limit, but starting in 1974 the pension index reflects full increases in living costs.

Survivor and disability benefits can be dealt with more briefly, since they are only marginally relevant to this study. A widow of sixty-five and over, regardless of when her husband died, receives 60 percent of the husband's retirement pension. In cases where the husband was not receiving the pension when he died, it is calculated in accordance with a prescribed formula. If a widow is also entitled to a pension in her own right, the two may be integrated within certain limits. A widow who is under sixty-five will receive a pension consisting of a flat-rate benefit and 37½ percent of her husband's retirement pension if she has dependent or disabled children, is herself disabled, or is widowed at forty-five or later. If she fits none of these categories, the pension is reduced by 1/120 for each month by which she is under forty-five at the time of her husband's death, from which it follows that she receives no pension if she is under thirty-five at that time. The same conditions govern the payment of pensions to disabled widowers who were substantially dependent on their wives. A disability pension, payable to a contributor who qualifies under a test of disability and employability, is a combination of a flat-rate benefit and 75 percent of what his retirement pension would be if he were sixty-five. Flat-rate benefits, additional to widows' and disability pensions, are payable for dependent children and orphans. When a contributor dies, a lump-sum benefit is also paid which is related to the amount of his retirement pension. All the above benefits, including those on flat rates, are adjusted at the time the awards are made and annually thereafter.

The Canada Pension Plan is administered by the Department of National Health and Welfare in regard to benefits and by the Department of National Revenue in regard to contributions. Appeals affecting benefits can be taken to the minister of national health and welfare, then to a review committee in the locality where the appellant lives, and finally to a Pension Appeals Board. Appeals relating to contributions may be made to the minister of national revenue, and failing satisfaction from him, to the Pension Appeals Board. An advisory committee representing employers, employees, the self-employed, and the general public periodically reviews and reports on the operation of the plan, the state of the investment fund, and the adequacy of coverage and benefits. Contributions and interest on investments are paid into a Canada pension plan account in the consolidated revenue fund, and benefits and administrative costs are financed exclusively from this account. The act specifically prohibits payments "in excess of the amount of the balance to the credit of the Canada Pension Plan Account." Contributions will exceed benefit payments substantially for some years. The resulting surpluses are paid into a Canada pension plan investment fund and are available as loans to the governments of those provinces where the plan is in effect in proportion to the contributions of their residents. Interest rates are determined by the minister of finance in accordance with detailed stipulations in the act. Contributions from the territories are invested in federal securities. So also are balances resulting from the failure of provinces to take up their full quota of loan capital, but the amount of such balances to date has been negligible.

Administration of the Quebec Pension Plan is in the hands of a board established specifically for the purpose (Quebec Pension Board) and the provincial Department of Revenue. Originally an advisory council assisted the board, but it was abolished in 1972 when the board itself was given a representative character. Appeals may be taken from either the board or the revenue minister to a Review Commission. By arrangement between the governments, the personnel of the Review Commission and the Pension Appeals Board under the CPP are identical, so as to ensure uniformity of interpretation of the Canada and Quebec plans.[7] Surpluses accumulated under the Quebec plan are paid to the Quebec deposit and investment fund established in 1965 and are available for investment by the fund under the terms of the statute governing its operations.

2. EMERGENCE OF EARNINGS-RELATED PENSIONS AS A POLITICAL ISSUE

As indicated in the previous chapter, section 4, the Canadian Congress of Labour, in its submission to the 1950 joint committee, proposed a two-level program consisting of a universal pension with a contributory earnings-related plan pyramided on it, the latter to be financed by contributions from employers, employees, and the federal government. The CCL's interest in this kind of arrangement is readily understood, since wage earners constituted the major group facing a sharp decline in living standards on retirement. After implementation of the 1951 program, however, the idea dropped into the background in labour thinking. That program was so inadequate in labour's view that its revision was seen as the most pressing need. Though a growing number of unions were making the establishment of pension plans in private industry a leading objective of collective bargaining and the CCL advocated a government-sponsored and -administered "industrial pension plan" at its 1953 convention,[8] the attention of all labour centrals in the legislative field was focused mainly on the 1951 program. The principal objectives were to eliminate the means-test plan by reducing to sixty-five the qualifying age for the universal pension and to increase the amount of the latter.[9] In 1960 the Canadian Labour Congress (formed in 1956 by the merger of the Trades and Labor Congress and CCL) revived the CCL proposal of a decade earlier and fleshed it out in some detail.[10] The new congress laid major stress on four points: that a contributory earnings-related plan should be compulsory and universal; that it should be grounded on a generous universal pension (the CLC advocated $75 a month at age sixty-five compared with the $55 at seventy then in effect); that state contributions were essential to mitigate the regressive taxation effects of employer-employee contributions; and that both earnings-related and universal benefits should be adjusted automatically to increases in the cost of living. By this time, however, the issue had entered the area of active political debate through other channels. The 1960 resolution can be interpreted essentially as labour's attempt to influence the specific shape of a policy proposal which had already gained substantial political acceptance in principle.

Such a proposal first emerged as an active issue in the 1957 election campaign. As shown in chapter 6, section 5, Conservative leader John Diefenbaker effectively attacked the Liberal government in that campaign for increasing the pension by only $6 a month. His promise of an additional increase, however, was only part of his total proposal on pensions. Indeed, one could say that it was the subordinate part—logically at any rate, if not in terms of its political impact. Diefenbaker was worried about the cost implications of efforts by political parties to outbid one another in their pension promises.[11] As a way out of the dilemma, he seized on the "old age and survivors' insurance" plan of the United States.

That plan was part of a larger old age pension program which was initiated by Titles I and II of the U.S. Social Security Act of 1935. Title I authorized federal sharing of the cost of state plans of "old age assistance" (needs- and means-test pensions). Several states already had such plans before the act was passed and coverage soon became nationwide, although there have been remarkably wide variations among states in both conditions and levels of benefit. Title II established a purely federal contributory earnings-related plan, which was broadened in 1939 to include benefits for survivors and dependants and was called "old age and survivors' insurance" (OASI) in its broadened form. In 1957 pensions became available to disabled contributors under certain circumstances, and the name was revised to OASDI. Though the total program consisted of two components, its structure was quite different from that of Canada's two-level program of 1951. In Canada age was the principal differentiating factor; in the United States it was a contribution record which satisfied certain prescribed conditions. A qualified contributor could claim his pension at sixty-five, although payment before seventy-two was subject to a retirement test, and women could qualify at as early an age as sixty-two for permanently reduced pensions (an option which became available to men as well in 1961). The qualifying age for old age assistance was also sixty-five, and this assistance was the permanent source of public income maintenance for those without the requisite contribution records. Coverage of the earnings-related plan was initially restricted to employees in industry and commerce, and it was some years before even continuously covered employees qualified for significant benefits. High employment, rising wages, and the built-in growth of accumulated credits would have resulted in some expansion of coverage and steadily rising benefits in the normal course of events. The process was greatly accelerated by a series of legislative amendments starting in 1950 which increased benefits sharply, broadened coverage to almost the entire work force (including most of the self-employed), and admitted the new categories on extremely generous terms. The concomitant was substantially increased contribution rates.

In a campaign speech of April 30, 1957, Diefenbaker claimed that the U.S. plan provided "far greater benefits" than the Canadian program at "only slightly increased costs" and promised that as prime minister he would commission a thorough study of it.[12] He added, however, that any new plan adopted as a result of the study would be supplementary to the existing Canadian program. It is doubtful if this injection of the U.S. plan into the Canadian election debate had any appreciable effect on the voters, few of whom had any knowledge of or even interest in it. Many newspapers gave Diefenbaker's declaration only minor coverage at the time, and the staunchly Conservative *Toronto Telegram* did not even mention it in its report of the April 30 speech. Even so, the declaration embodied an idea which had been gradually gaining some currency in Conservative thinking, owing initially to the work of the Ontario Department of Public Welfare (under a Conservative government).

J. S. Band was appointed deputy minister of public welfare in 1953 after extensive and broad experience in the department. A long-time believer in the "social insurance" approach to income maintenance, he regarded Canada's universal pension as inadequate even to cover basic necessities. This inadequacy not only had unfortunate consequences for the pensioners themselves, but it also gave rise to worrisome implications for provincial and municipal welfare costs. At the time, the Ontario government was under considerable pressure to follow the lead of some of the other provinces in providing financial supplements to federal old age security and assistance. As noted in chapter 6, section 5, Ontario established a joint provincial-municipal plan of supplementation in 1956, but this was largely ineffective for lack of municipal cooperation. Band saw a contributory earnings-related plan of the U.S. type as offering the best possible solution to the problem of old age security and the additional advantage of providing benefits to other categories. His position was stated publicly in his introduction to the department's annual report for the 1954–55 fiscal year, which criticized Canada's universal pension severely and held up the U.S. plan as a superior alternative.[13] The argument was repeated and elaborated on in subsequent annual reports and in ministerial speeches.[14] Information accumulated in the Ontario department found its way into the hands of a few federal M.P.'s. One of these was George Hees, a prominent opposition member who was to become a leading minister in the Diefenbaker governments of 1957 to 1963. As the member for Broadview, a working-class constituency in Toronto's east end, Hees had personal knowledge of the hardship suffered by people of modest means whose incomes were suddenly reduced to $40 a month. He was attracted by the U.S. system and publicly advocated the adoption of something like it in Canada as a supplement to the existing program.[15] All this was grist to the Diefenbaker mill in the 1957 election campaign.[16]

The CCF also became interested in earnings-related pension supplements, though it was influenced more by the United Kingdom Labour party (then in the process of developing what it called a "national superannuation plan")[17] than by the United States experience. In common with the trade unions and others, CCF policy-making bodies and elected members had persistently advocated increases in the amount of the universal pension and reduction of the qualifying age to sixty-five. The party research director, however, had growing doubts that this approach was adequate by itself. During 1957 he prepared a detailed study which was considered at length between October, 1957, and January, 1958, by the National Council and a committee appointed by it.[18] The upshot was that the council issued a new policy statement on pensions on January 6, 1958. Since the subject was considered to be timely and there were strong indications that a new election would be held in the near future, the council decided to incorporate the statement in the party's election program even though, in normal procedure, a major policy departure of this kind would have required approval of the national convention.[19] In essence, the new policy was for a two-level program of which a universal pension of $75 a month at age sixty-five was to form the first level and an earnings-related pension the second. Survivor benefits were proposed but there was no reference to disability benefits. The first level was to be financed out of general revenues rather than by the old age security tax to which the CCF objected (see chapter 9, section 1), and the second by employer-employee contributions with optional coverage for the self-employed. Contributions and benefits were to be related to incomes up to a "reasonable," but in the public statement unspecified, maximum—the research paper stated a maximum of $5,000 a year—and benefits were to be weighted somewhat in favour of lower income groups. A feature of the contributory principle which commended itself to the CCF was that certain investment funds would accrue to the state rather than to insurance companies and other financial institutions.

The CCF was thus the first party to offer a detailed proposal for a combined universal and earnings-related pension program. At the time, however, the newly elected Diefenbaker government occupied centre stage on pensions as on most other matters. The CCF proposal received scant and inaccurate coverage in the press, and it is doubtful if it made any impact on the public, favourable or otherwise. It was taken over in essence by the New Democratic Party upon its formation in 1961 under the joint sponsorship of the CCF and CLC.[20] There were, however, two differences of some consequence in the NDP program. First, the reference to funds for public investment was dropped, the emphasis in party thinking now being on keeping contributions at the lowest possible level and raising investment funds in other ways. Second, sickness, disability, and survivor benefits were to be provided through a separate plan.

In February, 1958, the Diefenbaker government honoured its election pledge by commissioning R. M. Clark, an economics professor at the University of British Columbia, to "conduct an inquiry into facts relating to old age security systems in Canada and the United States, with particular reference to those features of the old-age and survivors' insurance program in the United States which make it possible for higher benefits to be paid covering a wider range of contingencies at an earlier age than is provided under present legislation."[21] With the assistance of an expert from the Department of National Health and Welfare and others, Clark produced an exhaustive report a year later.[22] His terms of reference did not authorize him to make recommendations, and he scrupulously avoided doing so, confining himself to a comprehensive analysis of both public and private provision of pensions in the two countries and to a presentation of arguments for and against universal and contributory pensions. His exposition of how the U.S. system actually worked made it hard to escape the conclusion that it was not transferable to Canada. Nor was it by any means crystal clear, as Conservative speeches and even the terms of reference had assumed, that old age pensioners were treated more generously on the whole in the United States than in Canada. The earnings-related plan was only part of the U.S. system. Although it was by then the most important part, many of the aged were still under the federal-state old age assistance plan. It was almost impossible to compare the total program with Canada's because of its quite different structure. Clark was able, however, to make two reasonably firm findings on the situation at the time of his study: (a) that the proportion of the population of sixty-five and over receiving some form of old age pension was larger in Canada than in the United States, although the margin was narrowing rapidly; (b) that, while the average level of benefits was higher in the United States, the difference was if anything less than the difference in per capita personal income in the two countries.[23] Those who qualified for maximum benefit in the United States were substantially better off economically than Canadian pensioners. On the other hand, the minimum U.S. benefit—$33 a month at the time—was well below the $55 pension then being paid in Canada to everyone of seventy and over and to a significant proportion of the sixty-five to sixty-nine age group. The Conservatives themselves had made it clear that they did not contemplate reducing that benefit. Under the circumstances, the U.S. program was not a useful model for new policy departures in Canada. The past history of pension legislation here had restricted the choice of design to a program which included the universal pension as an integral part.

The Conservative campaign pledge and the Clark report, in focusing attention on the U.S. program, injected a new issue into Canadian policy discussions, namely, the incorporation of survivor and disability benefits in the public pension program. A number of public plans providing such benefits were in operation in Canada by 1960—federal-provincial plans covering the blind and other "totally and permanently" disabled, provincial workmen's compensation and mothers' allowances, and a plan in Alberta under which the province in effect made old age assistance available to widows at age sixty[24]—but these plans were uncoordinated and lacking in comprehensiveness. Those who did not qualify under them had to fall back on provincial-municipal general welfare assistance.

Though some work was done within the public service on an earnings-related plan during the Conservative tenure of office,[25] next to nothing was ever revealed as to what the government had in mind for the design of the plan. For reasons which are not now clear, the government apparently made a firm decision that inclusion of survivor and disability benefits was a *sine qua non* of any action in the field. This gave rise to a constitutional difficulty. The 1951 amendment to the BNA Act (inserting section 94A) was couched exclusively in terms of "old age pensions," and the government's constitutional experts were in little doubt that this would not be interpreted to include survivor and disability benefits, even if they were ancillary to an old age pension program.[26] It was not until January 17, 1962, with the time for another election drawing near, that Diefenbaker wrote to the provincial premiers, seeking an amendment to enlarge the scope of section 94A.[27] The reason given for this seemingly long delay was that the government had been hoping to receive provincial concurrence in Justice Minister Davie Fulton's formula for amending the constitution in Canada in time to make it unnecessary to apply to Westminster for a specific amendment to section 94A.[28] Eight of the ten provinces replied quickly and favourably to Diefenbaker's request. Newfoundland ignored it until December for reasons unrelated to the merits of the proposal as such, but finally assented. Quebec, however, refused assent in January, 1963, after exchanges between Diefenbaker and Premier Jean Lesage in which the two talked at cross-purposes: Lesage argued that his government could not consider a constitutional amendment without having before it details of the proposed federal plan, and Diefenbaker countered that legislation to be dealt with by Parliament could not be submitted to a province in advance. The government was defeated in a general election in April, 1963, after having been reduced to a minority position in Parliament in the election of 1962.

The Liberal party, finding itself in the unaccustomed role of opposition after the 1957 election and reduced to its smallest House of Commons representation in history by the Conservative landslide of 1958, entered a period of self-examination and reconstruction. New figures rose to prominence in the party, with the aim of restoring to it the reform image which they conceived it had once had but had lost in the latter years of the St. Laurent period. The process started tentatively at the leadership convention of January, 1958 (at which Lester Pearson was chosen to succeed St. Laurent as leader), with a resolution vaguely promising "immediate consideration of a national contributory pension scheme coordinated with existing provisions for retirement and old age security."[29] In the interval between a "national rally" (policy conference) in January, 1961, and a meeting of the party's National Council in January, 1962, the party first gave serious study to earnings-related pensions.[30] Although the pension issue was not dealt with at the rally's plenary sessions, a policy committee was appointed to complete the work initiated at the rally, and that committee sponsored a detailed study of a new pension program. The product of this study was a "bulky, black-bound book" setting forth a proposed plan in detail for internal party use.[31] For public consumption, the main outlines were digested in a policy pamphlet first issued on January 9, 1962. Essentially the proposal was to add a third level to the existing two-level program so that there would be (a) a means-test plan for the sixty-five to sixty-nine age group, (b) a universal plan for the seventy-and-over group, and (c) an additional earnings-related plan which would provide survivor and disability benefits as well as old age pensions.

By the time of the 1962 and 1963 elections, then, the Liberal, Conservative, and New Democratic parties were all committed to the principle of contributory earnings-related pensions, and the Liberals and NDP had set forth their proposals publicly in some detail. The Liberals were returned as a minority government in the 1963 election. During the campaign they had used the slogan "sixty days of decision"—to indicate that they would tackle the nation's problems with vigour and dispatch, in contrast to the procrastination and indecision of which the Diefenbaker government had often been accused—and Pearson's campaign speeches had promised that the pension program was to be one of the priority items.[32] The promise could not be carried out. Although the Department of National Health and Welfare had done preliminary work on the announced programs of the various parties in the belief that it might be called upon to implement one of them, and the deputy minister of welfare quickly assembled and put to work an impressive interdepartmental committee of experts when the new government gave the go-ahead signal,[33] it was simply impossible to prepare a bill on so complex a matter on short notice. The government temporized by introducing a resolution on June 21, 1963, about a month after the new Parliament opened,[34] and by tabling a more detailed explanation of its proposal on July 18.[35]

The resolution and explanatory statement were based on the Liberal party's election platform, but with some refinement of detail which reflected the preliminary work of the interdepartmental committee. This early formulation of what eventually became the 1965 program contained a radically new departure from the pre-1965 program, namely, a proposed third level under which earnings-related benefits were to be stacked on the universal pension (second level). Also involved, however, was an increase in the universal pension from $65 to $75 a month. Both this increase and the earnings-related benefits were to be financed by contributions, with the old age security tax being retained to finance the first $65 of the universal pension. Participation was to be compulsory for employees, with the requisite contributions being shared equally by themselves and their employers, but it was to be voluntary for the self-employed. A ceiling of $4,000 a year was established on the earnings on which both contributions and benefits were to be calculated. Full earnings-related benefits were to become payable in ten years. In the interim, reduced benefits would be payable where contributions had been made for at least a year. Financing was to be on a pay-as-you-go basis in order to prevent accumulation of "huge investment funds in the hands of the federal government." The method also had the incidental effect of permitting a low contribution rate—2 percent of earnings (1 percent each for employers and employees) up to the $4,000 annual maximum. Since the universal pension was not payable until seventy, full earnings-related benefits were to be available only at that age. The option was offered, however, of claiming both the universal and earnings-related pensions in reduced amounts at any time after the claimant reached sixty-five. The earnings-related pension payable after the ten-year transition was to range from 20 percent of average monthly earnings if claimed at sixty-five to 30 percent if claimed at seventy. The actual amount for a person who had contributed continuously at the maximum earnings level of $4,000 a year would thus range from $800 to $1,200 a year, or $66.67 to $100 a month. This amount would be additional to the universal pension, which in turn would range from $51 to $75 a month, depending on the age of the claimant. Earnings-related benefits paid to qualified claimants during the transition and/or on the basis of a lower level of contributions would be proportionately lower. A surviving spouse of sixty-five or over was to receive 60 percent of the earnings-related benefits for which the couple had qualified.

The proposed $10 increase in the universal pension was intended mainly to improve the position of those already receiving the universal pension or those close enough to the qualifying age that their entitlement to earnings-related pensions would be negligible. The increase was tied inextricably to the earnings-related plan, however, because of the decision to finance it out of contributions. That decision was based on financial considerations. To a considerable extent, the future beneficiaries of the earnings-related plan were to be given a lower overall level of benefits so that the universal pension could be increased immediately. The Liberals had consistently rejected as "irresponsible" the long-standing CCF-NDP and trade union proposal that the universal pension should be raised to $75 and paid at sixty-five. The Liberals were satisfied that they had devised a "responsible" formula for financing the increased pension. They did not at the time regard reduction of the qualifying age as financially feasible, except on the basis of a permanently reduced benefit level. Increasing the means-test pension required provincial participation, and no reference was made to that increase in the resolution of June, 1963. The explanatory statement of

July indicated, however, as did the preelection policy pamphlets, that the government would pay its share of the cost of increasing the maximum to $75 a month and of making the pension available to women at sixty, if the provinces concurred. In addition, the statement and the pamphlets suggested the desirability of including a complete range of survivor and disability benefits, but the resolution did not go beyond proposing benefits for surviving spouses of sixty-five and over. The Liberals made a point of the fact that they would not wait for provincial assent to a constitutional amendment before proceeding with as much of the program as was already within Parliament's legislative competence.

Chapter Eight

Shaping the 1965 Design

THOUGH AN ENORMOUS AMOUNT OF TECHNICAL WORK remained to be done, the government undoubtedly believed that the 1963 resolution and explanatory statement contained all the essentials of a program which could be implemented. In fact, the bill eventually placed before Parliament (Bill C-75) and the accompanying *Canada Pension Plan: White Paper* contained important revisions of the original proposal. Even the revised proposal, however, was inadequate to accommodate the varied and complex pressures bearing upon the government,[1] and a new bill (C-136) was substituted for Bill C-75. Bill C-136 was a far cry from the 1963 formulation: yet, as originally introduced, it too represented only a stage in the total process.[2] It was debated at great length in the House of Commons,[3] and was the subject of extensive hearings by a joint committee of the two Houses after second reading.[4] Several amendments were made in the process. As far as the earnings-related plan was concerned, these changes affected details rather than basic principles, but in the universal plan a change of major significance was made before the bill passed and again in 1966 by an amendment to the Old Age Security Act. Thus, three years elapsed from the presentation of the original formulation to Parliament in 1963 before the shaping of the new program was complete in all its aspects.

During that period the program was the subject not only of lengthy debates in Parliament but also of prolonged negotiations with the provinces, extensive discussion in the press, and innumerable representations, formal and informal, by interested groups and individuals. In this welter of conflicting influences, two were of particular significance in determining the final shape of the program. First, it proved to be politically impossible to project a substantial upward revision of the benefits of future pensioners without doing considerably more than originally planned for those already at or near pensionable age. Quite broadly based pensioners' associations were actively bringing the needs of their constituency to the attention of Parliament.[5] They had a ready spokesman there in Stanley Knowles, the inveterate champion of the pensioner, who had been temporarily retired from the House of Commons in the Conservative landslide of 1958 but had returned in 1962. And he was by no means alone. All opposition parties espoused the cause of the pensioner, and this at a time when the government was in a minority position in the House. Second, the two largest provinces, Ontario and Quebec, either had or were working on legislation of their own regarding earnings-related pensions. Ontario's legislation was considerably less comprehensive than Ottawa's and was abandoned eventually. Quebec's proposed plan, however, was more comprehensive (in that it included survivor, death, and disability benefits) and substantially different in some of its main features. In the end, the Ottawa and Quebec plans were mutually adapted so that there would at least be portability of benefits between Quebec and the rest of Canada. The first of the above influences was significant for the universal plan, the second for the earnings-related plan.

1. RESTRUCTURING THE UNIVERSAL PLAN

During the 1962 and 1963 election campaigns, Liberal publicity gave considerable prominence to the party's proposal for a $10 increase in the universal pension. Less clearly communicated was the fact that this increase was contingent on implementation of the earnings-related plan. The condition probably did not seem important at the time, for the Liberals were convinced that their program could be put into effect quickly. When the 1963 resolution and explanatory statement appeared, however, it became obvious that a substantial delay was inevitable. National Health and Welfare Minister Judy LaMarsh estimated that the earliest possible time for commencing payment of contributions would be October, 1964, and stressed that even this would require prompt action by Parliament once the bill was introduced.[6] The opposition parties pounced on this delay in the brief but spirited debate on the resolution, and John Diefenbaker, then leader of the official opposition, moved an amendment asking the government to make the increase in the universal pension effective immediately.[7] Neither the amendment nor the resolution came to a vote, but Knowles pursued the point in the remaining days before Parliament recessed on August 2, 1963.[8] The matter came to a head during the recess, especially after it was injected into a provincial general election campaign in Ontario. John J. Winter-meyer, Liberal leader in the province, berated the Conservative government for failing to accept the Canada Pension Plan. Premier John Robarts countered by criticizing the federal government for not making the increase in the universal pension effective immediately. Duff Roblin, Conservative premier of Manitoba, and Diefenbaker hammered the same point. Knowles predicted that the government would be defeated on the issue when Parliament resumed.[9]

The tie-in between the increase and the earnings-related plan was becoming untenable in any case. Quebec had announced that it was determined to proceed with its own earnings-related plan. It was hardly feasible to finance an increase in the universal pension out of the earnings-related contributions if the federal government was not to collect such contributions in the whole country. Though the Quebec decision was not accepted as final at this stage, there was nevertheless a strong possibility that the increase in the universal pension would have to be separated from the earnings-related plan sooner or later.

Political exigencies favoured early action. Not only had the matter become a leading issue in Ontario, but provincial election campaigns were also in progress in British Columbia and Nova Scotia where it was being used to the detriment of the Liberal cause. At the end of August, 1963, Ontario Liberal leader Wintermeyer made public a telegram he sent to Pearson, asking for an immediate increase in the universal pension. Behind the scenes, LaMarsh—herself an Ontario M.P. who had become involved in the provincial campaign—urged her colleagues to act immediately. The Cabinet approved the increase early in September. On the day on which Parliament resumed after its recess (September 30), a resolution was introduced—the required notice having been waived by unanimous consent—authorizing introduction of the necessary bill.[10] This bill also increased the income tax component of the old age security tax from 3 percent of taxable income up to a total tax of $90 a year to 4 percent up to $120.[11] The bill received quick action from Parliament, being assented to on October 16,[12] with the result that the increase was effective from October 1. The Old Age Assistance, Blind Persons, and Disabled Persons Acts were also amended to raise to $75 a month the maximum means-test pensions in which the federal government would share, with corresponding increases in maximum allowable income: $1,260 a year for a single pensioner, $2,220 for one who was married, and $2,580 for one whose spouse was blind in the Old Age Assistance and Disabled Persons Acts, and at higher levels in the Blind Persons Act. Seven provinces and the Yukon made these increases effective from December 1, 1963, and Newfoundland, Prince

Edward Island, Quebec, and the Northwest Territories from April 1, 1964.

The retreat from the 1963 resolution had only begun, however. LaMarsh commented ruefully in retrospect:

> Most people forgot about it [the increase to $75 a month], for when it was introduced, at once the clamour to make it $100 per month began. And Stanley Knowles, in the House, and groups of little old retired ladies and gentlemen who had nothing else to do but hold meetings, and ask for bigger benefits for themselves outside the House, kept up the clamour. They ignored the increase and during subsequent debates on the Canada Pension Plan complained that there was nothing in it for those already on pension![13]

In truth, "$100 a month" became a rallying cry, but a "clamour" also arose, albeit with narrower participation, in regard to the qualifying age for the universal pension. Knowles raised the point in the debate on the bill to increase the pension,[14] and Réal Caouette, leader of the Ralliement des Créditistes, followed up with an amendment (ruled out of order) to provide the universal pension at sixty-five and the means-test pension at sixty.[15] The NDP and Créditistes were the chief protagonists in Parliament of the reduced age, but all opposition parties pressed for the higher amount. Both points were raised in questions, in the estimates of the Department of National Health and Welfare, and in the debates on Bills C-75 and C-136.

Matters were brought to a head on February 8, 1965, in the executive session of the joint committee on Bill C-136 at which the committee's final report was considered.[16] All members were agreed, and included a paragraph in the report recommending, that the government should "give consideration to further measures regarding the position of those people who . . . will not be substantial contributors to, or beneficiaries from, the Canada Pension Plan." The Conservative and NDP members attempted to amend the report to indicate the specific ways in which they thought the objective should be achieved. The Conservatives would have provided an increase of up to $25 a month in the universal pension and a minimum guarantee on the earnings-related pension, both to be financed by the earnings-related contributions. The NDP, through Knowles, proposed simply that the universal pension be increased to $100 a month and the eligible age reduced to sixty-five. Both amendments were defeated, whereupon Knowles moved a further amendment proposing an unspecified increase in the universal pension and "progressive lowering of the eligible age" until it reached sixty-five. This too was defeated.

On February 17, however, Pearson announced that the government would sponsor an amendment in committee of the whole to reduce the qualifying age for the universal pension progressively over a five-year period.[17] This took the steam out of the agitation regarding the qualifying age, but the clamour for a $100 pension continued unabated. The case was strengthened by the fact that the Canadian economy had again entered an inflationary phase. The consumer price index (1949 = 100) increased from 128.3 in 1961 to 142.5 in 1964, 148.9 in 1965, and 154.4 in 1966. Few people were prepared to argue that a $75 pension was adequate if the pensioner had little or no other income. A study by the Age and Opportunity Bureau of Winnipeg, for example, concluded that in 1965 a minimum of $112 a month was needed for "a single retired person to live with a measure of independence and self-respect, allowing for some active participation in the life of the Greater Winnipeg community."[18] On the motion for third reading of Bill C-136, the Conservatives and NDP moved without success essentially the same amendments as they had presented to the joint committee.[19] The bill was passed without further change in the universal plan, but two major concessions had already been made. The pension was now $75 a month and it was only a matter of time until it would be payable at sixty-five. Only two or three years earlier the Liberals had argued that proposals for changes of this kind were irresponsible. The government was determined not to make any further concessions, notwithstanding the considerable pressure to which it was subjected to increase the amount of the pension still further.

The government was undoubtedly strengthened in its determination by the fact that it was ready to unveil the outlines of a new social welfare measure which could be represented as providing additional income to pensioners in need. On April 6, 1965, Pearson announced in the House of Commons the government's intention to proceed, in consultation with the provinces, with what was henceforth to be called the Canada Assistance Plan (CAP).[20] This measure, which was enacted into law in July, 1966 (with effect from April 1, 1966), was the product mainly of the growing dissatisfaction of welfare specialists with the uncoordinated nature of Canada's approach to social security.[21] The purpose was to overcome the problem in one area of the total social security field, namely, the provision of public assistance to those whose eligibility was determined under a means or needs test. Such assistance was available at the time under a combination of "categorical" plans— so called because benefits were paid to people who were categorized according to the causes of their need—and under general assistance plans for those in need who did not fit into any of the designated categories. The categorical plans offered four distinct classes of benefit: means-test old age pensions (though in this case the plan was being phased out in favour of the universal plan), pensions for the blind, pensions for the permanently and totally disabled, and mothers' allowances. The federal government shared with the provinces the cost of providing the first three classes of benefit (but not the last) under the Old Age Assistance and Blind Persons Acts of 1951 and the Disabled Persons Act of 1954. It also shared the cost of general assistance by virtue of the Unemployment Assistance Act of 1956. Under the Canada Assistance Plan these various plans would be merged into unified provincially administered programs in which eligibility and the level of benefits would be determined by a needs test rather than a means test. The federal government undertook to share the cost of all benefits, including mothers' allowances, and of a number of additional services which it had previously claimed were exclusively a provincial responsibility.

The proposed CAP did not affect the universal pension directly, but the government argued that it would be of substantial benefit to pensioners who had little or no outside income since it would provide them with supplementary income in accordance with their need. Actually, supplements were already being provided in many cases under general assistance. The government's contention in effect was that the CAP, with its emphasis on needs testing, would relate the supplements more realistically to need. Since CAP administration was to be entirely a provincial matter, Ottawa had no clear idea of how pensioners in need would fare. It nevertheless relied on the CAP as its answer to the advocates of a $100 pension when it called an election in the fall of 1965 in an effort to gain a clear majority of seats in the House of Commons. The most comprehensive campaign statement on the subject was made by Pearson in a free-time CBC political telecast on October 15. He claimed that under the CAP (then still in the gestation stage) a pensioner would receive whatever additional income was required to meet his needs, and specifically mentioned $125 a month as the total pension and supplement which could conceivably be paid in some cases. The cost of raising the pension to $100 a month across the board would be prohibitive, he said, and would not meet actual need as successfully as the CAP. The government was returned in the election, though the majority of seats it sought eluded it, and it proceeded to process the CAP through Parliament. That, however, did not still the demand for a $100 universal pension. The CAP, whatever other merits it might have had, was not a plausible alternative to an increase in the old age pension. Notwithstanding optimistic prognostications about possible benefits, it was by no means clear that the treatment of pensioners would be substantially different from what it had been. The battle for the $100 pension continued in the new Parliament, being the subject of the main amendment in the Throne Speech debate.[22]

At this juncture, the outline of a quite different design was offered by a special committee of the Senate which had been established in 1963 on the initiative and under the chairmanship of David Croll to study the broad spectrum of social and economic problems associated with aging.[23] The committee members and advisers were hardly unaware of the controversy raging over the amount of the universal pension at the time their report was being prepared. They had been impressed during the hearings with the importance old people themselves attached to financial independence. The basic finding of the portion of the report devoted to economic security was that poverty continued to be a major problem of old age. Emphasis was laid on the growing inequality which would arise between people currently drawing the universal pension and younger people who would subsequently receive both the pension and an earnings-related pension which would become larger year by year as the Canada Pension Plan matured. A flat increase in the universal pension was rejected as not reducing this inequality (since the CPP beneficiaries would be eligible for it too) and as being too costly. At the same time, a needs test was declared to be "utterly unacceptable" except "to meet residual needs and to deal with special circumstances." What the report called a "guaranteed income program" was suggested as a way to avoid both Scylla and Charybdis. The committee, however, shied away from making a firm recommendation—out of the chairman's apprehension that the government might be embarrassed, according to a private interview—and contented itself with endorsing the idea "in principle" and recommending it as a subject for "immediate study." Specifically, the report suggested the income ceilings then in effect for the means-test pension ($1,260 for a single person and $2,220 for a couple) as the incomes to be guaranteed. It proposed that all people of sixty-five and over with at least ten years' residence in Canada should receive allowances sufficient to bring their incomes up to those figures. The allowances would be the responsibility of the federal government and would be paid on the basis of simplified income declarations completed annually and subject to sample checks.[24]

The nation's press gave this aspect of the committee's report front-page coverage and interpreted it as the first step to a guaranteed annual income program. The government, far from being embarrassed, soon brought in legislation to make the proposal effective in modified form from January 1, 1967. Knowles and others continued to battle for a universal pension of $100 a month, but public interest was waning. Old age pensions were not a significant issue in the federal election of 1968.

To finance both the new supplement and the progressive reduction of the age of eligibility for the universal pension, the ceiling on the income tax component of the old age security tax was raised to $240 a year, effective January 1, 1967. In other words, the tax was levied thereafter on the first $6,000 of annual taxable income rather than $3,000 as in the past. Finance Minister Mitchell Sharp claimed that this change would only partly meet the new demands on the old age security fund. He therefore announced an increase in the general sales tax, except for building materials and production machinery and equipment, from 11 to 12 percent which, he said, was intended to cover the balance.[25] The increase was not earmarked for old age security, however, and there was no immediate prospect of a deficit in the fund which would have to be covered from general revenues. It would appear that the liberalization of the old age security plan was the sugarcoating on the pill of an increased sales tax, the yield of which was used for other purposes. The base of the sales tax component of the old age security tax was eroded somewhat by the removal of the general sales tax from drugs in September, 1967, and its progressive removal from production machinery and equipment during 1967 and 1968.

2. EVOLUTION OF THE EARNINGS-RELATED PLAN

There were three main formulations of the earnings-related plan, embodied successively in the 1963 resolution, Bill C-75, and Bill C-136, the last of which was enacted with some changes. The 1963 resolution was sketchy but the accompanying explanatory statement filled in enough detail to indicate the main shape of the plan then envisaged, while the two bills were elaborated on in white papers. Further information was provided in two actuarial reports prepared at different points in the evolution of the plan.[26] Table 12 shows the principal characteristics of the successive formulations. The "final formulation" refers to the plan as enacted. Important differences between it and Bill C-136 as introduced are indicated in footnotes.

Several points are worthy of attention. First, coverage of the self-employed, originally conceived as voluntary, was ultimately made compulsory. Second, the transition period during which less than full benefits were to be paid remained unchanged at ten years in all formulations. Third, though the plan was at first intended to be on a pay-as-you-go basis, a degree of funding was introduced in Bill C-75 and was increased in the final formulation. The table shows the estimated size of the fund only at the end of the transition but, in both Bill C-75 and the final formulation, it was projected that the fund would continue to grow for about another decade. Fourth, the funding envisaged in Bill C-75 was to be accomplished by a reduction in the benefit level, with the contribution rate remaining unchanged. Ultimately, however, the benefit level was restored to approximately the average of that envisaged in the original formulation. Fifth, the earnings ceiling was increased in each formulation, which meant that there was a corresponding increase in maximum contributions and benefits. Sixth, survivor, death, and disability benefits were added in the final formulation. This was possible because of a constitutional amendment secured under circumstances described in section 3. Seventh, the addition of those benefits, coupled with the increase in both the old age benefit and the degree of funding over Bill C-75, necessitated a substantial increase in the contribution rate. The burden on those with very low incomes was eased by the introduction of a basic exemption. That made the contribution schedule progressive at the lowest ranges of the earnings scale, while the ceiling made it increasingly regressive at higher ranges.[27] Eighth, it was envisaged from the beginning that both the ceiling and the average earnings used in calculating the amount of the benefit at the time of the award would be subject to adjustment. The technique for doing so was refined from formulation to formulation, and it was made more restrictive between Bill C-75 and the final formulation (assuming, as seemed reasonable, that average earnings would continue to rise more rapidly than the cost of living). On the other hand, the final formulation extended the principle of adjustment to the amount of the pension after the original award. Ninth, the idea of permanently reducing the earnings-related old age benefit when claimed before seventy was abandoned in favour of a retirement test. The permanently reduced pension was to have been available at sixty-five from the beginning in the original formulation. Bill C-75 introduced the idea of a progressive reduction of the qualifying age for the retirement-tested pension so that it could not be claimed at sixty-five until 1970. This principle was extended to the universal pension, unconditioned by a retirement test in that case, under circumstances described above.

To an extent, revisions of the plan were initiated internally in the government as a team of experts and the minister of national health and welfare acquired a full understanding of all the complexities involved. To an extent also, these revisions were in response to arguments advanced by organized interest groups in their numerous submissions and by M.P.'s in the House of Commons. An example in this area was the decision to make coverage of the self-employed compulsory. That

TABLE 12

EVOLUTION OF THE 1965 PROGRAM

	Initial Formulation June–July, 1963	Bill C-75 Spring, 1964	Final Formulation Spring, 1965
	Earnings-Related Pensions		
Coverage	Compulsory for employees; voluntary for self-employed	Compulsory for employees; voluntary for self-employed	Compulsory for employees earning more than $600 a year and for self-employed earning at least $800
Transition	10 years	10 years	10 years
Funding	Negligible; pay-as-you-go financing intended[a]	Estimated fund of $2.5 billion at end of transition;[b] half to be available for investment in provincial securities	Estimated fund of $4.5 billion at end of transition (Quebec excluded);[b] all to be available for investment in provincial securities
Earnings ceiling	$4,000 a year, subject to "annual adjustment"	$4,500 a year in first 5 years; adjustable thereafter (see adjustments category)	$5,000 a year in 1966 and 1967; adjustable thereafter (see adjustments category)
Basic exemption	Nil	Nil	$600 a year
Employee contribution rate	"Initial rate" of 1 percent of earnings up to ceiling[c]	1 percent of earnings up to ceiling for first 15 years; upward revision thereafter[d]	1.8 percent of earnings between basic exemption and ceiling[e]

Qualifying age for old age benefit	Unconditional at 70; permanently reduced pension 65–69	Unconditional at 70; retirement test 65–69[f]	Unconditional at 70; retirement test 65–69[f]
Rate of benefit	30 percent of average adjusted earnings at 70; proportionate reductions for lower ages until 20 percent at 65	20 percent of average adjusted earnings	25 percent of average adjusted earnings
Other benefits	Pension for surviving spouse at 65	Pension for surviving spouse at 65	Broad range of survivor, death, and disability benefits
Adjustments	Earnings ceiling adj. "in line with changes in the general level of salaries and wages"	Earnings ceiling adj. to earnings index after first 5 years[g]	Earnings ceiling adj. to pension index 1968–75, to earnings index thereafter[g]
	Average earnings on which pension awarded adj. on same basis as earnings ceiling	Average earnings on which pension awarded adj. to earnings index[g]	Average earnings on which pension awarded adj. to pension index until 1975, to earnings index thereafter[g]
	No adj. of amount of pension after award	No adj. of amount of pension after award	Amount of pension after award adj. annually to pension index

continued over

TABLE 12 (*continued*)

	Initial Formulation June–July, 1963	Bill C-75 Spring, 1964	Final Formulation Spring, 1965
Exclusion of low earning periods	Unspecified number of "years of lowest earnings"; each year's earnings after 65 substitutable for earlier year	10 percent of total number of months; pensionable earnings after 65 substitutable for equal period of earlier earnings[h]	15 percent of total number of months;[i] pensionable earnings after 65 substitutable for equal period of earlier earnings[h]
		Universal Pensions	
Qualifying age	Unconditional at 70; permanently reduced pension 65–69	Unconditional at 70; permanently reduced pension 65–69[j]	Progressively reduced from 70 in 1965 to 65 in 1970[j]
Amount	Ranging from $75 a month at 70 to $51 a month at 65	Ranging from $75 a month at 70 to $51 a month at 65	$75 a month;[k] GIS added in 1966
Adjustment	None	None	Basic amount and GIS adj. annually to pension index[k]

[a]Even under pay-as-you-go financing, there would necessarily have been a surplus of contributions over benefits while the plan was maturing. It had originally been envisaged that much of this surplus would be used to finance the $10 increase in the universal pension. Abandonment of that device would have resulted in the accumulation of a somewhat larger fund, but not of the same magnitude as that envisaged in Bill C-75. To be specific, it was estimated in the first actuarial report (Aug. 30, 1963) that there would be a fund of $300 million after the 10-year transition. This was on the assumption that the $10 increase would be a charge on contributions. Elimination of that charge would have increased the fund to somewhat more than $700 million.

[b]Estimate based on "intermediate" cost assumptions and interest rate of 4 percent compounded annually.

[c]In view of the pay-as-you-go method of financing, it was anticipated that upward revision of the rate would be necessary in time, but no details were given. Employee contributions were to be matched by equal employer contributions; participating self-employed were to pay aggregate rate in full.

[d]The bill specified a rate of 1¼ percent from 1980, 1½ percent from 1990, 1¾ percent from 2000, and 2 percent from 2015, but provision was made for reducing 1980 and later rates by order in council if such reductions were justified by actuarial reports. Employee contributions were to be matched by equal employer contributions; participating self-employed were to pay aggregate rate of 2 percent in full during first 15 years, but thereafter their rate was to be the sum of the applicable employee rate and 1 percent.

[e]Matched by equal employer contributions; aggregate rate of 3.6 percent payable in full by self-employed.

[f]Qualifying age not to be 65 immediately, but to be reduced progressively until 65 in 1970.

[g]Earnings index structured differently in Bill C-75 and final formulation, but designed in each case to base adjustments on changes in general level of earnings rather than cost of living.

[h]Exclusions and substitutions applicable only after transition and subject to condition that total number of months not reducible below 120.

[i]Ten percent in Bill C-136 as introduced. Joint committee recommended 20 percent and government compromised at 15 percent.

[j]In Bill C-136 as introduced, provision was the same as in Bill C-75. Final formulation was introduced when bill was in committee of the whole, under circumstances described in the text.

[k]For subsequent changes in amount of pension and in adjustment procedure, see section 4 of this chapter.

resulted in part from representations by the Canadian Federation of Agriculture that many farmers would not take advantage of the opportunity for voluntary coverage and would therefore be disadvantaged when they reached retirement age.[28] The inclusion of adjustment features was influenced by persistent representations by the Canadian Labour Congress. In its policy resolution of 1960, the CLC spoke in terms of automatic adjustment of pension benefits to the cost of living. It subsequently adopted the position that pensioners should not merely be protected against increased living costs but should participate in improvements in the community's standard of living,[29] and it was critical of the government's final decision to relate some important adjustments to the cost of living based pension index.[30] Business organizations, on the other hand, tended to oppose adjustment factors of any kind, because of the unpredictability of their cost implications.

Influences of this kind were operating continuously as the plan went through its successive formulations, but in the main the final shape was the product of prolonged interaction between the federal government on the one hand and the provinces, more particularly Quebec, on the other. The successive federal proposals were an important topic of discussion, mainly behind the scenes, at plenary federal-provincial conferences on July 26–27, 1963, November 26–29, 1963, and March 31 to April 2, 1964.[31] These proposals were also discussed at a conference of welfare ministers held specifically for the purpose on September 9–10, 1963, and in numerous meetings of federal officials with their Quebec and Ontario counterparts. In addition, they were the subject of extensive correspondence between Pearson and the provincial premiers.[32]

Strictly speaking, Parliament was constitutionally competent to proceed with a plan providing old age benefits without provincial cooperation or consent. It was widely believed, however, that the inclusion of survivor, death, and disability benefits was desirable, and it was government policy now, as it had been on earlier occasions, that constitutional amendments affecting the federal-provincial distribution of power should be assented to in advance by all the provinces. Moreover, under the constitution as it then stood, legislation relating even to old age benefits would probably be inoperative in any province where comparable provincial legislation was enacted. The Quebec government left little doubt that it intended to proceed with such legislation, and the possibility could not be excluded that Ontario might do the same. There was general agreement that the federal plan would lose seriously in effectiveness, or would even be reduced to a nullity, if it was not to apply in the two largest provinces. The government and most Anglophone M.P.'s and national organizations regarded it as important that any plan should be nationwide in scope. In any case, the Liberal party was now espousing the principle of "cooperative federalism," and in general the government regarded consultation with the provinces as essential, especially in a field of concurrent jurisdiction.[33] Provincial influences on the final shape of the plan will be examined in section 3. First, some consideration should be given to a campaign to block enactment of the legislation altogether.

Among the first visitors to call on LaMarsh after she became minister of national health and welfare was a deputation from the life insurance industry seeking an assurance that the government did not intend to proceed with contributory pensions as promised in the 1962 and 1963 election campaigns.[34] When this assurance was not forthcoming and instead the resolution of June, 1963, was introduced, the industry mounted a campaign of growing intensity to prevent implementation of the plan. The Canadian Life Insurance Officers Association published a memorandum at the end of July attacking the plan in detail. Great West Life Assurance Company distributed a pamphlet entitled *Let's Raise a Storm!* (the text of a speech delivered by its president, D. E. Kilgour, in September) among agents, policy-holders, and others. Similar material was issued by other companies. Industry-inspired letters and resolutions flooded in on ministers and private members and were reinforced by personal contact and frequent statements to the press.[35] The government's successive formulations were attacked as economically and actuarially unsound, inequitable, and ill-designed to meet the most pressing welfare needs of the country. The industry's basic position was that the government was already playing its proper role in old age security by providing an income maintenance floor through the universal pension, and that if further intervention was considered necessary, it should take the form of Ontario's Pension Benefits Act of 1963, designed to regulate private pension plans and to compel establishment of such plans by employers with fifteen or more employees. The Canadian Chamber of Commerce supported the industry, as it had done in regard to annuity and pension legislation in the past, and it invited its provincial chambers to urge the legislatures of their provinces to cooperate in establishing uniform legislation across the country along the lines of the Ontario act.[36] Several provincial chambers accepted the invitation,[37] and many local chambers joined vigorously in the campaign to prevent enactment of the federal plan.[38]

The campaign provoked a countercampaign by the Canadian Labour Congress. In October, 1963, the congress circularized its provincial federations, local labour councils, and affiliated unions, urging them to forward resolutions to the government supporting the Canada Pension

Plan in principle and advocating revision of the government's proposal of the time in line with CLC policy. In January, 1964, the congress launched a postcard and petition campaign, using the federations and labour councils as distributing and collection agencies. A circular of February, designed to keep up the momentum of the campaign, used the reduced benefits envisaged in Bill C-75 as evidence of the need for renewed effort.[39] Of the 200,000 cards distributed, it would appear from reports submitted to CLC headquarters that about 100,000 were sent in, together with petitions bearing about 35,000 signatures. These figures probably fell well short of the number of cards and coupons mailed in in the 1950 campaign against the means test. Part of the reason was, no doubt, that the CLC did not direct a substantial publicity campaign to the general public as the Canadian Congress of Labour had done in 1950. It is also possible that so complex a matter as a contributory pension plan did not generate the same emotional reaction as the abolition of the means test. Nevertheless, the campaign undoubtedly helped to offset the insurance industry's efforts.[40]

LaMarsh has implied that there were moments of doubt as to whether the Canada Pension Plan would proceed. Indeed, she gave a small private luncheon after it was enacted "to honour Stan Knowles for his unremitting nagging in the House, which had helped me to keep the Prime Minister from wavering when the legislation was under heavy attack."[41] But the insurance industry was unable to drum up support for its campaign beyond the Chamber of Commerce. Other national organizations—business, labour, and welfare—supported or at least accepted the plan in principle, although they had many and varied objections to specific features of it.[42] In the House of Commons, only the Ralliement des Créditistes opposed it in principle.[43] By the time of the joint commitee's hearings, even the Chamber of Commerce appeared ready to acquiesce in the inevitable. Arguing that the committee "must decide whether the further development of our country's social security system should conform to the principles contained in Bill C-136 or . . . the principles of universal coverage through suitable modification and reformation of the Old Age Security Act," the chamber contented itself in the main with outlining the specific courses of action it thought should be followed in either case.[44] Only the life insurance spokesmen remained implacable to the end.

3. The Ottawa-Quebec Compromise

The Quebec government posed a more serious obstacle to the fruition of the federal plan. A new era in policy-making was inaugurated in that province by the provincial election of 1960. Duplessis had died in 1959, and the demoralized and discredited Union Nationale government was defeated by a resurgent Liberal party. This generation of educated elites were repudiating the conservative, defensive nationalism of the past, which had not only failed to adapt the province's social and educational policies to modern needs but had also left provincial economic development largely to corporations run by Americans and Anglophone Canadians. Jean Lesage left the federal Cabinet in 1958 to take over the leadership of the provincial Liberal party. Only forty-six at the time, he personified the spirit emerging in the province and was able to attract to the party people who rebuilt it and refurbished its image. He campaigned on an old slogan, *Maîtres chez nous*, but gave it fresh content. A positive nationalism saw the people of Quebec taking control of their own destiny through the instrumentality of the state. Government was viewed as having a dynamic, modernizing role to play, and no longer as a potential threat to the French-Canadian way of life. Naturally, it was the provincial government which was to assume the responsibility for modernization, since it alone understood and cherished the distinctive values of Quebec culture.

Social welfare policy was considered to have a particularly intimate relationship to that culture. The government wanted the predominantly Anglophone Cabinet and Parliament at Ottawa out of the field, at least in Quebec. Previous administrations, too, had usually been resentful of federal intrusions into the social welfare field. The difference was that they had rarely had alternative policies of their own: it was a field where, failing federal initiative, only minimal action would have been taken. The new government wanted a well-developed social security system, but it was to be a Quebec system devised by Québecois for Québecois. This position did not apply only to shared-cost programs, some of the more important of which related to welfare. It applied equally to three major areas—unemployment insurance, family allowances, and universal old age pensions—where the federal government had been exercising exclusive jurisdiction for years, to the satisfaction of the other provinces. In the case of the universal pension, Lesage presented a claim at the federal-provincial conference of July 26–27, 1963, for federal withdrawal in Quebec, with financial compensation through removal of the old age security tax in the province or payment of a fiscal equivalent.[45] Constitutionally, the province could probably have preempted the field simply by putting a universal plan of its own into operation. This was rendered impractical, however, by the fact that the federal government was levying taxes in Quebec which were earmarked for the national plan. The Quebec government wanted a free hand to develop a complete old age security program conforming to its own assessment of the needs of the aged in the context of the total social security requirements of the province.

Even apart from this stated purpose, a provincially operated contributory plan was attractive as an instrument for achieving the government's total objectives.[46] On the one hand, it could be represented as an important advance in social welfare. On the other hand, it could provide the government with capital for development. In the latter case, a substantial degree of funding would be required. Funding was justified on the ground that it would stabilize contribution rates for a prolonged period, but its primary attraction was that it would mobilize savings for investment purposes determined by the government.[47] Lesage had always favoured the contributory approach, even though he had had to settle for something less when he chaired the joint Senate and House of Commons committee in 1950. When he was chosen leader of the Quebec Liberal party in 1958, he had a clause regarding "a general retirement fund" inserted in the party's platform.

Shortly after his government assumed office in 1960, the provincial Labour Department embarked on a study of earnings-related pensions. The study was given a more formal status in the fall of 1962 when an interdepartmental committee, buttressed by four prominent actuaries serving as consultants, was appointed to take it over.[48] The committee made little progress in the next several months. Notwithstanding the potential significance of a contributory plan, the government was at the time too preoccupied with more immediately pressing matters. What galvanized it into action was the federal resolution of June, 1963, and the resulting prospect that Ottawa would be in a position to proceed with a national plan before Quebec was ready to preempt the field in its own territory. Just as the provincial government now found itself blocked out of universal pensions, so also preemption of the earnings-related pension field might well have been impractical once Ottawa started to levy contributions in Quebec for the national plan. Not until July, 1963, did the interdepartmental committee receive sufficiently narrow and precise policy directives from the Cabinet to enable it to come to grips with its task.[49] To stake out the province's claim, Lesage introduced this resolution at a special session of the Legislature in late August: "That it is expedient . . . to pass as soon as possible an act to establish a public and universal retirement fund based on actuarial calculations, and maintained by compulsory contributions from every employer and employee as well as from every independent worker and applicable to all salaries or earnings, up to a stated amount."[50] The only criticism from the Union Nationale opposition was that the government was not moving fast enough. Opposition leader Daniel Johnson moved an amendment calling for immediate establishment of a committee of the Legislature to prepare a bill before the federal Parliament, then in recess, resumed its sittings. When the amendment was defeated, the main resolution passed unanimously.[51]

In the meantime, the Ontario government had gone off on a tangent on earnings-related pensions. Since Ontario is the most industrialized of the provinces, it is not surprising that the question of portable pensions evoked growing interest there during the 1950s. The opposition parties attempted to make it an issue in the 1959 provincial election and continued their efforts in the first (1960) session of the new Legislature. The Liberals introduced a resolution asking the government to "make available facilities for the development of a province-wide scheme of portable pensions for all workers," while the CCF (later NDP) group introduced a bill calling for full and immediate vesting in private pension plans.[52] In addition, a government backbencher and a CCF member both raised the cognate question of discrimination against older workers in employment by introducing bills to outlaw it.[53] The question was related in that private pension plans were regarded by many as an important factor in the unwillingness of employers to hire workers of more than forty or forty-five years of age. Premier Leslie Frost countered on April 7 by announcing the establishment of a technical committee "to explore ways and means by which retirement pension plans can be made more effective, provide more security for our older people, and minimize these inhibitions which militate against the employment of the older worker."[54]

The end result of the committee's investigations and recommendations was the enactment of the Pension Benefits Act in the spring of 1963. This act was designed to serve three main purposes. First, it provided for the establishment and enforcement of minimum standards of solvency in private pension plans. Second, it guaranteed a limited measure of portability in such plans by laying down certain modest conditions governing vesting of employer contributions and locking in of employee contributions.[55] Third, it required all employers with fifteen or more employees to institute and/or maintain plans providing not less than prescribed minimum benefit levels. These employers could choose among three options, but essentially the minimum requirement was for a pension of $80 a month at age seventy for an employee who was covered continuously for forty years after the requirement was to come into force (January 1, 1965) and earned $400 a month or more during the entire period. The minimum for an employee with a shorter period of coverage or lower earnings was correspondingly less.

The first two of the above requirements are not relevant to this study since they were concerned purely with the regulation of private plans. The third, however, was presented as an alternative to a public contributory plan as a means of making earnings-related pensions more widely available. At the federal level, all three parties which were also represented in the Ontario Legislature were committed to a public plan in principle. In the Ontario House, though the official (Liberal) opposition was inclined to accept the government's approach, the CCF-NDP group presented the alternative point of view. It condemned the third requirement of the Pension Benefits Act as a poor substitute for a public plan, and proposed restriction of that act to the regulation of private plans with more stringent portability provisions.[56] A public plan was being advocated even within the Ontario public service. As discussed in chapter 7, section 2, the Department of Public Welfare had for some years been promoting the idea of public contributory pensions on the U.S. model. Despairing of federal action in the near future, that department turned its attention in the late 1950s to a provincial plan for Ontario and produced an outline of such a plan in July, 1961.[57] Its efforts were brushed aside by the portable pensions committee. One of the committee's two joint chairmen was George Gathercole, at the time deputy minister of economics and probably the government's most influential adviser. He was philosophically opposed to state invasion of the insurance field, and most of the committee members shared his point of view.[58] The committee recommended flatly against a provincially administered public plan and limited its attention to "ways and means by which [private] pension plans for employees can be improved, broadened and strengthened."[59] Such improvement, broadening, and strengthening included compulsory extension of private plans. This approach struck a responsive note in the thinking of John Robarts, who succeeded Frost as premier in the fall of 1961.[60]

When the first federal formulation went before the federal-provincial conference of July 26–27, 1963, Lesage announced that although Quebec would not stand in the way of the federal plan in any provinces that wanted it, it would itself proceed with its own plan which would be funded.[61] Robarts, who had piloted the Pension Benefits Act through the Ontario Legislature only a few months earlier, was characteristically cautious and noncommittal. More detailed information would be required, he said, before the province could arrive at a definite conclusion.[62] The search for an acceptable compromise devolved on federal officials, whose discussions with their Quebec and Ontario counterparts became almost continuous by the end of the year.[63] The officials hoped that Quebec might still be induced to accept the federal plan and that

166

even if it insisted on its own plan, the two could be coordinated. Either way, it would be necessary to revise the federal plan to provide substantial funding. Ontario for its part was objecting, among other things, that the benefit-contribution ratio in the federal plan was so favourable as to discourage private plans. The problem faced by the officials was to find an intersection between what Quebec and Ontario might accept and what could be sold to the federal Cabinet.

The plan was reformulated in the manner indicated in column 2 of table 12, and the new formulation, which became Bill C-75, was communicated in detail to the provinces by Pearson on January 11, 1964.[64] The basic benefit level was to be reduced with the result that a substantial fund would be accumulated. Pearson offered half of this fund to the provinces for their capital purposes. Woodrow Lloyd, CCF premier of Saskatchewan, objected strenuously to the reduction of benefits,[65] as did the CLC and NDP M.P.'s. Robarts, on the other hand, attacked the new formulation from the opposite side.[66] There should, he said, be a stricter relationship between benefits and contributions; otherwise, integration with private plans would be extremely difficult. Therefore, he objected to the adjustment feature in the plan and even more to the ten-year transition which would permit almost a generation of beneficiaries to receive pensions higher than the actuarial value of their contributions. In addition, he put in a claim for 90 percent of the fund for the provinces, arguing that 10 percent would provide the federal government with a reserve fund of the same magnitude as had been envisaged in the original formulation.

The objections of both Lloyd and Robarts paled into insignificance when the matter came before the federal-provincial conference of March 31 to April 2, 1964. Quebec's interdepartmental committee had been working feverishly to elaborate the full details of a provincial plan. Although its report had not yet been published, Lesage outlined the main features of its proposed plan informally to the conference. The effect was electric. To most of the other provinces, Quebec's formulation seemed far superior to that of the federal government.

For one thing, Quebec's plan made extensive provision for survivor, death, and disability benefits. The federal government's problem in this regard had been and continued to be Parliament's constitutional incapacity in the field. At the federal-provincial conferences of July and September, 1963, spokesmen for Quebec, the only holdout when Diefenbaker had first broached the subject of constitutional amendment, had indicated that their province would not stand in the way of a plan for the rest of Canada. It became clear at the conference of November 26 to 29, however, that Quebec was prepared to use concurrence in a constitutional amendment as a bargaining weapon. Lesage offered such concurrence "on the express condition that the text thus modified includes for each province (insofar as old age security, aid to widows, orphans and invalids are concerned) the option of withdrawing completely from the federal programme with full financial compensation."[67] Acceptance of that condition would have meant that if Quebec had established its own universal pension plan, as it clearly wanted to do, the long-established federal plan would have had to be withdrawn in that province. The Liberal government was no closer to getting agreement on a constitutional amendment than Diefenbaker had been, but the need to include the additional benefits in its earnings-related plan was becoming more pressing.

Beyond providing these additional benefits, the Quebec formulation also provided higher maximum old age benefits than Ottawa's, less regressivity in the contributions structure, and substantially greater funding. The last feature attracted particular attention among the other provinces. In ten years the fund for Quebec alone would be of about the same size as that envisaged in the Ottawa formulation for the whole country, and it would continue to grow for a longer period. All the provinces and their municipalities were encountering difficulty in financing the investment in social capital they were being called upon to undertake. Compulsory savings generated by a pension plan and segregated for provincially directed investment had attractions for governments which usually proclaimed their devotion to the free market.

The conference ended in a major break between Ottawa and Quebec, which was almost universally described by the press as a "crisis of Confederation." The proximate cause was not the pension plan but failure to agree on fiscal arrangements. The former was intimately involved, however, especially since Robarts now took the position that Ontario like Quebec would have to think in terms of its own plan.[68] The crisis was averted when several days of feverish behind-the-scenes negotiations between federal and Quebec representatives produced agreement in principle on a package settlement of outstanding issues.[69] The pension plan was part of the package. Quebec was to have its own plan, but a compromise was struck between its formulation and Ottawa's so that coverage, eligibility, contributions, benefits, and funding would be identical in the two plans. In addition, Quebec assented to a constitutional amendment on additional benefits, without attaching the condition of November, 1963.[70] On April 16, Pearson notified the provincial premiers of the terms of settlement on both fiscal matters and the pension plan,[71] and on June 4 he provided them with a statement of the details of the new pension formulation which had been hammered out in the interval.[72] To put the other provinces on the same footing as Quebec, Pearson offered them the option either of administering the common plan themselves or, if they chose federal administration, of receiving all the investment funds generated by contributions in their territories. Thus, Quebec asserted successfully the paramountcy of its jurisdiction, while Ottawa was able to hold out the prospect that the terms if not the administration of the new formulation would be nationwide in application.

Table 13 sets forth the main features of the Quebec formulation as embodied in the report of the interdepartmental committee. For convenience, the comparable provisions of the federal government's second formulation (Bill C-75) are reproduced from table 12 in a parallel column. A compromise of these two formulations produced the final plans of both the federal and Quebec governments. In the Quebec formulation, coverage was to be compulsory for the self-employed as well as for employees, and the ceiling was to be substantially higher than in the federal formulation. As a result, total contributions would have been relatively much larger. In addition, the contribution rate was to be considerably higher, though there was an offsetting factor in the $1,000 basic exemption.[73] To an extent, the higher old age benefit and the inclusion of other benefits required a higher contribution rate. That, however, was only part of the story. The rate was sufficiently higher that, in combination with the twenty-year transition, it was to produce a level of funding far in excess of Ottawa's. Indeed, comparison of the sizes of the estimated funds after ten years understates the true situation. Since the transition was to be ten years in the Ottawa formulation, it was expected that the growth of the fund would level off after another decade. In the Quebec formulation, on the other hand, the transition would not end until then. It was estimated that the fund would continue to grow for still another decade until it reached $7.8 billion in 1996. The Quebec formulation proposed adjustments related to changes in the cost of living rather than in general earnings levels. It also proposed, however, that the benefits themselves, as well as the earnings on which they were initially based, should be so adjusted.

Comparison of table 13 with column 3 of table 12 indicates the main lines of the compromise. The federal government, which was in any case receiving representations for the inclusion of the self-employed, conceded the point, while Quebec made a sizeable concession on the ceiling. The old age benefit was set at 25 percent of average adjusted earnings, which was precisely the Quebec figure, and at the same time enabled Ottawa to claim that it had reverted in principle to its original intention of a benefit ranging from 20 to 30 percent of earnings (see

169

TABLE 13
FEDERAL AND QUEBEC FORMULATIONS
EARNINGS-RELATED PENSIONS
SPRING, 1964

	Federal Bill C-75	Quebec Committee Report
Coverage	Compulsory for employees; voluntary for self-employed	Compulsory for employees and self-employed earning more than $1,000 a year
Transition	10 years	20 years
Funding	Estimated fund of $2.5 billion at end of transition;[a] half to be available for investment in provincial securities	Estimated fund of $2.4 billion at end of 10 years, $5.6 billion at end of transition;[a] all available for Quebec investment
Earnings ceiling	$4,500 a year in first 5 years; adjustable thereafter (see adjustments category)	$6,000 a year in first 2 years; adjustable thereafter (see adjustments category)
Basic exemption	Nil	$1,000 a year
Employee contribution rate	1 percent of earnings up to ceiling for first 15 years; upward revision thereafter[b]	2 percent of earnings between basic exemption and ceiling[c]
Qualifying age for old age benefit	Unconditional at 70; retirement test 65–69[d]	Unconditional at 70; retirement test 65–69
Rate of benefit	20 percent of average adjusted earnings	25 percent of average adjusted earnings
Other benefits	Pension for surviving spouse at 65	Broad range of survivor, death, and disability benefits[e]
Adjustments	Earnings ceiling adj. to earnings index after first 5 years	Earnings ceiling adj. to consumer price index after first 2 years

TABLE 13 (*continued*)

	Federal Bill C-75	Quebec Committee Report
	Average earnings on which pension awarded adj. to earnings index	Average earnings on which pension awarded adj. to consumer price index
	No adj. of amount of pension after award	Amount of pension after award adj. "periodically" to consumer price index within limits of 1 and 2 percent
Exclusion of low earning periods	10 percent of total number of months; pensionable earnings after 65 substitutable for equal period of earlier earnings[f]	Ascending scale ranging from 1 year for 21 to 25 years of contributions to 5 years for 41 to 47 years; no provision for substituting earnings after 65 since no contributions after that age

[a]Estimate based on "intermediate" cost assumptions and interest rate of 4 percent compounded annually.

[b]See table 12, n. *d.*

[c]Matched by equal employer contributions; aggregate rate of 4 percent payable in full by self-employed.

[d]Qualifying age not to be 65 immediately, but to be reduced progressively until 65 in 1970.

[e]Disability benefits not payable initially before 60.

[f]Exclusions and substitutions applicable only after transition and subject to condition that total number of months not reducible below 120.

table 12, column 1). The survivor, death, and disability benefits, which Ottawa was now constitutionally competent to legislate, were taken over in substantial measure from the Quebec formulation, except for disability benefits.[74] Ottawa accepted a large increase in the level of contributions. Though the rate finally chosen was somewhat lower than Quebec's, the substantial reduction in the basic exemption ($600 compared with $1,000 a year in the Quebec formulation) resulted in higher absolute contributions in all but the top earnings range.[75] In regard to adjustments of the earnings ceiling and of the average earnings for calculating the initial amount of the pension, the cost of living (preferred by Quebec) was chosen as the base for the transition period but will be replaced by general earnings levels (Ottawa's preference) in 1975. An important additional feature not in Ottawa's formulation was taken over from Quebec, namely, adjustment of the amount of the pension after it is first awarded (on the basis of the cost of living). This adjustment was also applied to the universal pension.[76] Ottawa's formula for excluding low earnings periods was adopted in preference to the less precise (and also less favourable) Quebec formula.

Ottawa managed to retain the ten-year transition. This was no mean achievement. Not only did Quebec take a strong stand in favour of twenty years, but Ontario, business organizations, and the Conservative opposition in Parliament all pressed for a long transition (even longer than twenty years in some cases). The rationale of a long transition advanced by its proponents was that it conformed to what was described as the principle of "individual equity." In the full application of this principle, the pension of each individual would be strictly related to the contributions made by him and on his behalf, which, to be fully realized, would require a transition of forty or forty-five years. This, it was argued, was justified where a universal pension was already being provided, as in Canada. The universal pension guaranteed a basic minimum for everyone by effecting transfers among individuals. It was therefore unnecessary and inequitable to use earnings-related pensions to make still further transfers. The other side of the coin was that, the longer the transition, the longer would be the time before full benefits were payable. Even under a twenty-year transition, which was well short of providing "individual equity" in full, those who were over fifty would not be able to qualify for full benefits and those who were well over that age would receive very small benefits indeed. The federal government, supported by the CLC and NDP, argued that the new plan should offer meaningful benefits to these people. That view prevailed.

In the matter of funding, the federal government retreated a long way from its original intention to establish a pay-as-you-go plan. The decisions to provide for funding in Bill C-75 and to double it in Bill C-136 were due entirely to the determination of Quebec, supported by other provinces, to make substantial investment funds available for provincial purposes. Business, labour, and welfare organizations all opposed funding, as did all parties in the House of Commons. The motivations of such diverse groups naturally varied. Some, including the federal government itself and business groups, were opposed to the accumulation of investment funds in government hands. Some also wanted to minimize costs, while others wanted to maximize benefits. Since funding is inimical to both cost minimization and benefit maximization, groups with contrary objectives found common ground in opposing it. They all pointed out repeatedly that, except for a contingency reserve, funding is unnecessary in a public plan, the solvency of which is ultimately guaranteed by the state itself. The necessity in the case of the Canada Pension Plan arose out of provincial hunger for investment capital.

When Pearson announced in April, 1964, that a basis of settlement had been reached with Quebec, Robarts responded with an amendment to the Ontario Pension Benefits Act which removed the requirement on employers with fifteen or more employees to establish private plans. Actually, it is far from certain that that requirement would have made the proposed federal plan inoperative in Ontario. Logically, the two were not mutually exclusive: it would have been possible for an Ontario employer with fifteen or more employees to both participate in the federal plan and provide an additional benefit under a private plan in accordance with the provincial legislation. It was hardly expedient politically, however, and certainly not in accord with the philosophy of the Robarts government, to impose this dual obligation. The Ontario legislation provided the insurance industry fortuitously with a talking point, but it was of little significance in the development of public pensions in Canada. That legislation probably did not even provide the provincial government with leverage in discussions with Ottawa, because it was not a politically attractive alternative to the federal plan in any of its formulations. The minimum benefit the Ontario plan guaranteed was not to be paid in full until the year 2005. "Individual equity" was satisfied, but it is doubtful if significant numbers of the public were prepared to embrace that tendentious abstraction in preference to the concrete advantages of a plan under which full benefits would be paid at a higher level after ten years. Thus, even if the courts were to hold that the Ontario legislation preempted the field in that province, it is hard to conceive of any government using it to block a plan which the public would almost certainly regard as superior. When Robarts sponsored the Pension Benefits Act amendment, he accepted the inevitable.

At the same time, Robarts was loath to accept a plan worked out by Ottawa and Quebec without reference to Ontario, especially in view of the large-scale violation of the principle of individual equity. Even as the Pension Benefits Act was amended, he again held out the possibility that the Ontario government might find it to be in the best interests of the province to establish its own public plan.[77] Robarts was uncommunicative about the terms of the plan and gave no assurance that they would not diverge from those of the federal plan. Federal officials could not but be concerned about this possibility after their supreme effort to secure common terms between the federal and Quebec plans. And even if Ontario accepted the federal-Quebec terms in full, separate administration by that province, with its relatively large number of high income earners, could vitiate the calculations on which some of the benefits in the federal plan were based. In spite of this, however, Robarts' bargaining position was inherently weak. If, on the one hand, the terms of an Ontario plan were substantially different from Ottawa's, the provincial government would suffer the opprobrium of excluding its constituents from the nationwide portability which had apparently been achieved by the federal-Quebec settlement. On the other hand, if the terms were identical, the government would have the difficult task of explaining why provincial administration was necessary. The difficulty would be compounded by the fact that entirely new machinery would have to be established to collect the necessary contributions, a problem not encountered in Quebec as it had been collecting its own income tax since 1954 and pension contributions could be integrated with that collection. A public opinion poll published in July, 1964, indicated that most respondents outside Quebec favoured federal administration.[78]

One of Robarts' stated objections to leaving the matter entirely in federal hands was that Ottawa could change the terms of the plan without reference to the provinces, even though their interests might be involved. The federal government conceded this point. When Bill C-136 was introduced, it included provisions whereby (a) amendments affecting benefit levels or contribution rates cannot come into force earlier than the first day of the third year following notice of such amendments, and (b) amendments affecting any financial provisions of the act require the consent of at least two-thirds of the provinces where the plan is in force, having at least two-thirds of the aggregate population of those provinces. Thus, while any four of the provinces other than Quebec can veto an amendment, Ontario alone can do so since it has well over a third of the Canadian population outside Quebec. A guarantee was also included in the bill whereby a province which might later decide to set up its own plan will be in the same financial position as if it had opted out initially.

Ontario negotiators continued to press for a closer relationship between benefits and contributions. Thus, they continued to oppose the short transition and the adjustment features and added their opposition to the basic exemption (a new element in the latest federal formulation). They were unsuccessful on all points, but the essay in brinkmanship continued throughout 1964. Not until January 21, 1965, did Robarts announce that Ontario would accept both the federal plan and federal administration.[79] Ten days later, provincial representatives made a last attempt to change some features of the federal plan by presenting a brief to the joint Senate and House of Commons committee.[80] By then, however, the game was lost. Ontario had no influence on the final shape of the plan except to limit the federal government's freedom of action in amending it.

The joint committee had little influence either. It was in a different position from that of the Commons committee of 1924 and even the joint committee of 1950. In each of the earlier cases, especially the first, the committee had had scope to make a positive contribution, because the government had still been searching for a policy. In the Canada Pension Plan, hard bargaining between Ottawa and Quebec had produced a fully developed policy. The government made some minor changes in the earnings-related plan as a result of the committee's recommendations, but it was not prepared to do anything which would upset the hard-won agreement with Quebec. The committee's voluminous proceedings are mainly of interest in providing a valuable compendium of the views of major organized interest groups and of the analyses of numerous government experts whose talents were applied to the composition of this complex legislation.

4. REVISION OF THE 1965 PROGRAM

It had been expected that politically charged demands for increased pension benefits would be quelled by the adjustment feature built into the 1965 program, but that expectation was belied by persistent inflation after 1965. As previously noted, increases in the pension index were restricted to 2 percent per year, but year by year the cost of living increased by more. By 1970 the universal pension had reached $79.58 and the maximum guaranteed income supplement $31.83. If these payments had fully reflected increases in the consumer price index, they would have been close to $84.50 and $33.50. Once again pensions began to rise to the surface as a significant political issue. M.P.'s were raising the financial problems of pensioners with increasing frequency, as were the press and organized groups. Pensioners' organizations in particular were becoming more vocal. Politically, it was impossible to ignore Canada's nearly 2 million pensioners, almost all of whom were eligible to vote.

Simultaneously, however, expenditures on public pensions were mounting rapidly under the combined impact of the progressive reduction of the eligible age, the introduction of the GIS, and increases arising from adjustment. Expenditures on the universal pension, including the GIS, increased from just over $1,000 million in the 1965–66 fiscal year to over $2,500 million in 1972–73.[81] As a result, concern over the cost implications of pensions came to occupy centre stage again. The principle of universality, which had not been seriously challenged for fifteen years after its adoption in 1951, came under growing attack in the late 1960s. Prime Minister Trudeau himself was an outspoken opponent of the principle, as indicated graphically by his comment during the 1968 election campaign that there would be "no more of this free stuff." The argument against universality was that it diverted resources from those who were genuinely in need to those with more than adequate incomes. The fact that even millionaires were technically eligible for the universal pension was often cited in support of this proposition. In fact, incomes of the pensionable age group are much below the average for the community, and few in the group are wealthy. In 1971, for example, over 85 percent of income recipients aged sixty-five and over were receiving less than $5,000 a year, while only about 3 percent were receiving $10,000 or more. The median income for the age group was $1,867 per year compared with $4,186 for all ages.[82] The symbolism was effective, however. Universality could readily be represented as militating against the realization of the "just society" to which the government claimed to be committed.

In 1970 the government's policy on income security was set forth in two white papers, one on unemployment insurance and the other on the broader aspects of the question.[83] In the latter, the government stated its welfare philosophy in the following paragraph, which was printed in italics:

> Greater emphasis should be placed on anti-poverty measures. This should be accomplished in a manner which enables the greatest concentration of available resources upon those with the lowest incomes. Selective payments based on income should be made, where possible, in place of universal payments which disregard the actual income of

the recipient. In addition, social insurance programs should be expanded in those areas where poverty alleviation or prevention can be achieved. The combined result should provide a more stable income base for low-income families.[84]

In pursuance of this philosophy, the report proposed inter alia significant changes both in the universal pension and GIS and in the earnings-related pension, with the overall objective of downgrading the universal pension and upgrading the GIS and earnings-related pension in relative importance. Because of the statutory conditions governing amendment of the Canada Pension Plan, described in section 3, the proposed changes in the earnings-related pension could not come into effect before January 1, 1973, at the earliest nor without the consent of at least six of the nine Anglophone provinces including Ontario. Further, if identity of terms between the Quebec and Canada plans was to be retained, the cooperation of Quebec was necessary. No such limitations applied to changing the universal pension and GIS, and the white paper proposals on these items were implemented almost immediately.[85] Living costs continued to rise rapidly, however, and a general election was drawing inexorably nearer. As a result, further substantial changes were made in the universal pension and GIS in 1972. Even this was not the end of the story. The Liberal government fared badly in the general election of October 30, 1972, being reduced to 109 members in the 264-seat House of Commons. This left the Liberals with a margin of only 2 over the Conservatives and made them dependent on the 30-member NDP contingent for a majority. To retain NDP support, the government twice amended the Old Age Security Act during 1973 in ways which represented significant backtracking from the philosophy of the 1970 white paper.

The 1972 changes in the universal pension and GIS were the occasion of a flare-up in a simmering dispute between Ottawa and Quebec regarding jurisdiction over welfare legislation. Successive Quebec governments through the 1960s had insisted that Ottawa should vacate the welfare field in Quebec. Failure to achieve an accommodation on this matter which was satisfactory to the provincial government resulted in Quebec's rejection of the Victoria Charter (on constitutional amendment) in June, 1971, after Ottawa and all the other provinces had accepted it;[86] and the dispute continued afterwards to be a source of friction between the federal and Quebec governments. Quebec Social Affairs Minister Claude Castonguay and his department were working actively on plans for a major overhaul of the province's income security system, based on a massive study of the subject as part of an even more massive study of health and welfare policy generally.[87] The federal government's unilateral announcement in May, 1972, of a major change in the universal pension and GIS exasperated Castonguay to the point where it was only with difficulty that he was dissuaded from resigning.[88] Whether as a consequence of this or for some other reason, he proceeded almost immediately with legislation amending the Quebec Pension Plan without consultation with Ottawa.[89] In the meantime, negotiations with the other provinces on Ottawa's proposed amendments to the Canada Pension Plan had been pursued in only a desultory fashion, but the question of amending the plan was revived in a comprehensive *Working Paper* issued by the federal government in April, 1973.[90] The paper was considered by federal-provincial conferences of welfare ministers held on April 25 to 27 and October 11 and 12, with agreement being reached on significant amendments at the October conference.

A brief summary follows of the revisions made in the universal plan and GIS in 1970, 1972, and 1973, of the amendments made in the QPP in 1972, and of the changes in both the CPP and QPP agreed to in October, 1973.

Universal Pension and GIS. The old age security amending act of 1970 eliminated upward adjustment of the universal pension. That pension had been scheduled to increase to $81.51 a month on January 1, 1971, by virtue of the operation of the pension index, but it was instead frozen at $80. Residence requirements were also made somewhat more restrictive. Previously an applicant who had lived in Canada for the year immediately preceding his qualifying date but had been absent for all or part of the previous nine years could use earlier residence at any time in his life to compensate for the absence on a two for one basis. As a result of the 1970 amending act, earlier residence must now be triple the total period of absence and only residence after the applicant reached the age of eighteen can be counted. On the other hand, the maximum GIS was increased by considerably more than the amount which would have resulted from the normal operation of the pension index. For the 1971–72 fiscal year, the maximum was fixed at $55 a month for a single pensioner or one with a spouse not in receipt of the universal pension and at $95 for a married couple both on universal pension. The combined universal pension and maximum GIS thus produced aggregate payments of $135 a month single and $255 a month married. The comparable figures for the 1971 calendar year under the unamended legislation were $113.61 single and $227.22 married. The new legislation converted the basis of payment of the GIS from the calendar to the fiscal year in order to allow greater time to calculate the benefits to which GIS applicants are entitled and thus to reduce the number of *ex post facto* adjustments. During the three transitional months between January 1 and April 1, 1971, GIS recipients were paid the benefits provided in the unamended legislation.

The amending legislation provided for adjustment of the GIS after 1971–72 on the basis of the pension index. The annual increment, however, was to be a percentage, not of the GIS alone, but of the combined GIS and universal pension. On the other hand, continued use of the pension index meant that there would continue to be a 2 percent ceiling on the overall increase in any year. Moreover, the conversion of the basis of payment from the calendar to the fiscal year increased by three months the lag between actual increases in the cost of living and their reflection in increased GIS payments. The effect of the adjustment provision was to increase the supplement of those entitled to maximum GIS to $57.70 a month single and $100.10 married for 1972–73. Coupled with the universal pension, these payments produced total benefits of $137.70 single and $260.10 married.

The new rates had hardly taken effect when they were superseded by an amending act of May, 1972. The principal effects of this act were to restore upward adjustment for the universal pension, to increase the maximum GIS substantially, and to replace the pension index by a new formula for adjusting both the universal pension and the GIS. The figure of $80 a month at which the universal pension had previously been frozen was now established as the base for that pension. For the future, it was provided that upward adjustment, where warranted by increases in the cost of living, would occur in relation to the fiscal year. For 1972, however, where an upward adjustment of $2.88 a month was indicated, the adjustment was made retroactive to the beginning of the calendar year (continuing for fifteen months to the end of the 1972–73 fiscal year). As for the GIS, a single person entitled to the maximum was provided with a combined universal pension and GIS of $150 a month and a married couple with $285, compared with $137.70 and $260.10 which they would have received without the amendment. These new figures were also made retroactive to January 1 and were made subject to upward adjustment after 1972 on a fiscal year basis.

A new adjustment formula was established, the most significant effect of which was to eliminate the 2 percent ceiling inherent in the pension index. Also of some significance was the fact that the time lag between the cost of living increase and the pension adjustment, which had been extended three months by the 1970 amending act, was restored to the original interval. As a result of these two changes, the universal pension and the GIS came substantially closer than in the past to retaining their purchasing power, but the fact that the adjustment continued to be made only once a year permitted considerable erosion during the rapid inflation of 1973. The amending acts of 1970 and 1972 left unchanged the original income test provisions under which the GIS is reduced by $1 per month for each full $2 of outside income.

The first of the 1973 amending acts raised the universal pension to $100 a month effective April 1. This was $13.39 a month more than would have become payable on that date under the adjustment formula established in 1972. Provision was also made for annual adjustment from the $100 figure (starting in 1974) on the basis of the 1972 formula. The GIS was automatically adjusted effective April 1, 1973, so that starting from that date pensioners qualifying for full GIS received a combined universal pension and GIS of $170.14 a month at the single rate and $324.58 at the married rate. The second 1973 act adjusted both the universal pension and GIS upward from October 1 of that year (although no adjustment would otherwise have been made until April 1, 1974), and for the future, the act converted the adjustment process from an annual to a quarterly basis. The October adjustment raised the universal pension to $105.30 a month, and for those qualifying for the full GIS, the combined universal pension and GIS were increased to $179.16 for single and to $341.80 for married pensioners. Quarterly adjustments started in January, 1974, and the nature of the formula now in effect is illustrated by its specific application in January: the pension amounts established in October were increased by the ratio of the average of the consumer price index for August to October, 1973, to the average for May to July, 1973. Appropriate changes in the months used are made in each subsequent application of the formula. A ratchet clause prevents downward adjustment.

The tripartite old age security tax was abolished effective January 1, 1972. The sales tax component was simply transferred to the regular sales tax so that there was in fact no change in what the taxpayer pays. The corporation income tax component, on the other hand, was not similarly offset, while the personal income tax component was swallowed up in a major revision of the overall income tax rate structure implemented by a new Income Tax Act of 1971. Notwithstanding the discontinuance of earmarked taxes for the old age security fund, the fund itself was not abolished. Instead, the law requires credits to be made to the fund periodically which are estimated by the minister of national revenue to be equal to the amounts which the earmarked taxes would have yielded if they had continued to be separately identified.

Earnings-Related Pension. The key change in the earnings-related plan proposed in the 1970 white paper was a substantial progressive increase in the earnings ceiling. The legislative conditions governing upward adjustment of the ceiling had become quite unrealistic. For reasons explained in chapter 7, section 1, the ceiling could not increase by more than $100 a year between 1967 and 1975, and without legislative change it would have been at most $5,800 in 1975. That figure bore little relationship to the rapidly rising living costs and even more rapidly rising general level of earnings of recent years. In the words of the white paper: "The result is that a larger and larger proportion of contributors are at or above the earnings ceiling. This process is steadily converting an earnings-related plan, in which the amount of benefits was supposed to bear some relationship to previous earnings, into another flat-rate benefit plan for all those contributors now above the ceiling."[91] Therefore the white paper proposed a legislated increase in the ceiling to $6,300 in 1973, $7,100 in 1974, and $7,800 in 1975, as well as some other changes including improved survivor and disability benefits.

The 1972 amendments to the Quebec Pension Plan speeded upward adjustment of the earnings ceiling in that province, but not to the extent envisaged in the federal proposals. Specifically, the figures in the amended Quebec legislation were $5,900 for 1973, $6,100 for 1974, and $6,300 for 1975. The retirement test was relaxed, and the ceiling on the pension index was raised from 2 to 3 percent. Survivor and disability benefits were liberalized, though to a smaller degree on the whole than those proposed by the federal government. Thus, after January 1, 1973, when most of the Quebec amendments came into force, the terms of the Quebec plan deviated to a not inconsiderable extent from those of the Canada plan.

Ottawa, however, was still aiming at a revised plan which would be acceptable to all provinces, including Quebec. The 1973 working paper contained a wide-ranging set of "propositions" for changing Canada's overall social security system, and offered these as subjects for "joint federal-provincial review."[92] In the specific case of the CPP, the paper revived the proposal for an increase in the ceiling to $7,800 by 1975 and added a proposal that the 2 percent limit on the annual adjustment of pension benefits inherent in the pension index be abandoned in favour of full adjustment in accordance with rises in living costs. Intensive negotiations with the provinces followed, which resulted in agreement at the October 11–12 conference on full cost of living adjustment of benefits, acceleration of upward adjustment of the earnings ceiling and basic exemption, and elimination of the retirement test. Quebec accepted the agreement, so that at the end of 1973 the Canada and Quebec plans were in the process of being brought into harmony again, except for some survivor and disability benefits which were left to later negotiation. The conference also agreed that "priority attention" would be given in future discussions to "a number of additional concerns about the Canada and Quebec Pension Plans including, for example, the equality between men and women with regards [*sic*] to contributions and benefits; non-contributing spouses; the suggestion that early retirement provisions should be built into the Canada and Quebec Plans; the level of survivors' and disability benefits."[93]

It was decided to implement the agreed changes in two stages, so that some which were regarded as particularly urgent could be made effective at the beginning of 1974 without waiting for legislation to be drafted on the entire package. Accordingly, a bill was introduced in the House of Commons on October 22, 1973, and it received third reading on December 7.[94] It removed the 2 percent limit on annual adjustment of benefits from January 1, 1974, on, and for those who had gone on pension before that date, benefits were recalculated as if the limit had never been in effect. In addition, the base was made more current: whereas the adjustment for any year had previously been based on the average of the consumer price index for the twelve months ended on the preceding June 30, it was based for 1974 on the average for the sixteen months ended on October 31, 1973, and it will in every future year be based on the twelve months ended on the preceding October 31. The new legislation also fixed the earnings ceiling at $6,660 for 1974 and $7,400 for 1975, compared with $5,700 and $5,800 which would have been reached under the unamended legislation. A side effect of the increase in the ceiling to $6,600 was an increase in the amount of annual earnings exempt from contributions from $600 to $700. The overall result of the increased ceiling and exemption was to increase maximum employee contributions (matched by equal employer contributions) to $106.20 a year in 1974, from the $91.80 they would have been under the old legislation. Increased contributions will of course be reflected in increased benefits in time.

Legislation scheduled for 1974, designed to enact the remaining terms agreed to at the conference of October, 1973, is to provide for future increases in the earnings ceiling of 12.5 percent a year until the ceiling reaches the average earnings indicated by the Statistics Canada industrial composite of wages and salaries. It was estimated at the conference that this provision would result in an increase in the ceiling to over $13,000 by 1980, with corresponding increases in maximum contributions and benefits. Under the new legislation, the basic exemption is to be 10 percent of the ceiling. The retirement test will be eliminated so that pensioners between sixty-five and sixty-nine will be able to collect the full benefits their contributions justify whether or not they are gainfully employed.

Chapter Nine

Public Pensions and the Policy Spiral

1. INTEREST ARTICULATION AND AGGREGATION

AS A RESULT OF THE ENVIRONMENTAL CHANGES outlined in chapter 2, three main "groups" emerged in Canada with an interest in public pensions. There were, first, those who had reached or were approaching the age of seriously reduced earning capacity; second, the children of such people who, in traditional thinking, were responsible for maintaining their aged parents but were increasingly unable or unwilling to do so; and third, those whose sympathies were engaged by the plight in which many of the aged found themselves. These were groups only in the categoric sense of the term—diffuse collectivities with certain common characteristics and resulting shared attitudes but with no structural basis for cohesive action which could impinge directly on policy-making. Nothing emerged in Canada resembling the Townsend movement, which attracted millions of supporters in the United States in the 1930s with its promise of pensions for all retired people over sixty. Part of the reason no doubt was that, by the time the Great Depression struck, legislation was already on the books under which pensions were being paid to at least the most needy of the aged in some provinces and the means could readily be identified by which such pensions could become payable in the others.[1] There are shadowy references in the historical record to an organized group in Ontario (possibly two) which tried to pressure governments on public pensions in the 1920s.[2] With this exception, there is no trace of any organizations devoted primarily to securing or improving public pensions until after the 1927 act had been implemented. The role of these organizations after they did appear will be dealt with in section 2; for the moment it is sufficient to say that their influence has been marginal though it is now growing.

The existence of the diffuse collectivities mentioned at the beginning of the preceding paragraph, however, was of central importance. Truman's term "submerged" or "potential" interest groups, defined as "interests that are not at a particular point in time the basis of interaction among individuals, but may become such,"[3] can be aptly applied to them in his less comprehensive sense of "potential groups representing separate minority elements." He said: "Obstacles to the development of organized groups from potential ones may be presented by inertia or by the activities of opposed groups, but the possibility that severe disturbances will be created if these submerged, potential interests should organize necessitates some recognition of these interests and gives them a minimum of influence."[4] One can go further and say that the possibility of disturbances may exist in certain circumstances even if there is no apparent prospect that the interests concerned will organize, and it may exist to a degree that confers more than a "minimum of influence." The members of the categoric groups now under consideration were eligible to vote and, taken together, they constituted a significant segment of the total qualified electors.[5] The importance of this obvious fact should not be downgraded merely because of its obviousness. True, a single issue rarely, if ever, determines the voting choices of many electors.[6] Nevertheless, there is considerable evidence that many M.P.'s in Canada were convinced that the pension issue was a significant, even decisive, factor in electoral choice, especially at certain critical junctures in the development of pension policy.[7] This was true also of provincial politicians in those periods when public pensions were a provincial issue, notably in the decade when one province after another was induced to implement the federal act of 1927. To say this is not to deny that many politicians supported public pensions on grounds of equity, but merely to assert that their subjective assessments of the salience of the issue provided a recurring incentive for action. Actually, these two factors were probably mutually reinforcing. To take an example, Canadian Institute of Public Opinion polls indicated that a majority of the population supported the means test until after the report of the 1950 joint committee recommending a universal pension had received wide publicity;[8] yet many M.P.'s had long been convinced that elimination of the test was essential on political as well as moral grounds. Their constant agitations (and those of other opinion leaders) contributed to growing public rejection of the means test, and this in turn reinforced their determination to eliminate it.

The increasing magnitude of the need for public pensions made articulation inevitable. In the initial stages, however, it was a slow process. Hennessy's schema, described in chapter 1, section 3, is useful in explaining the prolonged time interval involved. At the turn of the century, public pensions had hardly emerged out of the sacrilege stage in Canada. The market ethos, reinforced by the experiences of a pioneer style of life which had disappeared not long before, did not envisage systematic income maintenance as a legitimate area of public policy. Even after the idea as applied to the aged received formal expression in the House of Commons and in the trade union movement, it was many years before public pensions became a salient issue. Long-term repetition of the demand was necessary before the resistance of the market ethos and the economic interests justified by it was overcome. The example of other countries contributed to the educative process. A policy which was already operative elsewhere, particularly in the British Empire countries of New Zealand, Australia, and the United Kingdom itself, could not remain in the category of an unthinkable thought. The international political system underlined the legitimacy of such a policy by its forthright support of public social security in part XIII of the Treaty of Versailles. Within Canada, the dislocations resulting from World War I created receptivity to new ideas. The reports of the Mathers Commission and the National Industrial Conference in 1919 indicated how far the erosion of the traditional norm had proceeded. As awareness grew among those who could benefit directly or indirectly from public pensions and those who sympathized with them that action to meet the needs of the aged was legitimately within the realm of public policy, the political salience of the issue grew. Throughout the process, articulation was performed preeminently by two main classes of actors: a relatively small number of M.P.'s acting as individuals and the trade union movement. These actors gave form and voice to the idea and kept it before Parliament and the public, while it gradually acquired legitimacy in the larger society.

It is not possible to generalize about or even to fathom entirely the motivations of those M.P.'s in the first quarter of this century whose concern for the aged was not matched in intensity or not shared at all by their fellow members. A few observations are appropriate.

J. H. Burnham, who induced the government of the day to establish Commons committees of inquiry with himself as chairman in the 1911–12 and 1912–13 sessions, had long manifested a broad interest in welfare matters and had played an active part in the establishment of Children's Aid Societies in Ontario. Biographical information now available about E. Guss Porter and R. A. Pringle, who placed the first resolutions on public pensions on the Commons order paper in 1906 and 1907, is too scanty to permit me to say much about them. Pringle represented a constituency (Stormont) which had a significant urban-industrial population, as did Burnham (Peterborough), but no more so than many other constituencies. It may be significant that all three men were Conservatives from eastern Ontario. It is possible that they represented those traces of philosophical toryism which Horowitz has argued was brought to Canada by the United Empire Loyalists and others.[9] One can only speculate about Porter and Pringle, but it is to be noted that Burnham proudly proclaimed his UEL origins and wrote books and articles on such patriotic subjects as *Canadians in the Imperial Service* (1891). The case is even clearer for T. L. Church who continued the battle for pensions in the 1920s. A man who dubbed himself towards the end of his life as "the last of the true-blue tories," Church had a long career in both municipal and federal politics marked by fervent devotion to the imperial connection and equally strong advocacy of state intervention in economic development, ownership of public utilities, and social welfare.

On the other hand, J. S. Woodsworth, William Irvine, and A. A. Heaps, whose role was decisive in the 1920s, represented the multifarious but lively labour and socialist tradition in Canadian politics[10] which, in the Horowitz hypothesis, was the natural and inevitable complement of the tory touch. Also representative of this tradition were the Labour members who pursued the issue in provincial legislatures. Their position on public pensions was similar to that of the tory traditionalists, but they arrived at it by the route of socialist egalitarianism. They were spokesmen of interests which were at best inadequately represented in the traditional party system. Woodsworth's own constituency of Winnipeg North-Centre, a polyglot mixture of impoverished workers, was in many respects a microcosm of such interests.

Other leading protagonists of public pensions in this early period appear to have taken their stand on pragmatic (perhaps opportunistic) rather than ideological grounds. E. M. Macdonald, G. W. Kyte, and W. F. Carroll, who tried to keep the issue alive in 1913 when party loyalty induced Burnham to drop it, were Liberals, and presumably therefore did not share in either the tory or socialist tradition. All of them, however, represented Nova Scotia constituencies with significant coal-mining populations, and the particular urgency of pensions in the case of coal miners was both obvious and vigorously expressed by their leaders. Another Liberal, J. E. Fontaine, who managed to get a resolution on pensions before the House in 1922, was a practising physician in industrial, low-income Hull. One can surmise that hard cases he encountered in his medical practice were enough to convince him of the need for public pensions. A. W. Neill, an Independent, usually supported the Liberal party in divisions in the House of Commons but resolutely avoided official identification with it. He represented a Vancouver Island constituency with a substantial working-class population, which later became something of a CCF-NDP stronghold. Combining intensive service to his constituency with support for progressive causes, he was successful in six consecutive general elections and retired undefeated after serving in the House for a quarter of a century—a unique achievement for an Independent in Canadian federal politics.[11]

Trade unions had an obvious direct interest in public pensions in that most of their members could hope to benefit from them, but their persistent advocacy was based on an additional pronounced element of altruism. From the earliest attempts to form a labour central in the 1870s, Canadian unions have included in their legislative programs a broad range of proposals intended to help the poor and dispossessed generally.[12] By themselves the unions were no more able than a handful of individual M.P.'s to force the issue on pensions. In 1926 their total membership was about 275,000, or less than 6 percent of the electorate.[13] If they could have delivered the votes of all their members to a single party, they might conceivably have determined the outcome of a close election, but there was no more evidence then than now that they could do so. In any case, there was considerable doubt in union circles immediately after World War I if either the Liberal or Conservative parties merited labour support. Frustration over what many unionists regarded as chronic governmental unresponsiveness to their representations led to forays into the field of independent labour political action.[14] The dismal failure of these ventures demonstrated the puniness of labour's political muscle. As working-class organizations, however, trade unions were peculiarly sensitive to the changing wants of the emerging urban-industrial society. They therefore provided an essential channel of communication between that society and its authorities.

Governmental responses to the earliest demands for public pensions were diversionary. An integrated demand by Nova Scotia coal miners led to provincial adoption in 1908 of the legislative authority for a public pension plan for them, but no plan in fact materialized. At the national level, Senator Cartwright deduced from the experience of other countries that public pensions could well become a salient issue in Canada in time. His strategy, accepted by the government, was to nip the issue in the bud by a publicly sponsored plan for the sale of annuities. The virtue of this plan in his thinking was that, on the one hand, it preserved the market ethos since it required the individual to "buy" his old age security through personal savings, while, on the other hand, it threatened no established business interests of the time. Neither Cartwright nor most of his contemporaries, however, appreciated the profound nature of the changes occurring in Canadian society. Two decades and one world war later, the market ethos in its pristine form had lost much of its force as applied to the aged poor. Some M.P.'s continued to expound that ethos in the debate on the old age pensions bill of 1926, but none was prepared to vote against the bill. This luxury was reserved for the nonelective Senate, and it was not long before that chamber too realized the folly of it.

In the four decades following the 1927 breakthrough, trade unions continued to play an important part in articulating demands both for incremental changes in existing pensions and for new policy departures. They were no longer alone, however. There was a striking difference between the Commons committee of 1924 and the joint committees of 1950 and 1964–65. Trade union spokesmen were the only representatives of organized groups to appear before the 1924 committee. In 1950 and 1964–65, the major business and welfare associations also appeared and presented well-researched briefs, as did many other organizations. Significant differences among these groups arose over cost factors and methods of finance, but there was also unanimity on the legitimacy of public pensions as such. Spokesmen before the 1950 committee, moreover, were in almost complete agreement that the means test should give way to a more inclusive policy. In 1964–65 the special interest of the insurance industry led to a short but sharp conflict over the desirability of once again restructuring the program. Supported by the Chamber of Commerce and indirectly by the Ontario government, that industry struggled vigorously to block public invasion of the contributory pension field. It found itself, however, in a quite different situation from that which had obtained on earlier occasions when it had successfully prevented the government annuities plan from becoming an important adjunct to public pensions. In that situation the industry had presented integrated opposition to a diffuse demand. In 1964–65 its opposition was also integrated, but it now faced a demand which was equally integrated and strongly articulated as well. The insurance men were finally isolated in the context of near unanimity on at least the principle that some kind of contributory public plan was needed.

Equally significant was the increasing attention political parties paid to public pensions in their policy statements and election platforms. Before 1927 the few M.P.'s who raised the issue in the House of Commons were acting as individuals. The Liberal leadership convention of 1919 had incorporated a broad social "insurance" plank in the party's platform, including protection against "dependence in old age." The resolution, however, was carefully hedged with reservations, and the party showed little disposition to act on it after taking office in 1921.

Moreover, Liberal M.P.'s were if anything somewhat less active than others in pushing the case for pensions. A more active role was played by the Independent Labour members, who had no more than an embryonic party base at the time. Conservative backbenchers were also quite prominent in the early 1920s and before; yet their party did not take an official stand on pensions until after the 1927 act became law. By the 1940s, in contrast, all parties were carefully defining their positions on pensions. As in the case of interest groups, there were important differences among them, but there was also agreement on certain fundamentals.

Increased emphasis by parties on the issue was paralleled by a large increase after 1940 in the number of individual M.P.'s raising it in the House of Commons, over the mere handful of the pre-1927 period. The outstanding example was Stanley Knowles of the CCF-NDP, who succeeded Woodsworth in Winnipeg North-Centre in 1942 and has been from that time by all odds the most persistent and consistent champion of the pensioner in Parliament. Though preeminent, his advocacy differed only in degree from that of many others. Opposition parties and members used the issue as a weapon against the government. A surprisingly large number of private members on the government side also criticized the Cabinet openly from time to time for its failure, as they saw it, to give high enough priority to the pension issue—or, if they refrained from direct criticism, urged the government on to new achievements. In their case, such public criticisms and exhortations were only part of the picture. Their representations behind the scenes were also a factor in inducing government action. Moreover, elected members on both sides of the House attributed enough salience to the issue that they were prepared on occasion to go beyond the literal terms of party policy. Thus, though both the Liberal and Conservative policy statements of the 1940s posited the contributory principle as the precondition of universal coverage, members of both parties on the 1950 joint committee abandoned the principle in order to reach the objective immediately.

In short, with federal adoption of the means-test plan in 1927 and its implementation by the provinces over the next decade, the principle of public pensions finally completed the long transition from sacrilege to public policy, and the transition to tradition was then under way. That development in turn provided the base for enlarged demands, especially a demand to universalize coverage, which could not be resisted outright. Concurrently an increasing gross national product and concomitant increases in governmental revenue potential enhanced capacity to meet enlarged demands. By the late 1940s hardly anyone was prepared to take a flat stand against more favourable treatment for the aged. Least of all were political parties and politicians in that category. To give evidence of one's concern for the aged came to be regarded as almost a *sine qua non* of political survival. Income redistribution in favour of the aged through the instrumentality of public policy became a fact between 1927 and 1936. Substantially greater redistribution became a necessity by 1950. The market ethos was adapted to this changing environmental requirement. It now became a rationalization of strategies to put as tight a limit as possible on the inescapable redistribution and more particularly on downward redistribution. This revised formulation was stated in terms of both moral principle and practical necessity.

The argument of principle led logically to a preference for contributory pensions. R. B. Bennett stated the rationale of that preference succinctly in his speech in the 1926 debate. While conceding that public pensions were desirable and inescapable, he argued that they would destroy "habits of thrift and economy" unless they were based at least in part on previous personal contributions by beneficiaries.[15] Over the next two decades, contributory pensions were given the blessing—with frequent repetition of Bennett's moralistic argument—of such prestigious actors as two commissions of inquiry (the Quebec Social Insurance Commission, the federal Rowell-Sirois Commission), the Canadian Manufacturers' Association, both major political parties, the federal Department of Finance, and the federal Cabinet. Moral fervour, however, was not accompanied by comparable zeal in coming to grips with the complexities of a contributory plan. When the crunch came in 1950, no study had been given to even the most elementary problems involved in applying such a plan to Canada. As a result, centre stage came to be occupied by the argument of practicality, which was stated in terms of cost control.

Such polarization of opinion as occurred on public pensions was in relation to this argument. On the one hand, there were actors who were primarily "cost conscious" and who gave expression at least implicitly to the market ethos in its revised form. On the other hand, there were those who were "welfare conscious," in whose minds the environmental want loomed larger than cost considerations. Broad generalizations applying this dichotomy to particular classes of actors are subject to exceptions. On the whole one can say that the traditional parties and especially business organizations were predominantly cost conscious over the years, while trade unions, the CCF-NDP, and to an extent the Social Credit and Créditiste parties were in the welfare-conscious group.[16] The differences between the Departments of Finance and National Health and Welfare before the 1950 joint committee suggest that there may also have been some such dichotomy in the public service.

The means test had been the central cost-control instrument of the 1927 plan. The administrative problems and inequities to which this instrument had given rise, however, had led to increasing dissatisfaction with it by administrators, politicians, and beneficiaries alike. Nor was the means test in reality compatible with the market ethos, because it penalized those whose old age had been provided for independently through personal savings or private pension plans. More and more the test fell into disfavour with active participants in the policy process. The prospect of its abandonment lent urgency to the cost-control argument. Even in the 1930s the Department of Finance had had grim forebodings that costs would get out of hand, a pessimism shared by other cost-conscious actors. There was an assumption that an irresponsible public would wreck the nation with its insatiable demands unless effectively constrained. The impelling need, it was argued, was to curb irresponsibility by inducing direct and immediate awareness of the costs involved. The contributory principle would have accomplished this by relating benefits to contributions, but it was not an available option in the exigencies of the situation and cost-conscious actors were divided as to the need for it. The insurance industry and its faithful ally, the Chamber of Commerce, rejected the contributory principle because of the threat which they believed was posed for the private sale of annuities and private pension plans. They argued that the laudable purposes the principle was intended to serve could be achieved in other ways. A universal plan with a minimal benefit and continuation of seventy as the eligible age would leave adequate incentive for individual thrift, while earmarked taxes would induce adequate public awareness of costs.

As it turned out, the government adopted a similar position, not because the insurance industry and the CCC had special influence, but because of the complete lack of preparatory work on a contributory plan. The benefit level in the 1951 program remained unchanged at $40 a month and eligibility for benefits below seventy was restricted by a means test. Provision was made to finance the universal pension, the costly part of the program, by earmarked taxes. It will be recalled that there were three of these taxes—a general sales tax and personal and corporation income taxes—all embraced under the rubric "old age security tax." The revenue from them was deposited in an "old age security fund" out of which benefits were paid. The establishment of a special fund was intended to convey to the public the idea that benefits would necessarily be limited by the yield of the three taxes. In the initial design all three were levied at 2 percent rates, but the income tax component applied only to the first $3,000 of annual taxable income.

In the actual operation of the plan the corporation income tax was a relatively insignificant source of revenue from the beginning. In the first fiscal year in which all three taxes were levied throughout the year (1953–54), it yielded only 19 percent of total revenue, and it subsequently declined until it brought in no more than 10 percent.[17] In the early years, the sales tax provided the largest amount of revenue: 50 percent in 1953–54 compared with 31 percent for the personal income tax. The latter, however, grew steadily in importance and accounted for 58 percent of total revenue by 1971–72, owing in part to changes in 1963 and 1967 which increased the relative importance of this component in the total old age security tax.

The old age security tax was the major source of cleavage in the House of Commons debates on the 1951 program.[18] CCF members argued that the universal pension should be financed by progressive taxes. In relation to the government's specific proposal, they directed their main fire at the ceiling on the income tax component because of its high regressivity in relation to incomes beyond the ceiling.[19] Though Social Credit members did not play a prominent part in these debates, they supported the CCF attack on the ceiling and also expressed some opposition to the sales tax component on the ground that it was regressive. The main concern of the Conservatives, on the other hand, was that the government had not adequately achieved the purpose of inducing public awareness of costs, because of the use of an indirect tax (the sales tax) as the most important single source of revenue.

Finance Minister Abbott's answer to the Conservatives' criticism was that the income tax component by itself would serve the purpose of inducing public awareness of costs. In response to the CCF and Social Credit criticism that the old age security tax imposed an unduly heavy burden on lower income categories, he asserted that in equity transfer payments such as public pensions should be governed by the benefit principle of taxation. Strict application of this principle to the new plan with its flat-rate benefits would have required identical contributions from all prospective beneficiaries and thus would have eliminated downward redistribution altogether. In other words, Abbott's definition of equity represented a full acceptance of the market ethos as modified. He noted, however, that the government was in fact tempering justice with mercy in two respects. First, he pointed out that the income tax component was progressive up to the ceiling and thus favoured those in the lowest income categories. Second, he claimed that the federal sales tax, because of its exemptions, was progressive at the lowest income ranges and proportional thereafter. Its inclusion in the old age security tax, he argued, would result in redistribution of income from those with taxable incomes of $3,000 a year or more to the rest of the population, since the annual income tax contributions of the former over forty years would by themselves about equal the actuarial value of the ultimate benefits. In short, the Conservatives appeared to favour little downward redistribution, while the dispute between the government and the other parties related to the appropriate degree thereof. Somewhat sharper differences on this point appeared among interest groups at the hearings of the 1950 joint committee. Business organizations favoured regressive taxes to finance universal benefits, trade unions proportional or progressive taxes.

The cost-conscious and welfare-conscious actors have also been divided over benefit levels and the eligible age. This division has been most marked between business organizations and trade unions. Emphasizing what they conceived to be the twin needs of minimizing costs and maximizing the incentive for private provision for old age, business organizations have argued for a relatively low benefit level and high eligible age. The trade unions have taken the opposite position. Political parties have exhibited a similar though less clear-cut dichotomy. The CCF-NDP, Social Credit, and Créditistes have consistently taken a more expansive position on benefit levels and the eligible age than the traditional parties. Crosscutting this cleavage has been a cost-conscious–welfare-conscious split between governments on the one hand and opposition parties as well as some government backbenchers on the other. An apparent exception to the usual cost-conscious role of governments was the substantial increase in benefits provided by the Diefenbaker government on its own initiative in 1957. This change, however, was a carry-over from a government-opposition dispute immediately before and during the election campaign of that year. At the same time, the increase marked the beginning of an accumulating erosion of government determination to hold the line on benefits and age. This reached a climax in 1963–65 when the Pearson government made large concessions on both points under heavy pressure from oppositionists and pension organizations and, having done so, found it necessary to alter the incidence pattern of the old age security tax by doubling the income tax ceiling. Concurrently, new strategies were devised to prevent similar breakthroughs in the future. One was the partial linking of benefits to rises in living costs, in the hope (forlorn as it turned out) that this would prevent a build-up of pressure for major upward revision at a later date. Another was the reimposition of an income test (though substantially modified in the beneficiary's favour from the earlier means test) to govern supplementary benefits (GIS). Most important of all was the establishment of a contributory plan.

2. SUBSIDIARY ACTORS IN THE POLICY PROCESS

Pensioners' Organizations. In Canada, pensioners' organizations were the product of pension plans, public and private. Although the aged have important interests in common, it took the shared experience of being pension recipients to create a perception of common interest sufficient to provide a basis for organized action. Even then, effective organization was inhibited for many years by geographic dispersion of potential members and activists and by late emergence in the life cycle of the common interest. For these reasons, formal organization was often easier among retired members of specific occupational groups where there had been previously established patterns of joint action. Nevertheless, more broadly based organizations appeared, starting in British Columbia and gradually spreading to other parts of the country. Though growth was slow for many years, it was cumulative so that membership and activity were reaching impressive proportions by 1970.[20]

The first provincewide organization, the Old Age Pensioners' Organization of British Columbia, was formed in 1932, five years after the means-test plan came into operation in that province. The precipitant was the increasingly rigid administration of the means test which characterized the period,[21] especially the practice then current of requiring proof, as a condition of receiving the pension, that a pensioner's children could not support him. A powerful factor in the organization's early battles was the keen publicity sense of its first president, E. R. Vipond, who provided the press with heartrending stories of harsh administration.[22] At the same time, the obstacles to unity among people with such diverse backgrounds as old age pensioners proved to be enough that a rival organization with similar purposes, the Senior Citizens' Association of British Columbia, was established a few years later. Both bodies continue to exist as separate entities, and together they now have close to 250 local branches or clubs with about 50,000 members. In 1958 they overcame their rivalry enough to establish, in conjunction with a number of organizations with occupational and other specialized bases, a Federated Legislative Council. This council, which now has twenty-two affiliates, continues to serve as a coordinating body for all pensioners' organizations in the province.

Provincewide organizations appeared on the prairies in the 1940s. The most active and best organized of these is the Pensioners' and Senior Citizens' Organization of Saskatchewan with about eighty local clubs. In Ontario large numbers of Golden Age, Second Mile, and other social and recreational clubs were organized during the 1940s and after, often under the sponsorship of outside organizations. It was not until 1956, however, that the United Senior Citizens of Ontario was organized with legislative purposes among its objects. The initial organizational impetus came from trade union retirement clubs, which continue to provide substantial leadership. Many of the social and recreational clubs have affiliated, so that the organization now embraces about 475 clubs with about 80,000 members.

The existence of central organizations in all of the provinces from Ontario west led to the establishment of the National Pensioners and Senior Citizens Federation, to which all of the provincial centrals, as well as some other regional and occupational groups, are affiliated. The national federation in turn stimulated further organizational activity not only in the provinces it originally represented, but also in the provinces east of Ontario. A Senior Citizens Federation was formed in New Brunswick in 1969 as an affiliate of the national federation, and by 1972 it embraced thirty local groups with a total membership of about 3,000. Similar provincial federations in Prince Edward Island and Newfoundland joined the national federation in 1971 and 1972, respectively. In Nova Scotia there is still no provincewide federation, but a Senior Citizens' Council in Cape Breton Island with six local groups and about 1,200 members is affiliated to the national federation, as are a number of local clubs in the province. In Quebec linguistic-ethnic differences have complicated the picture. A Senior Citizens' Forum with nearly 100 local groups and 15,000 members in Montreal joined the national federation in 1971, after having been in existence for fifteen years as an independent body. A Jewish Senior Citizens' Association with thirteen clubs and about 2,000 members is also affiliated. Both of these organizations are predominantly Anglophone. Some progress has been made in forming a provincial federation of French-speaking clubs, but it has not associated itself with the national federation.

The provincial organizations and the national federation follow the practice of many other organized groups of determining their policy objectives at regular conventions. The resolutions passed at these conventions are forwarded to the appropriate governments and have been supported increasingly in recent years by lobbying. The subject matter of the resolutions extends beyond better pensions to a wide range of social and welfare policies, especially though not exclusively those from which benefits will accrue to pensioners such as health insurance, public housing, nursing home care, control of drug prices. Until recently this legislative activity was effective, to the extent that it was effective at all, almost entirely at the provincial level and especially in British Columbia. In view of that province's long history of aggressive activity by pensioners' organizations, it is by no means entirely coincidental that

British Columbia has provided the most generous provincial supplementary benefits over the years. At the federal level, the lack of a national organization and inadequate financial resources made direct lobbying impractical. The provincial organizations were reduced in the main to mailing copies of their resolutions and other submissions to the government and M.P.'s. Some of the M.P.'s, especially Stanley Knowles, used the material provided as ammunition from time to time, although they used the wealth of material available from other sources more frequently.

It is fair to say that before 1960 pensioners' organizations had a significant influence on federal pension policy on only one occasion. That was in the early 1940s, and the influence was exerted indirectly through the British Columbia government. It will be recalled that pensioners of the time were caught in a squeeze between a fixed pension and rapidly rising living costs. The B.C. pensioners' organizations exploited the publicity techniques developed earlier by Vipond to create such a hue and cry that the provincial premier was at length reduced almost to begging the federal government to increase the pension. Correspondence of the period between the province's pension administrators and their opposite numbers at Ottawa betrayed a marked sense of harassment on the part of the former.[23] This unique episode left no apparent legacy. The influence of pensioners' organizations was negligible in the major restructuring of old age pensions in 1951 and in the pension increases of 1957.

There are indications that this situation has been changing during the past decade as organized activity among pensioners has increased. The first major indication came during the 1963–65 consideration of the Canada Pension Plan from which existing pensioners were to receive little benefit. The national federation undertook extensive lobbying at Ottawa and elicited vocal support in the House of Commons. The national health and welfare minister of the time has attested to the vigour of the campaign. Undoubtedly it was a factor in the substantial changes made in the universal plan, not originally contemplated by the government, culminating in the guaranteed income supplement in 1966. Continued agitation after that, especially as living costs mounted, was unquestionably a factor in the 1970 and 1972 changes in the universal pension and GIS, referred to in chapter 8, section 4.

The last few years have witnessed not only a rapid growth of organizations affiliated to the national federation, but also some tendency for pensioners to engage in lobbying activities beyond those sponsored by the federation and its affiliates. For example, ad hoc groups sprang up in 1972 under the name of Pensioners for Action Now, involving members of groups affiliated to the national federation and others in Vancouver, Saskatoon, and Hamilton. Their purpose was to organize a march on provincial capitals followed by a march on Ottawa. Marches were held on Victoria and Regina but the proposed march on Ottawa did not take place, partly because of the announcement in the 1972 federal budget of improvements in pensions. The Vancouver group, however, continued its activity at a high pitch. It played a prominent part in making pensions an issue in the British Columbia provincial election campaign in August, 1972, and it continued its efforts during the immediately following federal election.

An attempt to involve individual pensioners and small groups of them in lobbying activity on a continuing basis is being undertaken by an organization called Pensioners Concerned (Canada) Inc., formed in 1970. This organization, of which the driving force are two individual pensioners in Toronto, does not have dues-paying members. Its aim is to encourage pensioners as individuals and in small groups to write frequently to elected politicians and to lobby them personally where possible. For this purpose, it proposes objectives for pensioners to strive for and provides factual and argumentative material which can be used in letters and other lobbying activity in support of those objectives. The two Toronto activists travel the country extensively in search of contacts to whom this promotional material can be sent. Their technique in an area in which they have no contacts is to solicit the support of a sympathetic organization in sponsoring a meeting of pensioners and to attempt to gain contacts for further expansion of activities from this meeting. Financial and other support has been provided by the Anglican and United Churches of Canada, and operating grants have been forthcoming from the federal departments of the Secretary of State and National Health and Welfare.

Canadian Welfare Council. As noted in chapter 2, section 4, professional welfare workers provided pre–World War I Commons committees with telling evidence of the need for public pensions. In subsequent years many such workers have made a case publicly for liberalized pension policies. Social welfare organizations have also done so from time to time and have compiled and published budgets intended to demonstrate the inadequacy of contemporary pension benefits. The fact remains that such organizations have not been significant articulators of demands for public pensions. Many of them are oriented to specific clienteles—children, families, the disabled, delinquents—and apart from some purely local organizations such as the Age and Opportunity Bureau of Winnipeg, there have been none which have made the aged their primary concern. Even organizations with a broader orientation have rarely provided initiatives in policy-making on public pensions. This point will be illustrated in the succeeding discussion of the role played by the Canadian Welfare Council (called the Canadian Council on Social Development since September, 1970), which more than any other can be regarded as the country's peak welfare organization.[24]

The council brings together a wide variety of interests—businesses, trade unions, religious organizations, service clubs, other citizens' groups, and individuals—in a single complex structure which studies, discusses, and organizes conferences on welfare issues, makes policy recommendations to governments and private agencies, and provides technical advice when requested. Its funds, other than those from specially financed projects, come in approximately equal proportions from government grants, community funds, and organizational and individual membership fees. Its broad base, while enabling it to foster substantial community interest and involvement in welfare problems, also gives rise to a certain tendency to immobility. Agreed policies are often difficult to arrive at and promote energetically because of the need to harmonize conflicting internal interests. This is not to say that the council has not shown initiative in many welfare policy areas over the years. Where it has done so, however, it has usually reflected the concerns of its full-time staff, particularly its executive director, and occasionally of lay officers.

Historically the Canadian Welfare Council came into being in 1935 as the successor to an organization, the Canadian Council on Child Welfare, formed in 1920. Initially the earlier organization's attention was directed almost exclusively to child welfare. Though this focus was expanded gradually to embrace the whole family, and was reflected in a change of name to the Canadian Council on Child and Family Welfare, it was the nuclear family of parents and young children in which the organization was primarily interested. A concomitant was a high degree of emphasis on the quality and availability of services, an emphasis which continued even as the organization's range of concern broadened to include groups beyond the nuclear family. To take an example related to the subject of this study, the council has played a prominent part in promoting study of the aging process in all its ramifications. Since income maintenance is basic to effective service, the council has been concerned with that too. Its concern, however, has tended to be broad, directed to the whole community, as exemplified in its activity in promoting public consideration and discussion of the guaranteed annual income approach. Programs providing income for specific groups, including old age pensions, are in essence inconsistent with this universalistic approach. Indeed, the council's emphasis over the last fifteen or

198

twenty years has been increasingly on the rationalization and coordination of the numerous fragmented forms of welfare policies, including both services and income maintenance. This was the central thrust of comprehensive policy statements issued in 1958 and 1969.[25] It was also the underlying philosophy to which expression was given, albeit imperfectly and tentatively, in the Canada Assistance Plan of 1966. The council's role in that policy departure was substantial, its influence being exerted both directly through submissions and indirectly through the large number of federal and provincial welfare administrators included in its membership.

In the case of public pensions, by contrast, the Canadian Welfare Council's role has historically been and continues to be mainly passive. It has reacted to the initiatives of others rather than taking the initiative itself. The scant references to public pensions in its official journal in the 1930s indicated acceptance of the conventional wisdom of the time that the problem could be dealt with satisfactorily only through a contributory plan.[26] G. F. Davidson, the council's executive director in the mid-1940s and subsequently Canada's first deputy minister of welfare, provided much of the basic material on old age pensions for the Marsh Report, but this was done in his personal capacity. The council presented cautious briefs to the parliamentary joint committees of 1950 and 1964–65, but its participation was essentially a response to the fact that the committees were in existence and were inviting briefs from interested parties.

In 1963, after the new Liberal government had tabled its resolution of June 21 looking to a restructuring of the then existing pension program to include contributory pensions, the council presented its views to Prime Minister Pearson in an unpublished but public submission.[27] Here it merely reiterated the position it had taken on public pensions in its 1958 policy statement, itself drawn substantially from the submission to the 1950 joint committee. In sum, the council advocated retention of seventy as the age of eligibility for the universal pension, restriction of benefits in the sixty-five to sixty-nine age group to unemployables, frequent review of the pension benefit level in the light of empirical studies of the minimum needs of the aged, and joint federal-provincial supplementation of benefits on the basis of need. The council took a neutral position, as it had also done in 1958, on the question of contributory pensions even though that had become a major political issue by 1963. It noted the complexity of the problems involved and called for a "searching" public inquiry into them. In 1966, while conceding that the proposal of the Senate Committee on Aging for a minimum guarantee for the aged had "much to commend it," the council wanted to know if similar guarantees would be available to other disadvantaged groups and how they would be fitted into total welfare policy.[28] This kind of approach has been characteristic of the council's policy statements and submissions on public pensions over the last twenty years. The proposals of others have been examined and evaluated in the light of society's broader welfare needs.

In short, the Canadian Welfare Council has been concerned with aggregation rather than articulation in the old age pension field. To an extent, this has been a reflection of its particular history and structure: income maintenance for the aged has never been one of its central concerns. In a larger sense, however, its preoccupation with aggregation has been the response of an organization whose focus of attention is on social welfare policy in its totality.

Provincial Governments. In 1867 social welfare was regarded as essentially a private and local matter and thus, by inference, under provincial jurisdiction. As discussed in chapter 2, section 1, the Canadian variant of the market ethos dictated that charitable and municipal relief should be the main recourse of indigents, though a role was recognized for institutions—private, municipal, and in special cases provincial. Given that framework, there were three provisions of the British North America Act, 1867, which could be said to have dealt with social welfare directly or indirectly. Section 92, head 8, assigned jurisdiction over local government to the provinces, and head 16 all matters of a merely local or private nature. In the only specific reference to social welfare in the entire act, head 7 placed "hospitals, asylums, charities and eleemosynary institutions" other than "marine hospitals" under the provinces.

By the mid-1920s when Canada's first public pension legislation was under consideration, the only cases involving legislative jurisdiction over social welfare before the Judicial Committee of the Privy Council related to what was then a new approach to workmen's compensation by some of the provinces. The new Compensation Acts were held to be *intra vires* the provincial legislatures, but that determination offered little or no guidance for other social welfare fields because of the special characteristics of the compensation plans.[29] At the same time, the thrust of Judicial Committee decisions generally since at least the 1890s had clearly been in the direction of confining the federal government to the enumerated powers of section 91 of the BNA Act (apart from the "emergency power" which was read into the "peace, order and good government" clause). An opinion of the federal deputy minister of justice in 1925 reflected this trend. While recognizing the possibility of federal participation in noncontributory public pensions, the deputy minister was careful to warn that such participation would involve Ottawa in "heavy expenditures with regard to a matter which does not fall specifically within the Dominion field of legislation" and which had in his opinion been "entrusted to the provincial legislatures."[30]

Yet, in spite of the traditional views regarding the paramountcy of provincial responsibility and the constitutional uncertainty surrounding federal participation, the provinces exercised minimal initiative at most in policy-making on public pensions. Articulators of demands for such pensions invariably looked to the federal government for action. One infers that they regarded a pension plan as fulfilling a national purpose. On the whole, provincial governments accepted or at least did not dissent from this viewpoint. It is necessary, however, to deal separately with Quebec and the other provinces because there have been important differences in their attitudes to federal involvement in public pensions.

When confronted with the federal act of 1927, the Anglophone provinces did not rush to the barricades in defence of their jurisdiction. On the contrary, their only real concern was over their own involvement in the plan. The maritime provinces delayed implementing it for several years because of their financial incapacity. To them the preferred course was for the federal government to assume full responsibility. Both then and later this was basically the attitude of all Anglophone provinces. Thus, at the federal-provincial conference of 1945–46, Premier George Drew of Ontario was as outspoken as Duplessis of Quebec in asserting provincial rights, especially in the division of tax revenues, but he also argued that Ottawa should take over full responsibility for public pensions.[31] At the conference of December, 1950, the Anglophone provinces welcomed federal assumption of responsibility for a universal plan and later agreed readily to a constitutional amendment to enable Ottawa to impose earmarked taxes to finance it. In 1962 they again concurred when Diefenbaker asked for a further amendment which he represented as a necessary prelude to a federal contributory plan. In the period from 1963 to 1965, when the federal government took steps to initiate such a plan, only Ontario demurred, and its hesitation was based more on doubts as to the appropriateness of governmental intervention in the field per se than on objection to federal occupancy. The Robarts government preferred to leave the underwriting of contributory pensions in private hands, a manifestation of a basic philosophy which was also apparent in the development of Ontario policy on medical care insurance through its successive permutations. The Robarts position proved to be untenable, and in the contributory pension case Ontario finally accepted the federal plan along with the other Anglophone provinces.

The long-term result of this provincial quiescence was a major assumption of power by the federal government in a field traditionally regarded as provincial. Public pensions are now entirely a federal responsibility, except for contributory pensions in Quebec. In terms of the effective exercise of governmental power, the situation was not inherently different even in the first stage, except with regard to administration. The 1927 act established a joint plan, but the provinces had no more discretion than to accept or reject it since the federal act laid down the basic terms. The sequel, described in chapter 5, section 1, proved that even the power to reject could not in fact be exercised, for political reasons. The only discretion left to the provinces was administrative. Since rules governing the application of a means test cannot begin to cover all contingencies, provincial governments and administrators had some scope to fill in the details of the 1927 design. Even there, however, the heavy hand of federal supervision was upon them.[32] The provinces' response was not to try to reclaim their jurisdiction but to encourage more complete federal involvement. With each new policy departure, public pensions became increasingly costly. The provinces were happy to transfer such costs to Ottawa. All important initiatives—whether for means-test, universal, or contributory pensions—were taken by the federal government. Provincial participation in policy-making was confined to some supplementation of the benefits paid under federal law and to occasional attempts to persuade the federal government to improve benefits. The most noteworthy example of these attempts was in 1940–43 when concerted representations by the provinces (including Quebec) were instrumental in inducing a stubborn finance minister to face the reality of rising living costs by increasing the maximum pension payable under the means-test plan. Here the role of the provinces was analogous to that of interest groups pressuring the federal government.

Quebec's position was never quite the same as that of the other provinces, and in time it became radically different. Though the Taschereau government's opposition to the federal initiative of 1927 was based as much as anything on its laissez-faire liberalism, that government also argued the uniqueness of Quebec society and the inappropriateness in that province of policies which might be suitable in the others. This argument became an increasingly important factor in the attitude of Quebec governments to federal initiatives. That it was not confined to governments and nationalist elites is illustrated by the concern expressed by the Catholic unions, proponents of governmental responsibility for social welfare, at the centralizing import as they saw it of the Marsh Report. By the mid-1930s, however, a purely negative stance on public pensions had become politically untenable in the province. Since the Quebec government of the day had no policy of its own in the field, it could only accept the federal plan. Indeed, the succeeding Duplessis regime, for all its emphasis on the defence of Quebec culture against the centralizers at Ottawa, sought kudos for itself in the hyperbolic claims that it had brought public pensions to the province and was responsible for the benefit increases of 1947 and 1949. Duplessis continued to indulge federal initiatives on public pensions even in the face of the major policy departure of 1951, the introduction of purely federal universal pensions. Like the province's Liberal government of 1937, the Union Nationale government of 1951 had no policy of its own to substitute for the federal plan, and it had long before learned the inexpediency of mere opposition to public pensions.

At the same time, Duplessis kept the way open for future provincial action by insisting that the constitutional amendment of 1951 provide to his satisfaction for the paramountcy of provincial over federal legislation in the pension field. This proved to be of central importance in policy-making on contributory pensions more than a decade later. Within the framework of the positive Quebec nationalism of the 1960s, the Lesage government was determined to have its own contributory plan. The federal government believed it had no choice but to adapt to that hard fact, with the result that Quebec was a proximate policy-maker on contributory pensions. This was the only occasion on which any province played a major policy-making role in the pension field.

3. CONVERSION TO POLICY

It was stated at the end of chapter 1, section 3, that the design phase of the policy cycle can be divided conceptually into commitment, information processing, choice, and implementation. These elements will be ordered and intertwined in many different ways in the real world. In particular, government commitment may sometimes precede and sometimes follow information processing. It is not, however, an inevitable consequence of such processing: sometimes an external precipitant is needed to induce a government to commit itself even after there has been substantial information processing.

In Canada's first policy innovation on old age pensions, the means-test plan, information processing was largely the work of the Commons committee of 1924, whose report contained the essence of what became the policy of 1926–27. This was a case where information processing did not lead directly to commitment. The appointment of the 1924 committee and of its successor in 1925 was a delaying tactic of the same nature as the appointment of similar committees before World

War I. Resistance to public pensions continued and the government temporized. Only the intervention of Woodsworth and Heaps, who fortuitously held the balance of power in the Commons, led to commitment. Even after the 1927 act was passed, a further intervention by Heenan and the British Columbia government was needed to bring about effective implementation. In view of the powerful environmental want, a public pension policy would undoubtedly have been implemented eventually. Without the interventions just mentioned, especially the first, there might well have been a delay of several years. Only after the government was committed did the 1924 committee's report become integral to the policy process. As the government found a policy suitable for implementation in that report, it was able to proceed without resort to significant additional information processing.

In the case of universal pensions, the government committed itself conditionally as early as 1945, in the Green Book proposals, to a design produced by an informal task force of key ministers and civil servants. With the failure of the federal-provincial conference of 1945–46, that commitment lapsed. To the extent that the government continued to consider the question at all, it reverted to its preference for contributory pensions. No further information processing of significance occurred until 1950 when the government implicitly committed itself to the principle of policy innovation, though not at that stage to a specific design. The commitment was not precipitated by a single dramatic occurrence, but was the culmination of mounting dissatisfaction with the means test, based in substantial measure on experience with administration of the 1927 plan. The demand for an end to that test involved in differing ways a variety of interest groups, especially trade unions, as well as civil servants and all parties in the House of Commons. The government looked to a joint committee of the Senate and House of Commons for needed information processing. The committee in turn revived and updated the policy of the 1945 task force. Both the committee and the task force, however, left the important question of financing vague. Further information processing within the civil service was needed to complete the policy design.

The case of contributory pensions differed from the two earlier cases in that commitment preceded information processing. The Liberal party lagged behind the CCF and the Conservatives in incorporating in its program a contributory plan pyramided onto the universal plan. Once the Liberals accepted this policy, however, they treated it as a leading issue in the 1962 and 1963 election campaigns. On their return to power in 1963, they regarded themselves as committed and symbolized their commitment in the resolution introduced by Health and Welfare

Minister LaMarsh in June, 1963. Information processing had been done previously by the party task force which produced the "bulky, black-bound book" referred to by LaMarsh. The required policy design was too complex, however, to be dealt with in anything but a preliminary way by a private group, and it can reasonably be said that information processing did not begin in earnest until the resources of the public service were applied to it under government direction.

Choice was a relatively simple matter in 1926–27. The 1924 committee eliminated other possibilities until nothing was left but a joint federal-provincial means-test plan. The matter became more complex in the next policy innovation. The joint committee of 1950 again eliminated other possibilities until only the two-level program of the Green Books was left. This program, however, represented one part of the required policy design. The question of how to finance the program had acquired high salience by then, a problem not encountered with the means-test plan for two reasons. First, expenditures under that plan were relatively small and overall redistribution of income was *ipso facto* limited. Second, federal-provincial taxation was highly regressive before World War II, so that financing of pension payments out of the general revenues of the two levels of government resulted in little downward redistribution. The universal pension recommended by the 1950 joint committee involved expenditures of an entirely different magnitude. Moreover, increasing resort to graduated income taxation during World War II had added a significant progressive element to the tax structure at the federal level (and the federal government was entirely responsible for financing the universal pension).

The financial design chosen by the authorities in 1951 consisted ostensibly of the old age security tax and fund, but this was a purely metaphorical way of describing it. From the inception of the universal plan, the proceeds of the tax were faithfully credited to the fund and pension payments debited. All that this involved was a bookkeeping operation, since the fund consisted of nothing more than a set of entries in the public accounts. In reality, the universal pension, like all objects of public expenditure, was a charge on the government's total revenues.[33] Allocation of the pension segment of those revenues to a mythical fund was a rationalization of certain specific tax increases, collectively described as the old age security tax in accordance with the metaphor. These tax increases shifted the burden of taxation in the manner set forth in section 4, and that shift was integral to the overall design of the universal pension.

Designing the 1965 program was a complex process of changing choices made by the authorities in response to strong political pressures and in the light of continuous information processing within the civil service. Initially a three-level program was chosen in which the old age assistance (means-test) part of the 1951 program was to be retained. After a series of adaptations which culminated in the adoption of the guaranteed income supplement in 1966, the choice which was finally implemented incorporated many material changes from the original choice. These, described in detail in chapter 8, included staged abandonment of the means-test plan, greater increases in the benefits of existing pensioners than originally envisaged, and considerable revision of the proposed contributory plan. Even the original choice would have resulted in a substantial increase in the cost of public pensions; the increase was significantly greater in the final choice. As in 1951, therefore, the financial design was of central concern. As in 1951, too, it was described in metaphors. The distinctively new element of the 1965 program was the Canada Pension Plan. Its contributory nature revived an old formulation of the metaphor which had been pressed into service on many occasions in the past, namely, that prospective recipients of public pensions should pay for at least part of their anticipated benefits. In actual fact, contributory pensions are no different from other public expenditures: they are paid for out of current public revenues, which in turn are increased by current contributions under the plan. As with the old age security tax, the metaphor was a rationalization of new taxes, called "contributions" in this case, and these contributions, too, shifted the burden of taxation.

4. Public Pensions and Income Redistribution

Three main kinds of income redistribution can arise from the transfer payments involved in a public pension program: geographic, intergenerational, and vertical (among income levels). Geographic redistribution was never at any time a deliberate objective of pension policy, and available evidence suggests that the contribution of old age pensions to such redistribution has been small.[34] It goes without saying that intergenerational redistribution has been the major result of old age pensions. It is extremely difficult to estimate the net transfer to the aged accurately, but it is hardly necessary to do so. In terms of the central theme of this study, the crucially important variable is vertical redistribution, and more specifically, downward redistribution.

To arrive at a precise measure of the redistributional effects of public pensions, it is necessary to correlate the sources of the federal government's revenues with its pension payments. Deutsch undertook this Herculean task with respect to the universal pension payments of 1961.[35]

Using three different measures of income redistribution, he arrived at substantially different results for vertical redistribution according to the measure used. For example, he variously calculated the proportion of pension benefits actually redistributed at 33.9 percent, 62.8 percent, and 71.0 percent. In spite of these discrepancies, the figures are all large enough to suggest that there was in fact substantial vertical redistribution. Deutsch's study leaves little doubt that it was in a downward direction and that it favoured mainly those in the income cell below $3,000. This conclusion, however, should be interpreted in the light of the fact that in 1961 the overwhelming majority of people of pensionable age were in that cell.[36] To say, therefore, that there was vertical redistribution to the income group below $3,000 is to say little more than that there was intergenerational redistribution. And saying that begs the significant question: How has the burden of providing income maintenance for pensioners been distributed among nonpensioners? To answer that question, it is necessary to consider the incidence of the old age security tax and CPP "contributions" which were integral parts of the universal and contributory pension designs.

It will be recalled that the old age security tax was a composite of increases in the personal income, sales and corporation income taxes, and that initially all three of these components were increased by two percentage points. The incidence of the increase can be readily calculated for the personal income tax component. It was influenced at one end of the income scale by the basic income tax exemptions and at the other end by the ceiling built into the design ($3,000 of annual taxable income, which at 2 percent limited the tax to $60 a year). To illustrate the overall effect of the two influences, I have calculated the percentage of gross income taken by the tax from a taxpayer with married status and two dependent children, at various income levels. I have credited the taxpayer in each case with only the standard exemptions in effect at the time the old age security tax came into effect. The results are:

Gross Annual Income	Percentage Paid in Tax
$ 2,000	nil
3,000	0.47
5,000	1.08
7,000	0.86
10,000	0.60
15,000	0.40
20,000	0.30

The income tax component was progressive in the example cited for gross annual incomes of up to $5,300, but was sharply regressive beyond that point because of the ceiling. At the $7,000 level a smaller proportion of the taxpayer's income was taken than at $5,000. At $15,000 the proportion was smaller and at $20,000 much smaller than at $3,000. Calculating the incidence of the federal sales tax is more difficult, but available studies suggest that it is probably regressive, though possibly proportional in middle income ranges.[37] It is impossible to estimate the incidence of the corporation income tax with any reasonable degree of confidence, but it accounted for only a small part of the yield of the old age security tax. It will therefore be ignored in the discussion of the overall effect of that composite tax.

The effect of the personal income tax component was to shift the burden of taxation to those whose incomes were at or somewhat above the level at which they were liable for income tax. For convenience, I will describe them as being in "the lower middle income range." Those with incomes too small to pay income tax will be described as being in "the lowest income range." A proportional sales tax would not have offset the shift of tax burden to the lower middle income range. A regressive sales tax, on the other hand, would have spread the burden to include the lowest income range as well. Either way the combined effect of the two important components of the old age security tax was to militate strongly against downward income redistribution in the universal pension plan. There is no question that the authorities of the day were aware of this at least in general terms. It is true that Finance Minister Abbott regarded the sales tax as progressive for the lowest income range. If more recently published incidence studies are closer to the truth than the internal studies on which he relied, then the sales tax component would appear to have placed a heavier burden on the lowest income range than Abbott intended. By the same token, however, the burden on the lower middle income range was not quite as heavy as intended. Abbott and his associates could not have been unaware of the incidence of the income tax component. Given that fact, together with their interpretation of the incidence of the sales tax component, it was clearly deliberate government policy to produce a shift of the tax burden to the lower middle income range. If the actual result deviated at all from the intention, it was only because there may also have been some shift of burden to the lowest income range.

Changes in the old age security tax were adopted in 1959, 1963, and 1966, and the tax was finally abolished from the beginning of 1972. The first change did not affect the basic pattern just described since each component was increased to 3 percent. The second increased the burden on those in the lower middle income range because the personal income tax component only was increased (to 4 percent). The third shifted the burden somewhat upwards by increasing the ceiling from $3,000 of annual taxable income to $6,000. This, however, was more than offset by a new set of taxes which had already come into effect, the "contributions" levied under the Canada Pension Plan. It is not possible to trace fully the effect on incidence of the abandonment of the old age security tax in 1972. In the case of the sales tax component, no change in incidence occurred since the component was simply incorporated into the regular sales tax. Abandonment of the income tax component, on the other hand, was accompanied by complete restructuring of personal income tax rates, as well as abandonment of federal estate and gift taxes, and it will be some time before the incidence of the new tax structure can be analysed adequately. Preliminary indications are that the shift of the tax burden to the lower middle income range and below occasioned by the old age security tax has been reversed to only a limited degree. According to one expert, "taking all tax changes into account, the net redistributive effect of Bill C-259 is to decrease taxes on individuals and families in the lowest income brackets, to increase taxes on families in the middle-income brackets and to decrease taxes for individuals and families in the highest income classes."[38]

The Canada Pension Plan is financed by two so-called contributions: a payroll tax and an earnings tax, each levied at 1.8 percent of an employee's earnings between $600 a year and a ceiling which initially was $5,000. For the self-employed, the entire levy of 3.6 percent is an earnings tax. Incidence can be calculated as readily for an earnings tax as for the personal income tax. In the specific case of the CPP contributions, the earnings tax is less progressive at the bottom of the income scale than the income tax component of the old age security tax and more sharply regressive in the upper ranges. This is so because, on the one hand, the basic exemption is substantially less than the basic exemptions of the income tax and, on the other hand, the earnings tax is not only limited by the earnings ceiling but is also deductible for income tax purposes. To arrive at the true tax burden, it is necessary to net out the income tax saving. To illustrate the incidence of the tax as it applied before 1974, I will again use the example of a taxpayer with married status and two dependent children.[39] The percentage of his income taken by the tax at various income levels is as follows:

Gross Annual Income	Net Percentage Paid in Tax
$ 2,000	1.25
3,000	1.28
5,000	1.34
7,000	0.91
10,000	0.60
15,000	0.33
20,000	0.23

Here there was a shift of the tax burden not only to the lower middle range but below as well. As noted in chapter 8, section 4, a large increase in the earnings ceiling was legislated for 1974, and the ceiling will continue to increase substantially in future years until it reaches the average of Canadian wages and salaries. This higher ceiling will raise the income level at which the CPP earnings tax becomes regressive, but the result will merely be to restore essentially the same incidence pattern as obtained when the tax was first imposed. What was happening before 1974 was that the upward adjustment of the earnings ceiling, restricted as it was to $100 a year, was proceeding at a snail's pace compared to the rapid rise of overall money incomes. As a result, the burden of the earnings tax relative to contemporaneous money incomes was being steadily shifted down the income scale. This trend to increasing regressivity has been reversed, but only to the extent of restoring approximately the original degree of regressivity.

The incidence of a payroll tax is as resistant to estimation as that of the corporation income tax, but it cannot be ignored because it provides about half the revenue accruing from CPP contributions. It is commonly assumed on theoretical grounds that, overall, about half of a payroll tax used for social security is shifted to employees—that is, half of an employer's contributions to employee benefits are in fact a form of wages—and that the other half is shifted to consumers as a disguised sales tax.[40] If this assumption is valid, then the incidence pattern just indicated for the earnings tax is applicable to about three-quarters in all of CPP contributions. The remaining one-quarter is also regressive because it is a general sales tax without exemption of even basic necessities.

In short, with the expansion of public pension programs, the market ethos provided a rationalization for new taxes or increases in old taxes which added significant elements of regressivity to the tax structure. The real effect of these tax changes has been that those in the lower middle income range and below have been required to assume a disproportionate share of the burden of income maintenance for those who have been reduced by age to the bottom of the income scale.

It is in the light of this reality that one must interpret the result to date of the long-term conflict between the environmental want and the cultural norm. To revert to Hennessy's terminology, it was not until 1936, when the 1927 means-test plan finally became operative in all provinces, that public pensions completed the transition from the realm of sacrilege to the realm of public policy. The limited expenditures involved in the 1927 plan indicated that the transition from public policy to tradition had only begun. The maturing of that transition was apparent in the large increases in expenditure required by the policy innovations of 1951 and 1965. The transition, however, also involved large-scale accommodations to the market ethos. The regressive earmarked taxes of 1951 and the even more regressive contributions of 1965 were integral to the incorporation of pension policy into tradition.

Notes

Abbreviations other than standard abbreviations used here are as follows:

DBS	Dominion Bureau of Statistics (now Statistics Canada)
HC	House of Commons of Canada
Nat. Accts.	*National Accounts, Income and Expenditure*, a DBS occasional publication
Nat. Fin.	*The National Finances: An Analysis of the Revenues and Expenditures of the Government of Canada*, produced and published annually by the Canadian Tax Foundation, Toronto
Pub. Arch.	Public Archives of Canada
Sen.	Senate of Canada
Sess. Papers	Sessional Papers

Notes to Preface

1. Theodore J. Lowi, "American Business, Public Policy, Case-Studies, and Political Theory," *World Politics* 16, no. 4 (July, 1964): 707.

Notes to Chapter 1, Framework of the Study

1. Richard M. Titmuss, *Income Distribution and Social Change: A Critical Study in British Statistics* (London: George Allen & Unwin, 1962); Herman P. Miller, *Income Distribution in the United States*, 1960 Census Monograph (Washington: U.S. Government Printing Office, 1966). For more recent studies with similar conclusions, see Andrian L. Webb and Jack E. B. Sieve, *Income Redistribution and the Welfare State*, Occasional Papers on Social Administration, no. 41 (London: G. Bell & Sons, 1971);

Herman P. Miller, *Rich Man, Poor Man* (New York: Thomas Y. Crowell Company, 1971).

2. Jenny R. Podoluk, *Incomes of Canadians*, 1961 Census Monograph (Ottawa: Queen's Printer, 1968), chaps. 10, 11.

3. See, e.g., Michael Harrington, *The Other America: Poverty in the United States* (New York: Macmillan Company, 1963), chaps. 6, 9; Margaret S. Gordon, ed., *Poverty in America: Proceedings of a National Conference held at the University of California, Berkeley* (San Francisco: Chandler Publishing Company, 1965), chap. 6; Herbert Krosney, *Beyond Welfare: Poverty in the Supercity* (New York: Holt, Rinehart & Winston, 1966), chap. 6; Sen. Special Committee on Poverty, *Poverty in Canada* (Ottawa: Information Canada, 1971), sec. 2.

4. Margaret S. Gordon, *The Economics of Welfare Policies* (New York: Columbia University Press, 1963), p. 24.

5. The definition proposed here does not embrace some of the arrangements to which pension has traditionally been applied, for example, annuities paid by rulers to court favourites, by patrons to artists or scholars, or by employers to aged or disabled employees who were deemed to have rendered faithful service. Some definitions attempt to include this kind of arrangement by making desert the distinguishing characteristic. Thus, pensions are annuities paid to those who in some way are deemed to deserve them— because of meritorious conduct, past service to either an employer or the country, previous contributions, age, disability, or simply poverty. Desert, however, is a slippery concept and, in some of the examples mentioned above, it was determined arbitrarily, even capriciously, by the benefactor. The thrust of the twentieth-century drive for both public and private pensions has been to establish objective criteria of eligibility, but that is possible only in a systematic group arrangement with clearly defined rules. It is this which distinguishes pensions in the twentieth century from other annuities. So-called informal pension plans (in which an employer may provide an annuity for a retiring employee if he thinks he deserves it) create no entitlement and are better classified as charity. In any case, they have never benefited more than an inconsequential proportion of the population.

6. Robert H. Salisbury, "The Analysis of Public Policy: A Search for Theories and Roles," in *Political Science and Public Policy*, ed. Austin Ranney (Chicago: Markham Publishing Company, 1968), p. 153; emphasis in the original.

7. See, however, Bauer's comment in his introduction to a collection of original articles: "We are not proposing 'hypothesis testing' . . . but rather the testing of the utility of some assumptions about the policy process. The assumptions are not likely to prove either 'right' or 'wrong.' " Raymond A. Bauer and Kenneth J. Gergen, eds., *The Study of Policy Formation* (New York: The Free Press, 1968), p. 26.

8. Gabriel Almond, "Political Theory and Political Science," *American Political Science Review* 60, no. 4 (Dec., 1966): 869.

9. C. Wright Mills, *The Sociological Imagination* (New York: Oxford University Press, 1959), p. 146.

10. Earlier programs dealing with agricultural instruction, employment offices, highway construction, and vocational training were for limited periods and involved relatively small expenditures.

11. The foregoing figures were derived from *Nat. Accts.*, 1926–52, tables 37, 44, 46; *Nat. Fin.*, 1973–74, pp. 33, 118.

12. Sen. Special Committee on Aging, *Final Report* (Ottawa: Queen's Printer, 1966), p. viii.

13. V. O. Key, Jr., *Southern Politics in State and Nation* (New York: Alfred A. Knopf, 1951), chap. 14, esp. pp. 307–10; Duane Lockard, *New England State Politics* (Princeton, N.J.: Princeton University Press, 1959), chap. 12.

14. Richard E. Dawson and James A. Robinson, "Inter-Party Competition, Economic Variables and Welfare Policies in the American States," *Journal of Politics* 25, no. 2 (May, 1963): 265–89.

15. For a succinct exposition of the Key, Lockard, and Dawson-Robinson models, see the first two pages of Charles F. Cnuddle and Donald J. McCrone, "Party Competition and Welfare Policies in the American States," *American Political Science Review* 63, no. 3 (Sept., 1969): 858–66.

16. Richard J. Hofferbert, "Ecological Development and Policy Change in the American States," *Midwest Journal of Politics* 10, no. 4 (Nov., 1966): 464–85; idem, "The Relation between Public Policy and Some Structural and Environmental Variables in the American States," *American Political Science Review* 60, no. 1 (Mar., 1966): 73–82; Thomas R. Dye, *Politics, Economics and the Public: Policy Outcomes in the American States* (Chicago: Rand McNally & Company, 1966).

17. Phillips Cutright, "Political Structure, Economic Development and National Social Security Programs," *American Journal of Sociology* 70, no. 5 (Mar., 1965): 537–50.

18. Cnuddle and McCrone, "Party Competition and Welfare Policies"; Ira Sharkansky and Richard I. Hofferbert, "Dimensions of State Politics, Economics and Public Policy," *American Political Science Review* 63, no. 3 (Sept., 1969): 867–79; Brian R. Fry and Richard F. Winters, "The Politics of Redistribution," *ibid.* 64, no. 2 (June, 1970): 508–22; John L. Sullivan, "A Note on Redistributive Politics," *ibid.* 66, no. 4 (Dec., 1972): 1301–5.

19. Sharkansky and Hofferbert, "Dimensions of State Politics," p. 867.

20. Adapted from Austin Ranney, "The Study of Policy Content: A Framework for Choice," in *Political Science and Public Policy*, pp. 3–21.

21. It is emphasized that they are used here for expository purposes only. The systems analysts' search for general theory and their consequent concern for "system maintenance," "system persistence," and the "life processes of systems" raise problems which are beyond the scope of this study.

22. David Easton, *A Framework for Political Analysis* (Englewood Cliffs, N.J.: Prentice-Hall, 1965); idem, *A Systems Analysis of Political Life* (New York: John Wiley & Sons, 1965).

23. Gabriel A. Almond and G. Bingham Powell, Jr., *Comparative Politics: A Developmental Approach* (Boston: Little, Brown and Company, 1966).

24. Almond and Powell, *Comparative Politics*, chaps. 4, 5. Cf. Easton's stylized representation of the U.K. system: "The infinite number of popular demands . . . is sharply reduced to a relatively smaller number by interest groups; these are then further reduced by parties; and in the legislature and executive they are still further winnowed out into an agenda from which policies are formed." *Systems Analysis*, p. 139.

25. This one category compresses two of Easton's major categories: support for the political community and support for the regime of basic values, political structure, and norms. *Systems Analysis*, chaps. 11, 12. It also embraces all of the examples given by Almond and Powell. *Comparative Politics*, p. 26.

26. Bernard C. Hennessy, *Public Opinion*, 2d ed. (Belmont, Calif.: Wadsworth Publishing Co., 1970), chap. 22.

27. Hennessy modified his original statement on this point by conceding that "in modern societies, very little is forbidden to ideas; sacrilege is almost an extinct commodity." Ibid., p. 397. The point is relevant to this study, however, because public pensions were unquestionably in the category of unthinkable thoughts in Canada in the nineteenth century.

28. Murray Edelman, *The Symbolic Uses of Politics* (Urbana, Ill.: University of Illinois Press, 1964), p. 153.

29. David Braybrooke and Charles E. Lindblom, *A Strategy of Decision* (New York: The Free Press of Glencoe, 1963); Charles E. Lindblom, *The Intelligence of Democracy: Decision Making through Mutual Adjustment* (New York: The Free Press, 1965); idem, *The Policy-Making Process* (Englewood Cliffs, N.J.: Prentice-Hall, 1968). See also Lindblom's "The Science of Muddling Through," *Public Administration Review* 19, no. 2 (Spring, 1959): 79–88.

30. The complementary criticism at the normative level is that the model is inherently conservative, both because it locks new policy to what has already happened and because the most powerful interests are those which will dominate mutual adjustment.

31. See Amitai Etzioni, *The Active Society: A Theory of Societal and Political Processes* (New York: The Free Press, 1968), chaps. 11, 12; idem, "Mixed-scanning: A 'Third' Approach to Decision-Making," *Public Administration Review* 27, no. 5 (Dec., 1967): 385–92; Yehezkel Dror, *Public Policymaking Reexamined* (San Francisco: Chandler Publishing Company, 1968), chap. 12.

Notes to Chapter 2, Market Ethos versus Environmental Want

1. C. B. Macpherson: *The Political Theory of Possessive Individualism: Hobbes to Locke* (London: Oxford University Press, 1962).

2. Karl Polanyi, *The Great Transformation: The Political and Economic Origins of Our Time* (New York: Farrar & Rinehart, 1944), chaps. 7 to 9.

3. A. V. Dicey, *Law and Public Opinion in England during the Nineteenth Century*, 2d ed. reissued with a Preface by E. C. S. Wade (London: Macmillan & Co., 1962), p. 233.

4. Royal Commission on the Relations of Labor and Capital in Canada, *Report* (Ottawa: Queen's Printer, 1889), pp. 13, 24–28.

5. Richard B. Splane, *Social Welfare in Ontario, 1791–1893: A Study of Public Welfare Administration* (Toronto: University of Toronto Press, 1965).

6. Esdras Minville, "Labour Legislation and Social Services in the Province of Quebec," app. 5 to *Report* of the Royal Commission on Dominion-Provincial Relations (Ottawa: King's Printer, 1939), pp. 45–46.

7. *HC Debates*, 1906–7, cols. 3386–87.

8. Leroy O. Stone, *Urban Development in Canada: An Introduction to the Demographic Aspects*, 1961 Census Monograph (Ottawa: Queen's Printer, 1967), chap. 2, pp. 201–3.

9. Ibid., pp. 26–30, app. A.

10. 1941 Census of Canada, vol. 1, *General Review*, pp. 35–36.

11. 1961 Census of Canada, Bull. 1.1-7, *Population: Rural and Urban*, table 13.

12. 1961 Census of Canada, Bull. 3.1-1, *Labour Force: Historical Tables*, table 3.

13. DBS, *Canada Year Book*, 1930 (Ottawa: King's Printer, 1930), pp. 386–89.

14. Ibid., 1922–23 (Ottawa: King's Printer, 1923), p. 219; 1930, p. 185.

15. See S. D. Clark, *The Employability of the Older Worker: A Review of Research Findings* (Ottawa: Dept. of Labour, 1959).

16. Frank T. Denton and Sylvia Ostry, *Historical Estimates of the Canadian Labour Force*, 1961 Census Monograph (Ottawa: Queen's Printer, 1967). The information used here is derived from tables 3 to 7 inclusive.

17. Actually the principle was established by a statute of 1920, but it was not until 1922 that a restriction on alien-born citizens was abolished. See Norman Ward, *House of Commons: Representation*, 2d ed. (Toronto: University of Toronto Press, 1963), p. 231. The eligible age was lowered to 18 in 1970.

18. Arthur Pedoe, *Life Insurance, Annuities and Pensions: A Canadian Text* (Toronto: University of Toronto Press, 1964), p. 256.

19. Splane, *Social Welfare in Ontario*, pp. 109–12.

20. Harry M. Cassidy, *Public Health and Welfare Reorganization: The Postwar Problem in the Canadian Provinces* (Toronto: Ryerson Press, 1945) contains inter alia informative discussions of welfare policy in the various provinces. Though they relate mainly to a later period than that with which I am concerned at this point, the conclusions stated here are based on Cassidy's discussions in part. Other support for my conclusions is provided by testimony before parliamentary committees immediately before World War I, which is outlined at the end of this chapter.

21. *HC Journals*, 1924, app. 4, p. 97.

22. *Sen. Debates*, 1926, p. 159.

23. See Royal Commission on Banking and Finance, *Report* (Ottawa: Queen's Printer, 1964), chap. 13; E. P. Neufeld, *The Financial System of Canada: Its Growth and Development* (Toronto: Macmillan Company of Canada, 1972), esp. chaps. 3, 11, 13; Pedoe, *Life Insurance*, passim.

24. J. R. Podoluk, "Income Characteristics of the Older Population," in Sen. Special Committee on Aging, *Proceedings* (Ottawa: Queen's Printer, 1964), p. 1258. See also Podoluk, *Incomes of Canadians*, 1961 Census Monograph (Ottawa: Queen's Printer, 1968), pp. 210–14.

25. Unless otherwise specified, the figures on annuities sold by insurance companies which are cited in this chapter are derived from Superintendent of Insurance, *Reports* (Ottawa: King's and Queen's Printer) for the relevant years. Figures on government annuities are from the Department of Labour, *Annual Reports* (Ottawa: King's and Queen's Printer). Superintendent of Insurance reports cover only federally licensed companies, but together such companies account for more than 95 percent of the life insurance business done in Canada (Pedoe, *Life Insurance*, p. 24) and probably an even higher percentage of annuities business.

26. *Survey of Pension and Welfare Plans in Industry, 1947* (Ottawa: King's Printer, 1950), table 13.

27. *Report on Phases of Employment Conditions in Canadian Industry* (Ottawa: King's Printer, 1937).

28. See *Retirement Plans in Canada, 1938* (Kingston, Ont.: Queen's University, Industrial Relations Centre, 1938), pp. 31–33; this was a detailed analysis of the terms of 120 plans in effect in private industry in the year indicated.

29. Before 1957 the information was published in the *Labour Gazette*; thereafter, in separate reports.

30. The DBS published a survey of trusteed pension plans in 1953 and such surveys were produced annually after 1957. For a summary of the results of all surveys up to 1957, see Robert M. Clark, *Economic Security for the Aged in the United States and Canada: A Report prepared for the Government of Canada* (Ottawa: Queen's Printer, 1960), vol. 2, pp. 77–85.

31. DBS, *Pension Plans, Non-Financial Statistics, 1960* (Ottawa: Queen's Printer, 1962). This survey was undertaken largely in response to Clark's

plea for more adequate information on private plans. *Economic Security for the Aged,* vol. 2, pp. 87–89.

32. DBS, *Survey of Pension Plan Coverage, 1965* (Ottawa: Queen's Printer, 1967); Statistics Canada, *Pension Plans in Canada, 1970* (Ottawa: Information Canada, 1972).

33. Beginning in 1946 the Department of National Revenue issued policy statements, commonly called Blue Books, setting forth the conditions under which pension plans would be recognized for income tax purposes. The last of the Blue Books was withdrawn in 1957, but in 1959 a new Information Bulletin no. 14 was issued. It in turn was withdrawn in 1960, but the principles it enunciated continued to be followed in departmental interpretations. The change of major significance in the proliferation of top hat plans was the elimination of a previous injunction against discrimination among classes of employees. See William R. Latimer, "Pension Plans and Income Tax," in *Pensions in Canada: A Compendium of Fact and Opinion,* ed. Laurence E. Coward (Don Mills, Ont.: CCH Canadian, 1964), pp. 102–13. For a historical survey of income tax provisions and interpretations relating to pension plans, see Clark, *Economic Security for the Aged,* vol. 2, pp. 45–55.

34. 1961 Census of Canada, Bulls. 4.1-1 to 4.1-6, *Population Sample.*

35. Podoluk, "Income Characteristics." Pololuk drew on data published in part in 1961 Census Bulletin 4.1-1 and on unpublished data of the 1952 *Survey of Consumer Finances.* She said that the resulting figures for 1951 and 1961 were "reasonably comparable." See also *Incomes of Canadians,* chap. 9. For more recent figures, see chap. 8, sec. 4.

36. *Labour Gazette,* 1924, p. 665.

37. The surviving records of this committee consist of: (a) a brochure entitled *Old Age Pensions System for Canada, Memorandum* (Ottawa: King's Printer, 1912) described as "Part of a Preliminary Report on the Information collected pursuant to Recommendation of the Committee on Old Age Pensions System for Canada, in Its Report to the House, dated 25th March, 1912"; (b) *Proceedings of the Special Committee on Old Age Pensions, comprising the Evidence taken during the Parliamentary Session of 1911–12, Statements, Exhibits, etc.;* (c) *Minutes of Proceedings and Evidence taken before the Select Special Committee on Old Age Pensions, Parliamentary Session of 1912–13.* Evidence referred to in the text is taken from these documents.

38. *Nat. Fin.,* 1973–74, p. 15.

Notes to Chapter 3, Early Pressures for Public Pensions and the Government Annuities Plan

1. See *Non-Contributory Pensions* and *Compulsory Pension Insurance: Comparative Analysis of National Laws, and Statistics,* Studies and Reports

Series M (Social Insurance) nos. 9, 10 (Geneva: International Labour Office, 1933).

2. The classic account of this campaign is Stead's own book, *How Old Age Pensions Began to Be* (London: Methuen & Co., 1909). A recent scholarly account appears in Bentley B. Gilbert, *The Evolution of National Insurance in Great Britain: The Origins of the Welfare State* (London: Michael Joseph, 1966).

3. *HC Debates*, 1906–7, col. 3390.

4. *HC Journals*, 1906–7, p. 196.

5. *HC Debates*, 1906–7, col. 3396.

6. *HC Journals*, 1906–7, p. 142.

7. This is how he described himself in *Canadian Parliamentary Guide*, 1908, p. 147. His speech on Pringle's resolution appears in *HC Debates*, 1907–8, cols. 2419–23.

8. Ibid., col. 12659.

9. *HC Journals*, 1911–12, p. 124. References to Macdonald's notice of motion were made in the debate on Burnham's resolution. *HC Debates*, 1911–12, cols. 1362, 1822.

10. *HC Journals*, 1911–12, p. 386.

11. Ibid., 1912–13, p. 170. A summary of some of the representations made to the committee in its two years of activity appears in chap. 2, sec. 4.

12. *HC Debates*, 1914, p. 1341.

13. *HC Journals*, 1914, p. 200.

14. *HC Debates*, 1914, pp. 1333–40, 1343–52.

15. Ibid., pp. 1354–58.

16. *Convention Proceedings*, 1905, pp. 44, 46.

17. Ibid., 1907, p. 32; *Labour Gazette*, 1907–8, p. 1349. In 1908 the NTLC changed its name to Canadian Federation of Labour.

18. *Convention Proceedings*, 1907, pp. 47, 68.

19. See, e.g., *HC Debates*, 1906–7, cols. 3375–76.

20. *Convention Proceedings*, 1908, p. 8; 1909, p. 10; *Labour Gazette*, 1907–8, p. 995; 1909–10, p. 691; 1910–11, pp. 673–74.

21. *Convention Proceedings*, 1908, pp. 65–66.

22. Ibid., 1911, p. 56.

23. Ibid., 1912, pp. 20–21.

24. Ibid., 1913, p. 74; 1914, p. 16.

25. Ibid., 1911, p. 56. The reference to "a handsome advertisement" appears to have been a comment on an argument frequently used that a public pension program would be tantamount to a declaration to the world that poverty was widespread in Canada and thus would be bad advertising for a country anxious to attract immigrants.

26. Ibid., 1907, p. 75.

27. Ibid., 1908, p. 66.

28. Ibid., 1907, p. 47; 1908, p. 66.

29. *Sen. Debates*, 1906–7, pp. 331–32, 795.

30. *N.S. Debates*, 1907, pp. 98, 234–35, 345–47.

31. The full text of the commission's report appears in ibid., 1908, pp. 156–65. It was also published as an appendix to *N.S. Journals*, 1908.

32. *N.S. Debates*, 1908, p. 431.

33. *Sen. Debates*, 1906–7, pp. 331–36, 520–22, 669–72, 701–14, 786–99.

34. "Imputed" in the sense that interest was used in the calculation of the rate structure under the act. Actually the government paid no interest, although the imputed interest rate was an element in the long-term liability it accepted.

35. Francis A. Carman, "Canadian Government Annuities: A Study of Their Relation to Poverty in Old Age," *Political Science Quarterly* 30, no. 3 (Sept., 1915): 425–47.

36. Unless otherwise specified, figures on government annuities cited in this chapter are derived from the Department of Labour, *Annual Reports*; on annuities sold by life insurance companies, from Superintendent of Insurance, *Reports*.

37. *HC Debates*, 1920, pp. 402–3.

38. Dept. of Labour, *Annual Report*, 1927, p. 88.

39. See, e.g., statement of Victor Smith, general manager of Confederation Life, *Financial Post*, July 20, 1935; *Life Underwriters' News*, June, 1936.

40. This comes out clearly in an internal memorandum initialled by Chief Actuary A. D. Watson. Bennett Papers, Pub. Arch., MG 26, K, vol. 540, pp. 334655–61. See also Watson's evidence to the 1936 Sen. committee referred to later in this chapter.

41. Feb. 5, 12, 19, 26, Mar. 5, 12, 19, 1931.

42. *Sen. Debates*, 1931, p. 194; *HC Debates*, 1931, p. 2918.

43. *Sen. Journals*, 1936, pp. 89, 107.

44. Of the eight members in addition to Black, one was a director of two insurance companies, a trust company, and a bank; a second was a director of a trust company and a former president of the Moncton Board of Trade; a third was an officer of a bank; a fourth was a retired life insurance agent; a fifth was a senior partner in a St. James St. law firm; and a sixth was first vice-president of the Canadian Chamber of Commerce, London. Information derived from *Canadian Parliamentary Guide*, 1936; the *Canadian Who's Who*, 1936–37; *Who's Who in Canada*, 1936–37; *Financial Post Directory of Canadian Directors and Officials*, 1937; *Martindale-Hubbell Law Directory*, 1936.

45. The committee's report appears in full in *Sen. Debates*, 1936, pp. 459–60. The evidence of Watson and MacKenzie was summarized in detail. Blackadar's appearance was merely noted.

46. *Sen. Debates*, 1936, p. 549.

47. Ibid., p. 461.

48. HC Sess. Paper 157 (1938). The a(f) and a(m) tables was the popular name of the tables contained in *The Mortality of Annuitants, 1900–1920* published by the Institute of Actuaries and Faculty of Actuaries of Scotland.

49. From the beginning the act permitted employers and voluntary associations to purchase fully contributory, partly contributory, or non-contributory annuities for their employees or members, but individual contracts had to be issued to beneficiaries and were subject to the full vesting requirements of the act. Under the new procedure a contract could be issued to an employer for the purchase of annuities for his employees in accordance with an agreed plan. The employees were provided with certificates but received contracts only when their annuities became due. At March 31, 1940, only four group plans, covering 1,240 employees, were in effect. There was a rapid expansion thereafter.

50. Based on private interviews.

51. PC 1713 and 1714, both dated Apr. 16 and effective Apr. 19, 1948. The rate continued at 4 percent for contributions refunded on the death of an annuitant prior to maturity of his contract. A statutory amendment would have been necessary to change that.

52. *HC Debates*, 1948, pp. 6143–45.

53. Ibid., 1951 2d sess., p. 384.

54. Standing Committee on Industrial Relations, *Minutes of Proceedings and Evidence* (*HC Journals*, 1951 2d sess., app. 7), pp. 36–85.

55. Ibid., pp. 185–211, 240–42.

56. William M. Mercer of the pension consulting firm bearing his name told the standing committee that the new mortality basis was "amply conservative." He attacked the 3 percent interest rate ("I could make money if I could borrow at 3 percent and so could the Government") and advocated an even greater relaxation of the restrictions than the bill proposed. He said that if the plan were placed on a "realistic" basis, "government annuities will sweep across this country." Ibid., pp. 87–98.

57. Royal Commission on Government Organization, *Report* (Ottawa: Queen's Printer, 1962), vol. 3, pp. 286–88.

58. Royal Commission on Banking and Commerce, *Report* (Ottawa: Queen's Printer, 1964), p. 257.

59. *Labour Gazette*, 1968, p. 6.

60. In the 1936–37 and 1948–49 fiscal years, when minor panics were created as to the alleged potential insolvency of the plan, these bookkeeping

transfers were $8.9 million and $11.4 million. In other years they were small and even zero or negative on a few occasions.

61. The acting director of the branch estimated that it will be approximately seventy-five years before the plan is completely ended. *Labour Gazette*, 1968, p. 6.

62. No trade union spokesmen appeared before the Standing Committee on Industrial Relations in 1951. The Canadian Congress of Labour tried to counter the insurance lobby with a letter which was not received until the last day of the committee's sittings. *Minutes of Proceedings and Evidence*, pp. 217–18.

Notes to Chapter 4, Means-Test Pensions, 1927

1. Francis A. Carman, "Canadian Government Annuities: A Study of Their Relation to Poverty in Old Age," *Political Science Quarterly* 30, no. 3 (Sept., 1915): 428.

2. Order in Council PC 1806. The board was reconstituted from time to time thereafter to allow for the entry of new provinces into the plan and for other reasons. For an evaluation of its contribution, see Joseph E. Laycock, "The Canadian System of Old Age Pensions" (Ph.D. dissertation, University of Chicago, Mar., 1952), chap. 5.

3. Order in Council PC 217, Feb. 1, 1932.

4. This paragraph is based on James T. Shotwell, ed., *The Origins of the International Labor Organization* (New York: Columbia University Press, 1934), vol. 1; quotation from p. 424.

5. *Convention Proceedings*, 1915, p. 18.

6. Ibid., 1906, pp. 83–87.

7. Ibid., 1917, pp. 43–44.

8. For a comprehensive account of the Canadian Labour party and its antecedents and left-wing competitors, see Martin Robin, *Radical Politics and Canadian Labour, 1880–1930* (Kingston, Ont.: Queen's University, Industrial Relations Centre, 1968).

9. The highly compressed account contained in this and the next paragraph is based on: H. A. Logan, *Trade Unions in Canada: Their Development and Functioning* (Toronto: Macmillan Company of Canada, 1948), chaps. 13, 18; D. C. Masters, *The Winnipeg General Strike* (Toronto: University of Toronto Press, 1950); W. L. Morton, *The Progressive Party in Canada* (Toronto: University of Toronto Press, 1950); Robin, *Radical Politics*, chaps. 11 to 13; Walter D. Young, *Democracy and Discontent: Progressivism, Socialism and Social Credit in the Canadian West* (Toronto: Ryerson Press, 1969). Here and elsewhere in the study, election results are taken from Howard A. Scarrow, *Canada Votes: A Handbook of Federal and Provincial Election Data* (New Orleans: Hauser Press, 1962).

10. Royal Commission appointed under Order in Council (PC 670) to Inquire into Industrial Relations in Canada, *Report, together with a Minority Report and Supplementary Report* (printed as a supplement to *Labour Gazette*, July, 1919).

11. *Labour Gazette*, 1919, pp. 1172–81.

12. *HC Debates*, 1921, p. 2.

13. W. L. Mackenzie King, *Industry and Humanity: A Study of the Principles underlying Industrial Reconstruction* (Toronto: Thomas Allen, 1918). This book is a curious mixture of Manicheism, self-justification, and humanitarianism. The world was seen as a battleground between the "law of blood and death" and the "law of peace, work, and health." The triumph of the latter would be achieved through joint control of industry by capital, management, labour, and the community, along the lines of the company union model King had established for the Rockefellers in Colorado Fuel and Iron Co. This policy was to be underpinned by protective labour legislation and state action to achieve the "national minimum" proposed by the U.K. Labour party. Old age pensions were an integral part of this program. Pp. 347–48. The hope was held out that "labour and management . . . will roll back the stone from the door of the world's sepulchre today, and give to Humanity the promise of its resurrection to a more abundant life." P. 529.

14. National Liberal Convention, Ottawa, Aug. 5–7, 1919, *The Story of the Convention and the Report of Its Proceedings* (Ottawa: National Liberal Federation, 1920), pp. 126–27. This paragraph is based on King Papers, Pub. Arch., MG 26, J1, vol. 31, pp. 27483–530; J4, vol. C28, pp. C19947–60, C20132–33, C20169–283; vol. C43, pp. C34095–107; subsequent references to the King Papers are to Pub. Arch., MG 26. See also R. MacGregor Dawson, *William Lyon Mackenzie King: A Political Biography*, vol. 1, *1874–1923* (Toronto: University of Toronto Press, 1958), chaps. 10, 11; Ross Harkness, *J. E. Atkinson of the Star* (Toronto: University of Toronto Press, 1963), chap. 7.

15. King to Mrs. Ralph Smith, Mar. 12, 1921. King Papers, J1, vol. 67, pp. 57738–39.

16. See H. Blair Neatby, *William Lyon Mackenzie King*, vol. 2, *1924–1932, The Lonely Heights* (Toronto: University of Toronto Press, 1963), chap. 4.

17. See, e.g., *Convention Proceedings*, 1920, p. 150; 1921, pp. 25, 209; 1922, pp. 19, 108; 1923, pp. 12, 47–48.

18. *N.S. Journals*, 1921, pp. 44, 69–71; *Ont. Journals*, 1921, pp. 380–81; *N.B. Journals*, 1922, p. 111.

19. *B.C. Journals*, 1921 2d sess., p. 152.

20. Macdonald to King, Feb. 9, 1922. King Papers, J1, vol. 79, p. 65222.

21. *HC Journals*, 1922, p. 151. Fontaine stated the next year, "I have received hundreds of letters from all over the country asking me to follow up on this project, and even lately I had the honour to join a Nova Scotia

labour delegation which . . . came here to impress upon the government the necessity for this old age pension." *HC Debates*, 1923, p. 2817.

22. *HC Debates*, 1922, pp. 184, 1069, 1375; 1923, pp. 733, 1646–47, 1652, 2517, 2518–19, 2817, 2827, 3046; 1924, pp. 353, 456, 1367, 2312, 4429, 4554; 1925, pp. 61, 408, 539, 592, 647, 961, 1918.

23. *HC Journals*, 1924, pp. 192–93.

24. Ibid., pp. 464–65.

25. Ibid., 1925, p. 235. The replies were published in the committee's report. Ibid., pp. 455–57.

26. W. H. Price to W. G. Raymond, June 22, 1925. Dept. of National Health and Welfare file no. 208-1-18, Pub. Arch., RG 29, vol. 127.

27. *B.C. Journals*, 1924, pp. 89, 165.

28. *HC Journals*, 1925, p. 457.

29. Ibid.

30. *B.C. Journals*, 1925, pp. 77, 102.

31. *HC Journals*, 1925, p. 457.

32. *HC Debates*, 1925, p. 4425.

33. Ibid., pp. 4425–34; *HC Journals*, 1925, pp. 470–71.

34. Based on an examination of the election material on file in the library of the Liberal Federation of Canada, Ottawa.

35. Neatby, *Mackenzie King*, chap. 6.

36. Woodsworth read the text of this letter and the replies into the record on Jan. 29. *HC Debates*, 1926, pp. 560–61. The original of the letter to King and the file copy of King's replies appear in King Papers, J1, vol. 165, pp. 119473–76.

37. For sidelights not included in the brief account given here, see Grace MacInnis, *J. S. Woodsworth: A Man to Remember* (Toronto: Macmillan Company of Canada, 1953), chap. 15; Kenneth McNaught, *A Prophet in Politics: A Biography of J. S. Woodsworth* (Toronto: University of Toronto Press, 1959), pp. 215–20; Neatby, *Mackenzie King*, chap. 7.

38. *HC Journals*, 1926, pp. 28–29.

39. Quoted from Neatby, *Mackenzie King*, p. 110.

40. *HC Debates*, 1926, pp. 1949–50, 1970–76. Bennett's position will be considered more fully in section 4.

41. Ibid., pp. 1953–57, 1963–64, 1966–69, 2490–92, 2495.

42. See speeches of Sir Henry Drayton (ibid., pp. 1940–46), H. H. Stevens (pp. 1980–81, 2478–83), Arthur Meighen (pp. 2473–76), and R. J. Manion (pp. 2484–89). Meighen charged that the measure "bears every evidence of being brought to this House for one purpose and one purpose only—to satisfy a compact entered into for the sake of getting votes on the Address; and the bill will not get us any closer to old age pensions."

43. *Sen. Debates*, 1926, pp. 132–36, 155–84.

44. Ibid., p. 176.

45. *Sen. Journals*, 1926, p. 282.

46. Only 116 had run as Liberals but an additional 11 successful Liberal-Progressive, Liberal-Labour-Progressive, and Liberal-Labour candidates, together with 1 Independent Liberal, were committed to support the Liberal party. Sixty of the 116 Liberals were from Quebec.

47. See, e.g., *The Parliament of 1926 and the Constitutional Issue* (Ottawa: National Liberal Federation, n.d.), p. 15. This was a forty-seven-page pamphlet reproducing the text of King's keynote speech in the campaign.

48. Aug. 17, 1926. Senator L. McMeans reported as follows on a meeting in Winnipeg he had attended during the campaign: "The Premier of this country, addressing an audience of 5,000 people, said: 'I have given you an Old Age Pensions Bill.' This was greeted with enthusiastic handclapping and cheers." *Sen. Debates*, 1926–27, p. 131. Senator W. B. Ross referred to "walls plastered with pictures showing the leader of the government standing with a big basket containing large quantities of money, to be handed out to men on reaching the age of 70, provided they will just defeat this Tory Party and return the Liberals to power." Ibid., p. 99.

49. Ibid., p. 159.

50. *HC Debates*, 1926–27, pp. 336, 337, 346, 347, 348, 445, 456, 458–62, 464, 470, 476–78, 483–84. Typical comments were: "If there was one question discussed more than the customs scandal, it was the old age pension scheme" (p. 336); "There was no measure presented to the people in my constituency at all events which contributed more to the success of myself and the Liberal candidates generally" (p. 347); "The old age pension bill was an important concern, if not the chief concern, of the masses of people during the recent general election" (p. 453).

51. Neatby, *Mackenzie King*, chap. 9.

52. *Sen. Debates*, 1926–27, pp. 95–100, 130–60, 164–78.

53. Ibid., pp. 157–58.

54. Senator John McCormick's phrase. Ibid., p. 151.

55. *Sen. Journals*, 1926–27, pp. 246–48.

56. Dandurand to King, Jan. 18, May 7, June 8, 1927. King Papers, J1, vol. 167, pp. 120951, 120955, 120957–58. Dandurand to Robb, Nov. 26, 1926, Apr. 19, May 2, 1927. Dept. of National Health and Welfare file no. 208-1-1, Pub. Arch., RG 29, vol. 125.

57. June 8, 1927. King Papers, J1, vol. 178, pp. 127418–19.

58. When King circularized Liberal candidates after the 1925 election for their explanation of the party's poor showing, Heenan replied that workers had voted Conservative to "demonstrate their resentment at the dilatoriness during the past four years in matters of important social legislation such as the old age pensions." Oct. 25, 1925. Ibid., J1, vol. 132, p. 98578. He attributed the electoral success of 1926 largely to the pension bill. *HC Debates*, 1926–27, pp. 335–36.

59. He had been appointed to the Cabinet only because, as an Irish Catholic from northern Ontario with a labour background, he fitted a number of categories whose combination was felicitous at the time. Neatby, *Mackenzie King*, pp. 172–73.

60. King Papers, J1, vol. 160, pp. 116082–83.

61. The B.C. bill was introduced on June 19, 1927, received third reading on Feb. 28, and was assented to on Mar. 7. *B.C. Journals*, 1926–27, pp. 23, 147, 194.

62. Aug. 23, 1927. King Papers, J1, vol. 169, pp. 122269–71.

63. Aug. 27, 1927. Ibid., J1, vol. 172, p. 123721.

64. *HC Debates*, 1926–27, p. 332.

65. National Liberal Conservative Convention, Winnipeg, Oct. 10–12, 1927, "Verbatim Report" (typewritten transcript), pp. 103–5. Pub. Arch., MG 28, IV-2, vol. 1. Ironically, the convention chairman at the session where this decision was taken was Senator C. P. Beaubien, one of the most intransigent opponents of the bill in both 1926 and 1927.

66. Bennett Papers, Pub. Arch., MG 26, K, vol. 44, p. 26572; subsequent references to the Bennett Papers are to Pub. Arch., MG 26, K.

67. *Winnipeg Free Press*, June 10, 1930.

68. *St. John Telegraph-Journal*, June 27, 1930.

69. Compared with its percentage in 1926, the Conservative percentage of the vote in 1930 increased from 53.9 to 59.4 in New Brunswick, from 47.3 to 50.0 in Prince Edward Island, but declined from 53.7 to 52.5 in Nova Scotia where the most strenuous efforts were made to exploit the issue.

70. See correspondence with these governments in Bennett Papers, vol. 540, pp. 334364–402.

71. *HC Debates*, 1931, p. 3944.

72. This paragraph is based on *Non-Contributory Pensions* and *Compulsory Pension Insurance: Comparative Analysis of National Laws, and Statistics*, Studies and Reports Series M (Social Insurance) nos. 9, 10 (Geneva: International Labour Office, 1933).

73. Dominion-Provincial Conference, Nov. 3–10, 1927, *Précis of Discussions* (Ottawa: King's Printer, 1928), p. 34.

74. This argument was advanced by the ministers piloting the 1926 and 1927 bills through both the Senate and House of Commons. *HC Debates*, 1926, pp. 1939–40; 1926–27, p. 325; *Sen. Debates*, 1926, pp. 135–36; 1926–27, p. 169. Premier MacLean of British Columbia also used it at the 1927 federal-provincial conference. *Précis of Discussions*, p. 34.

75. See *HC Journals*, 1924, p. 464; Special Committee appointed to Make an Inquiry into an Old Age Pension System for Canada, *Proceedings* (*HC Journals*, 1924, app. 4).

76. Charles Booth, *Pauperism, A Picture, and the Endowment of Old Age, an Argument* (London: Macmillan & Co., 1892); idem, *Old Age*

Pensions and the Aged Poor: A Proposal (London: Macmillan & Co., 1899).

77. *Proceedings*, p. 52. There was, however, a wide divergence between Moore's view of what constituted a "reasonable amount" and that of most of the committee. Moreover, he argued that an applicant should not have to demonstrate need as a matter of course but that, instead, the administrative authorities should have to prove that an applicant who was to be excluded was not in need.

78. *HC Debates*, 1926, pp. 1970–76.

79. Ibid., pp. 1976–80.

80. *Sen. Debates*, 1926–27, pp. 96–97.

81. *HC Debates*, 1926–27, pp. 448–49.

82. *Convention Proceedings*, 1927, p. 113; 1928, pp. 59, 123.

83. A thick segment of the Bennett Papers (vols. 541–42, pp. 335094–817) consists of resolutions and other written representations Bennett received on this subject during his term as prime minister. They came from provincial legislatures, municipal councils, and a host of voluntary organizations, as well as private individuals.

Notes to Chapter 5, Implementation of the 1927 Plan

1. The plan was made operative in the Northwest Territories in 1929 and in the Yukon in 1949. Newfoundland implemented it immediately upon entering Confederation in 1949.

2. *Sask. Journals*, 1927, pp. 52–53.

3. *HC Journals*, 1925, p. 456.

4. *Man. Journals*, 1926, pp. 199–200, 218, 240; 1927, pp. 178, 192–93.

5. Dominion-Provincial Conference, *Précis of Discussions* (Ottawa: King's Printer, 1928), p. 34.

6. Except as otherwise indicated, the account of events in the various provinces is based on contemporary press reports. The *Winnipeg Free Press, Regina Leader*, and *Edmonton Bulletin* were used for the prairie provinces; the *Toronto Globe, Mail and Empire*, and *Star* for Ontario; the *St. John Telegraph-Journal* for New Brunswick; and the *Charlottetown Patriot* for Prince Edward Island. In the case of Nova Scotia, the highly partisan approach of the newspapers made it necessary to consult two to obtain a balanced picture, namely, the *Chronicle* (Liberal) and *Herald* (Conservative) of Halifax. The *Montreal Gazette* and *La Presse* were used for Quebec. *La Presse* was particularly valuable, since its detailed reports of debates in the Legislature were tantamount to a condensed Hansard, and its reports on political developments outside the House were thorough.

7. *Alta. Journals*, 1926, pp. 123–24, 132, 147.

8. Ibid., 1927, pp. 33–38.

9. Ibid., 1928, pp. 58–64.

10. *Labour Gazette*, 1924, p. 1021.

11. It is not entirely clear that the organization circulating the petition was the same as that formed in 1924, though the name was the same. A petition from the residents of Preston was tabled in the Legislature on Mar. 4, 1928. *Ont. Journals*, 1928, p. 91.

12. See the resolution of the Ontario section of the Union of Canadian Municipalities of Jan. 25, 1928 (*Labour Gazette*, 1928, p. 283); resolution of York County Council (*Toronto Star*, Feb. 3, 1928); petition of York Township Council (*Ont. Journals*, 1928, p. 116). York Township was a low-income dormitory municipality on the edge of Toronto. Immediately after the 1927 act was passed at Ottawa, the Conservative M.P.P. for the area made a strong plea in the Legislature for provincial participation.

13. See chap. 4, sec. 2.

14. *Ont. Journals*, 1928, p. 25.

15. See Dept. of National Health and Welfare file no. 208-5-5, Pub. Arch., RG 29, vol. 137.

16. Data supporting the latter statement are not available but it is a reasonable assumption in view of the consistently low level of overall personal per capita income in the maritime provinces relative to the others. See *Nat. Accts.*, 1926–56, table 29. For figures on the seventy-and-over population as a percentage of the total in 1931, see table 6, chap. 2, sec. 2.

17. *N.S. Journals*, 1928, p. 14. The much larger Liberal opposition in the 1929 and 1930 sessions also made pensions the subject of the Throne Speech amendment. Ibid., 1929, p. 20; 1930, pp. 13–14.

18. The reports were published in ibid., 1929, app. 31; 1930, app. 29.

19. Mothers' allowances and minimum wages for women were often linked to old age pensions in both Nova Scotia and New Brunswick. No action had been taken on the former in either province, although the pioneering measure in the field had been adopted in Manitoba as far back as 1916. Legislation to set minimum wages for women had been passed in Nova Scotia in 1920, but the board to administer it had never been appointed. There was no such legislation in New Brunswick.

20. An interesting exchange of letters took place between Premier J. B. M. Baxter and Bennett early in 1931. It was precipitated by a press report of a promise by Bennett to the prairie premiers that Ottawa would assume 95 percent of the cost. Baxter argued that nothing short of this would make it feasible for New Brunswick to adopt the plan but that it would be dangerous to leave administration in the hands of the provinces if their financial obligation was to be so slight. The obvious solution would be for the federal government to take over the whole plan. Bennett said that he had an opinion from the law officers that Ottawa could not constitutionally

undertake the administration of the plan. When Baxter suggested that he ignore this opinion, Bennett replied that he had discussed the matter with his colleagues and they did not want to get involved in administration. Baxter to Bennett, Jan. 8; Bennett to Baxter, Jan. 26; Baxter to Bennett, Jan. 28; Bennett to Baxter, Feb. 4. Bennett Papers, Pub. Arch., MG 26, K, vol. 540, pp. 334370–74.

21. *P.E.I. Journals*, 1933, p. 10.

22. During the depression, some other provinces administratively limited the total pension awarded to a married couple to $30 a month. Bennett Papers, vol. 540, p. 334673.

23. See Herbert F. Quinn, *The Union Nationale: A Study in Quebec Nationalism* (Toronto: University of Toronto Press, 1963), chaps. 2, 3; Pierre-Elliott Trudeau, "La Province de Québec au Moment da la Grève," in *La Grève de l'Amiante: Une Étape de la Révolution industrielle au Québec*, ed. Trudeau (Montréal: Éditions Cité Libre, 1956), pp. 1–91; Mason Wade, *The French Canadians, 1760–1967*, rev. ed. (Toronto: Macmillan Company of Canada, 1968), vol. 2, chaps. 13, 14.

24. See Esdras Minville, "Labour Legislation and Social Services in the Province of Quebec," app. 5 to *Report* of Royal Commission on Dominion-Provincial Relations (Ottawa: King's Printer, 1939).

25. Even when he was finally forced to accept the 1927 plan, he looked back with regret at the old system. Thus, the 1936 Speech from the Throne stated: "Up to the present, the Province has deemed it inadvisable to avail itself of the Federal Old Age Pensions Act, considering that our admirable charitable institutions, with the good will of our population, would meet the situation. But hard times belied our hopes, and the Government will request you to pass an Act enabling the Province to share in the Federal Old Age Pensions System." *Que. Journals*, 1936, p. 7.

26. He ultimately found his way into H. H. Stevens' shortlived Reconstruction Party and was defeated as its candidate in Hull in the 1935 federal election.

27. *Que. Journals*, 1929, p. 104.

28. Ibid., p. 315.

29. Ibid., 1930, p. 41.

30. Social Insurance Commission, Que., *First and Second Reports* (Quebec: Dept. of Labour, 1933), p. 13.

31. Social Insurance Commission, Que., *Fifth Report*. A minority report proposed that Quebec should proceed with a contributory plan of its own if the federal government did not do so and that Ottawa should pay to the province the total amount which its residents would be entitled to under the 1927 plan.

32. *Que. Journals*, 1933, pp. 272, 355–56; 1934, pp. 40, 124, 143–46; 1935, p. 393.

33. Ibid., 1935, pp. 81–83. The reference to new federal legislation was based on a statement by R. B. Bennett in his "new deal" radio broadcasts of Jan., 1935, that he was considering a contributory pension plan.

34. The Sunday Observance Act prohibited work on Sunday except in cases of necessity or mercy, but one section permitted those who conscientiously observed the seventh day of the week to work on the first if they did not disturb others. The demand was for repeal of this section.

35. *HC Debates*, 1941, p. 4428.

36. HC Sess. Paper 35D (1943–44).

37. *HC Debates*, 1941, pp. 4423–29.

38. See Speech from Throne, *Man. Journals*, 1943, p. 16.

39. A large selection of material of this kind appears in the personal files of Stanley Knowles, M.P.

40. See, e.g., comments during the Finance Department estimates in 1943 by these Liberals: F. W. Gershaw (Medicine Hat), Rev. Dan McIvor (Fort William), Harry Leader (Portage La Prairie), Ralph Maybank (Winnipeg South), D. A. McNiven (Regina), R. W. Mayhew (Victoria). *HC Debates*, 1943, pp. 110, 155, 184, 381–82, 438, 442.

41. *Man. Journals*, 1943, pp. 41–43.

42. HC Sess. Paper 89M (1944–45).

43. *HC Debates*, 1943, pp. 5355–56. The order in council was PC 6367, Aug. 10, 1943.

44. PC 3377, May 29, 1944. Ilsley's reluctance to increase the ceiling arose out of objections to the move by the Liberal government of his home province of Nova Scotia. Unfavourable reactions from some of the other provinces induced him to change his mind. Sess. Paper 89M (1944–45).

45. Actually, the previous statutory provision relating to both the five-year and twenty-year periods had been relaxed somewhat by regulation. See Joseph E. Laycock, "The Canadian System of Old Age Pensions" (Ph.D. dissertation, University of Chicago, Mar., 1952), pp. 262–71; Dept. of Finance, *Report on the Administration of Old Age Pensions in Canada, 1937–38*, pp. 12–13.

46. The last figure harmonized the limit where there was a blind spouse with the limits established for blind pensioners by the same act.

47. Where a province wanted to pay a higher pension than the maximum in which the federal government would share, the most satisfactory method continued to be the payment of a supplement, since the limits of allowable income were still inflexible in the 1947 amending act. Thus a provincial increase in the pension proper would be offset in part by the operation of the means test.

48. Even a $30 pension was a noteworthy improvement in Newfoundland. Under the plan in effect there before 1949, maximum benefits were $72 a *year* for single and widowed pensioners and $120 a year for couples.

The qualifying age was seventy-five, except that a widow who was sixty-five at the time of her husband's death was also eligible.

49. Based on examination of the circulars and amplified by information from private sources.

50. *HC Debates*, 1926–27, p. 467.

51. An extensive analysis of the administration of the act is contained in Laycock, "Canadian System of Old Age Pensions," esp. chaps. 3 to 7 incl. Administrative developments as seen from the federal point of view were reported on annually in varying degrees of detail. See Dept. of Labour, *Annual Reports* up to and including the 1934–35 fiscal year, and for the period from 1937–38 until the plan was abandoned the *Reports on the Administration of Old Age Pensions and Pensions for the Blind* (subsequently referred to as *Administrative Reports*) which were issued by the Department of Finance until 1944–45 and thereafter by the Department of National Health and Welfare. (The first of these reports covered only old age pensions since pensions for the blind were not then in effect.) Provincial authorities also issued annual reports but many of them are not now readily available and those which are are rarely illuminating on administrative policies.

52. Order in Council PC 1732, May 1, 1947. The revised regulations had the dual objective of systematizing investigatory and other procedures and of reducing rigidity in the conditions imposed by the act and regulations. Included in the latter category was the power to disregard general welfare payments by provinces or municipalities in calculating a pensioner's income. Thus, there was at least the possibility of tailoring benefits to need as a substitute for the rigid ceilings of the means test. In addition, provisions on the commencement of the pension, temporary absence from Canada, determination of income from property, and recovery of overpayments were made more flexible.

53. Auditor General, *Report*, 1929–30, vol. 1, p. xxvii.

54. Ibid., 1930–31, vol. 1, p. xxxvii.

55. An account of the meeting and more particularly of its results in terms of amended regulations is contained in the 1937–38 *Administrative Report*, pp. 10–15.

56. PC 1/3050, Dec. 9, 1937.

57. See, e.g., this comment by the Ontario Old Age Pensions Commission: "Our experience in endeavouring to enforce the maintenance of Parents Act has not been at all satisfactory. We have found that in over 90% of cases brought before magistrates no order was made against the children." Dept. of Public Welfare, Ont., *Annual Report*, 1933–34, p. 14.

58. See presentation by Dept. of National Health and Welfare, in Joint Committee of the Senate and House of Commons on Old Age Security, *Minutes of Proceedings and Evidence* (Ottawa: King's Printer, 1950), pp. 34–36. The regulations were amended in 1944 to give the provinces dis-

cretionary authority to exempt the first $2,000 of an estate from recovery.

59. Ibid., pp. 30–32.

60. Ibid., pp. 33–34.

61. Based on figures published annually in *Administrative Reports.*

Notes to Chapter 6, Universal Pensions, 1951

1. See opening to chap. 4.

2. Precise figures on total provincial expenditures on pension benefits are not readily available. However, net ordinary expenditures on "aid to aged persons" (which included pensions, supplements, grants paid to homes for the aged, and administration) totalled $32.7 million in 1952–53, the first full fiscal year in which the Old Age Assistance Act was in force, compared with $43.1 million in 1950–51, the last full year of operation of the Old Age Pensions Act of 1927. DBS, *Financial Statistics of Provincial Governments, Revenue and Expenditure,* 1950, 1952 (Ottawa: Queen's Printer, 1953, 1954), table 6 in each case.

3. Bennett Papers, Pub. Arch., MG 26, K, vol. 540, pp. 334644–51. The memorandum was unsigned, but it appears to have been prepared by A. D. Watson, chief actuary of the Department of Insurance.

4. A descending scale of bonus was to be offered according to the amount of premium paid by the purchaser of an annuity in any year. For the first $50 of premium, the bonus annuity was to be 90 percent of the annuity purchased by the premium, and was to decline with each additional $50 of premium until it reached 10 percent for the fifth $50. A prerequisite was to be amendment of the Government Annuities Act to establish premiums at a level sufficient to cover both the calculated cost of annuities and administrative expenses. It was also suggested that the bonus arrangement might be made applicable to private pension plans and to annuities purchased by individuals from private carriers.

5. A proof appears in Bennett Papers, vol. 540, pp. 334686–90.

6. *Attorney General for Canada* v. *Attorney General for Ontario et al.,* 1937 AC 355.

7. "Perhaps the best hope of success is through employers of labour. A bonus pension should interest them, and insurance companies might stimulate that interest." Watson to R. K. Finlayson (Bennett's personal secretary), Feb. 12, 1935. Bennett Papers, vol. 540, p. 334680.

8. Dept. of National Health and Welfare file no. 208-1-1, Pub. Arch., RG 29, vol. 125. The commission incorporated the substance of the brief in its report. Royal Commission on Dominion-Provincial Relations, *Report* (Ottawa: King's Printer, 1940), vol. 2, pp. 31–32.

9. See, e.g., Watson to W. C. Clark, deputy minister of finance, Feb. 2, 1937; Clark to Watson, Feb. 8, 1937. File no. 208-1-1.

10. H. Mitchell, "What Will Old Age Pensions Cost Canada?" *Industrial Canada*, Feb., 1928, pp. 41–43. The gist of Mitchell's argument was that once public pension plans are adopted, their terms are always liberalized and costs "prove year by year a heavier burden to carry."

11. *Industrial Canada*, July, 1929, pp. 145–46.

12. Ibid., July, 1930, p. 152. The committee's minutes (unpublished) indicate that during 1930 and 1931 representations were made on several occasions to both the Liberal government and, after the 1930 election, the Conservative government to have pensions paid under private plans excluded from the calculation of income under the 1927 act.

13. *Fifth Report*, p. 149.

14. Ibid., p. 155.

15. *Report*, vol. 2, p. 41.

16. *Convention Proceedings*, 1931, p. 61.

17. Ibid., 1930, p. 197; 1931, p. 17; 1937, p. 80; 1938, p. 138; 1939, p. 25; 1940, p. 24.

18. The actual phrase used was "national non-contributory social insurance." CCF records are now in Pub. Arch., MG 28, IV-1. Proceedings and minutes of conventions and council meetings from 1934 to 1936 inclusive are in vol. 10 and the records for the 1937 convention in vols. 11, 12.

19. *HC Journals*, 1936, pp. 48–49.

20. *HC Debates*, 1936, pp. 356, 315–20.

21. Ibid., pp. 336, 361.

22. *HC Journals*, 1938, p. 122; 1939, p. 163.

23. The act provided unemployment benefits, medical and related coverage, family allowances, and old age, disability, and widows' pensions from a single social security fund, which was financed by a 5 percent income tax supplemented by grants from general revenues. The levy on income provided approximately half the receipts of the fund.

24. Sir William Beveridge, *Report on Social Insurance and Allied Services* (London: HM Stationery Office, 1942), 2 vols.

25. Advisory Committee on Reconstruction, Special Committee on Social Security, *Report on Social Security prepared by Dr. L. C. Marsh* (Ottawa: King's Printer, 1943). The Advisory Committee on Reconstruction was set up in 1941 to advise the Cabinet on postwar problems. Its chairman, F. Cyril James, principal of McGill University, was constantly in conflict with influential civil servants, and in the latter part of 1943 the committee was instructed to wind up its inquiries and prepare its report. Effective Jan. 1, 1944, the committee's functions were transferred to the Advisory Committee on Economic Policy, an interdepartmental committee of senior civil servants.

26. Dept. of Labour, *Annual Report on Labour Organization in Canada*, 1945 (Ottawa: King's Printer, 1947).

27. *Convention Proceedings*, 1940, pp. 70–71. The precise wording quoted here is from the second annual convention. Ibid., 1941, p. 52.

28. *Convention Proceedings*, 1942, pp. 294–95.

29. Ibid., 1948, pp. 345–46.

30. *Procès-Verbal*, 1943, p. 30.

31. *Convention Proceedings*, 1941, p. 112.

32. *Procès-Verbal*, 1945, p. 61; 1947, pp. 195–96.

33. *Convention Proceedings*, 1944, p. 71.

34. *Canadian Unionist*, Mar., 1950, p. 53.

35. See J. L. Granatstein, *The Politics of Survival: The Conservative Party of Canada, 1939–45* (Toronto: University of Toronto Press, 1967).

36. "Report of the Round Table on Canadian Policy" (mimeo.), item 25.

37. "National Conservative Convention, Winnipeg, Dec. 9, 10, 11, 1942," pp. 201–2; Progressive Conservative Association of Canada, "National Convention, Ottawa, Sept. 30, Oct. 1, 2, 1948," pp. 211–12. These are stenographic reports deposited in Pub. Arch., MG 28, IV-2, vols. 3 and 4. Election material is on file in the Macdonald Cartier Library in Ottawa.

38. Pub. Arch., MG 28, IV-1, vols. 13 to 16 incl.

39. Cf. N.Z. Social Security Act of 1938.

40. See J. W. Pickersgill, *The Mackenzie King Record*, vol. 1 (Toronto: University of Toronto Press, 1960), index references to "social security" and "industry and humanity."

41. *HC Journals*, 1943–44, pp. 3, 126, 133; 1944–45, p. 161.

42. Except as otherwise indicated, the information presented on the work of this group was derived from private interviews.

43. See Taylor Cole, *The Canadian Bureaucracy: A Study of Canadian Civil Servants and Other Public Employees, 1939–47* (Durham, N.C.: Duke University Press, 1949), pp. 268–71, for an account of the relatively small "group" (whose personnel duplicated that referred to here to a considerable extent) which in reality determined Canada's economic policy from 1939 to 1945.

44. See Pickersgill, *Mackenzie King Record*, chap. 20; *Politics and the War: Address by the Rt. Hon. W. L. Mackenzie King to National Liberal Federation, Sept. 27, 1943* (Ottawa: National Liberal Federation, n.d.).

45. These resolutions were published as a pamphlet entitled *The Task of Liberalism: Resolutions approved by the Advisory Council, National Liberal Federation, Ottawa, Sept. 27 and 28, 1943* (Ottawa: National Liberal Federation, n.d.).

46. Dept. of Reconstruction, *Employment and Income with Special Reference to the Initial Period of Reconstruction* (Ottawa: King's Printer, 1945). Tabled in the House of Commons on Apr. 12, 1945. *Journals*, 1945, p. 86. This document was prepared by and on the initiative of W. A.

Mackintosh. For a discussion of its role in the policy-making of the period, see Mackintosh, "The White Paper on Employment and Income in Its 1945 Setting," in *Canadian Economic Policy since the War*, by Canadian Trade Committee (Private Planning Association of Canada, 1966), pp. 9–21.

47. No constitutional problem was considered to exist in this case since it was generally believed that Parliament could distribute largesse in any way it saw fit as long as it did not attempt to impose contributions.

48. *HC Journals*, 1944–45, p. 4.

49. See, e.g., *Mackenzie King to the People of Canada: A Series of Addresses by Rt. Hon. W. L. Mackenzie King, Prime Minister of Canada, May–June 1945* (Ottawa: National Liberal Federation, n.d.), p. 92.

50. Dominion-Provincial Conference on Reconstruction, *Proposals of the Government of Canada* (Ottawa: King's Printer, 1945). For my purposes the most important reference book was that on health, welfare, and labour.

51. *Proposals*, p. 52. Actually, this principle had been enunciated even earlier in the Rowell-Sirois Report. That report and the Green Books differed substantially in the nature of their proposals but both were inspired by Keynesian thinking.

52. Ibid.

53. The task force's criticisms of the pension plan were set forth in ibid., pp. 37–39, and in *Health, Welfare and Labour*, pt. 2.

54. *Proposals*, pp. 37–39. J. W. Pickersgill and D. G. Forster, *The Mackenzie King Record*, vol. 2 (Toronto: University of Toronto Press, 1968), suggests at pp. 14–15 that the principle of the two-level program was approved by the Cabinet as early as May 29, 1944. The actual extracts quoted from King's diaries, however, do not support this inference. On the contrary, they indicate that at that time King, the Cabinet, and Finance Department were still wedded to the contributory principle.

55. *Proposals*, pp. 38–39.

56. Ibid., p. 42.

57. See Conference of Federal and Provincial Governments, Ottawa, Dec. 4–7, 1950, *Proceedings* (Ottawa: King's Printer, 1953), p. 44.

58. See, e.g., statements of National Health and Welfare Minister Paul Martin, *HC Debates*, 1947, pp. 4283–84, 4643–44.

59. *HC Debates*, 1947, p. 3139.

60. National Liberal Convention, Aug. 5, 6, 7, 1948, *Report of Proceedings* (Ottawa: National Liberal Federation, n.d.), pp. 175–76.

61. *HC Debates*, 1950, p. 60.

62. Ibid., 1949 2d sess., p. 3019.

63. Mar., 1950, p. 100.

64. *The Canadian Liberal*, Summer, 1951, p. 5.

65. *HC Debates*, 1950, p. 62.

66. *HC Journals*, 1949 2d sess., p. 26.

67. Based on private interviews.

68. *HC Journals*, 1950, pp. 95–96, 198, 199, 202. The willingness of the Senate to participate in this inquiry was in marked contrast to its attitude in 1926–27. The old age assistance and security bills passed all stages in the Senate without formal division. A few senators expressed misgivings at "the trend toward the welfare state and away from encouragement of thrift and industry," but there was no real opposition to either bill. One senator remarked on "the change of heart that has taken place here." *Sen. Debates*, 1951, pp. 677–80, 696–701, 709; 1951 2d sess., pp. 79–85, 94–96, 101–5, 113–18, 133–39, 157–63, 168–71.

69. *Canadian Unionist*, Mar., 1950, p. 53.

70. Joint Committee of the Senate and House of Commons on Old Age Security, *Minutes of Proceedings and Evidence* and *Report* (Ottawa: King's Printer, 1950).

71. Based on private interviews.

72. U.S. experience was seen by both Davidson and the committee as providing a particularly significant object lesson. Though the earnings-related contributory plan of that country had been in operation for fifteen years, intergovernmental means-test plans were still the major source of income maintenance for the aged.

73. See pp. 191–93. There is no reference in the report to the Green Book proposal and interviewees did not remember its being a factor in the committee's discussions. Though it is no doubt possible that the committee arrived at the same conclusion independently, it is hard to believe that the Green Book proposal had been completely forgotten in a matter of only five years. A more probable explanation is that it had become a conditioning factor in almost everyone's thinking.

74. *Report*, p. 111. A specific suggestion was included, but only as "one possibility among many" and "an idea worthy of consideration rather than as the final view of the committee." It was for a combination of (a) a levy on income or earnings from which those with very low incomes would be exempt, (b) a payroll tax on employers, and (c) continuance of the existing level of payments out of general revenues.

75. *HC Debates*, 1951 2d sess., pp. 382–83.

76. Ibid., p. 415.

77. This paragraph is based on private interviews.

78. *Minutes of Proceedings and Evidence*, pp. 1161–72.

79. Conference of Federal and Provincial Governments, Ottawa, Dec. 4–7, 1950, *Proceedings* (Ottawa: King's Printer, 1953), p. 8.

80. Most of this correspondence was tabled in the House of Commons and printed as an appendix to Hansard. *HC Debates*, 1951, pp. 2726–42.

81. The amendment inserted a new section 94A in the British North

America Act providing that "the Parliament of Canada may from time to time make laws in relation to old age pensions in Canada, but no law made by the Parliament of Canada in relation to old age pensions shall affect the operation of any law present or future of a Provincial Legislature in relation to old age pensions." It had been originally envisaged that the new section would be numbered 95A, following immediately after section 95 which provides for concurrent jurisdiction over agriculture and immigration. Duplessis, however, objected to that sequence on the ground that it might give rise to an inference that the paramountcy given to federal legislation by section 95 extended also to old age pensions.

82. *HC Debates*, 1951, p. 3663.

83. Dept. of National Health and Welfare, *Annual Report*, 1954, p. 107; idem, *Report on the Administration of Old Age Assistance in Canada*, 1952, p. 6; 1953, p. 9.

84. Public awareness of the hardship suffered by those who had to rely exclusively on the public pension was no doubt heightened by newspaper features, which were common in the mid-1950s, describing in graphic detail what it was like to live on $40 a month. A memorable example was a series by William MacEachern, at the time a young *Toronto Star* reporter, who personally lived on a pensioner's income for two weeks and recorded his experiences day by day for his newspaper and its readers. The series was subsequently published as a pamphlet entitled *Fourteen Days as an Old Age Pensioner* (Toronto: *Toronto Star*, 1956).

85. *HC Debates*, 1957, pp. 2222–23.

86. As income maintenance programs increased in number and coverage, governments more and more had to face the difficulty that it was politically inexpedient to grant increases under one plan without also giving consideration to beneficiaries under the others. Moreover, since some of the plans involved provincial participation, successive federal governments could not be entirely unmindful of the cost implications for the provinces (even though they did not consult the provinces in advance).

87. Canadian Institute of Public Opinion release, May 8, 1957.

88. Based on private interviews.

89. For a discussion of the issues in the 1957 election, and of the significance of old age pensions among them, see John Meisel, *The Canadian General Election of 1957* (Toronto: University of Toronto Press, 1962), chaps. 3, 13.

90. For a discussion of the operation of the fund, see chap. 9, sec. 3.

Notes to Chapter 7, Contributory Pensions, 1965

1. For example, a major policy statement of the Canadian Welfare Council argued against reduction of the eligible age for the universal pension "in view of the higher priority the Council would give to other uses of the

large sums involved." *Social Security for Canada* (Ottawa: Canadian Welfare Council, 1958), p. 5.

2. This is the official short title of the act. The long title is "An Act to Establish a Comprehensive Program of Old Age Pensions and Supplementary Benefits in Canada Payable to and in Respect of Contributors."

3. It should be noted in passing that five of the provinces brought the means-test pension under the Canada Assistance Plan. The declared purpose was to convert it from a means-test to a needs-test pension in those provinces for the few years during which it was to continue to be paid.

4. Changes in the adjustment procedure effected by the amending act of 1972 are described in chap. 8, sec. 4.

5. The last mentioned are excluded whenever an employer pays them less than $250 cash or for less than twenty-five working days in a year. Members of the armed forces and Royal Canadian Mounted Police were excluded initially but were brought in in 1967. Provincial civil servants outside Quebec are covered by agreement with the provincial governments concerned. Employees of a foreign government or international agency in Canada may be included by agreement with the government or agency concerned. Members of religious orders who have taken vows of perpetual poverty are excluded, as are exchange teachers. An employment unit may be excluded under the terms of a reciprocal agreement with a foreign country where the employer covers all his employees under a plan in that country, and conversely, employees in a foreign country may be included under certain conditions. Reciprocal agreements may be entered into with foreign countries regarding transfer of benefit rights.

6. To illustrate, let us assume that a retirement pension commenced in Jan., 1970, that is, five years or sixty months after contributions first become payable, and that the contributor was continuously employed in pensionable employment during the five-year period. His "average monthly pensionable earnings" were arrived at by dividing his aggregate adjusted earnings by 120 rather than 60, and his pension is 25 percent of the quotient. In other words, his pension is half as large as it would have been if he had received pensionable earnings of the same magnitude for ten years.

7. See Dept. of National Health and Welfare, *Annual Report*, 1966–67, pp. 143–44.

8. *Convention Proceedings*, 1953, p. 51. The proposal was for government action to establish "industrial pensions" for all wage earners and to make them fully portable through complete and immediate vesting of benefits rights.

9. See, e.g., convention resolutions and reports throughout the 1950s. TLC, *Convention Proceedings*, 1952, pp. 44, 169–70; 1953, p. 25; 1954, p. 17; 1955, pp. 33, 196; CCL, *Convention Proceedings*, 1953, pp. 63–64; 1954, pp. 43–44, 98; 1955, pp. 89–90; CLC, *Convention Proceedings*, 1956, pp. 55–56; CTCC, *Procès-Verbal*, 1955, p. 221; 1956, p. 159; 1957, p. 132;

1958, p. 62; 1959, pp. 248–49. The labour centrals also advocated that the amount of the pension should be tied to the cost of living and that special provision should be made for pensioners in regard to medical and related benefits, and housing.

10. *Convention Proceedings*, 1960, pp. 32, 39.

11. Based on private interviews.

12. *Toronto Globe and Mail*, May 1, 1957.

13. Dept. of Public Welfare, Ont., *Annual Report*, 1954–55, p. 4.

14. Ibid., 1955–56, pp. 5–6; 1956–57, p. 8; 1958–59, p. 9; 1959–60, p. 13. The 1955–56 report called the universal pension a "modified Townsend plan" and a "handout method" which "in both scope and value to the wage earner . . . is inferior to the insurance plans of the U.S. and other advanced countries." In 1959–60 it was asserted that portable pensions were not a problem in the U.S. as they were in Canada. For the ministerial speeches, see especially the paper presented by Public Welfare Minister Louis P. Cecile to the 1958 conference of the Institute of Public Administration of Canada. "The Social Security Systems of Canada and the USA," in *Proceedings*, 1958, pp. 23–29.

15. His views were set forth succinctly in a speech in the House of Commons on July 26, 1956. *HC Debates*, 1956, pp. 6507–8.

16. Except as otherwise indicated, statements in this paragraph are based on private interviews.

17. *National Superannuation: Labour's Policy for Security in Old Age* (London: Labour Party, 1957). This was a comprehensive and detailed statement of a proposed new pension program for England, which was published in May, 1957, for consideration by the Labour party's conference later in the year. It was based on technical studies by no less expert a committee than Richard M. Titmuss, Brian Abel-Smith, and Peter Townsend.

18. National Council minutes for the period are contained in Pub. Arch., MG 28, IV-1, vol. 3, and records relating to the pension study in vols. 109, 174.

19. It was approved retrospectively with some changes by the convention of July 23–25, 1958. *Convention Report*, 1958, p. 26.

20. See *The Federal Program of the New Democratic Party*, 3d ed. (Ottawa: New Democratic Party, 1967), pp. 14–15.

21. Order in Council PC 1958-8/307, Feb. 25, 1958.

22. Robert M. Clark, *Economic Security for the Aged in the United States and Canada: A Report prepared for the Government of Canada* (Ottawa: Queen's Printer, 1960). The report was submitted on Feb. 17, 1959, and tabled on Mar. 5. *HC Journals*, 1959, p. 201.

23. Vol. 2, chaps. 16, 21.

24. Quebec adopted a similar plan in 1961 and applied it to unmarried women as well as widows. Ontario did the same in 1962.

25. Based on private interviews.

26. In an opinion furnished for Clark's benefit, the acting deputy attorney general said: "While it is impossible to express an opinion with any assurance . . . I am of opinion that a law enacted by Parliament under s. 94A supra could not provide pensions or similar benefits for persons on any ground other than their attaining 'old age.' " Clark, *Economic Security for the Aged*, vol. 2, p. 218.

27. Copies of Diefenbaker's letter and the provincial replies were tabled in the House of Commons and printed as appendices to Hansard. *HC Debates*, 1962, pp. 76, 619–21; 1962–63, pp. 1741–43, 2219, 3059–60.

28. Ibid., 1962, pp. 74–75, 531.

29. *Report of Proceedings* (Ottawa: Liberal Federation of Canada, n.d.), p. 185.

30. Based on private interviews.

31. Judy LaMarsh, *Memoirs of a Bird in a Gilded Cage* (Toronto: McClelland and Stewart, 1969), pp. 58, 78. According to LaMarsh, the plan was worked out by "Toronto economists and actuaries for Walter Gordon."

32. See, e.g., *Montreal Gazette*, Feb. 28, 1963; *Toronto Globe and Mail*, Mar. 9, 12, 16, 1963; LaMarsh, *Bird in a Gilded Cage*, p. 78.

33. Based on private interviews. See also LaMarsh, *Bird in a Gilded Cage*, pp. 58–59, 78–82.

34. *HC Journals* 1963, p. 124.

35. Printed as an appendix to Hansard. *HC Debates*, 1963, pp. 2431–36.

Notes to Chapter 8, Shaping the 1965 Design

1. The resolution was introduced on Mar. 11, 1964, and adopted on Mar. 17, whereupon the bill was introduced and received first reading. *HC Journals*, 1964–65, pp. 84–85, 100–101; *HC Debates*, 1964–65, pp. 778–79, 1161–65, 1174–96. The white paper was tabled on the same day and printed as an appendix to Hansard. Ibid., pp. 1197–1202. On Nov. 9, the bill was withdrawn. *HC Journals*, 1964–65, p. 861.

2. Advance information on the contents of Bill C-136 was given in a revised *Canada Pension Plan: White Paper*, which was tabled on Aug. 10, 1964, and printed as an appendix to Hansard. *HC Debates*, 1964–65, pp. 6635–47. The resolution was introduced on Oct. 28. *HC Journals*, 1964–65, pp. 829–30. The bill received first reading on Nov. 9, second reading on Nov. 18, third reading on Mar. 29, 1965, and was assented to on Apr. 2. Ibid., pp. 860–61, 883–84, 1189, 1228.

3. These debates took place at the resolution stage, on second reading, and especially in committee of the whole. *HC Debates*, 1964–65, pp. 9898–9930, 10118–51, 10163–203, 10224–45, 11581–614, 11634–68, 11696–

705, 11721–32, 11741–57, 11770–99, 11832–68, 11885–922, 11979–84, 11989–12011, 12028–54, 12088–121, 12134–72, 12201–19, 12232–46, 12254–73, 12286–92, 12351–84, 12402–13, 12690–722, 12752–61, 12775–87, 12796–813.

4. Between Nov. 24, 1964, and Feb. 8, 1965, i.e., between second reading and consideration in committee of the whole, the joint committee heard expert evidence and representations, filling more than 2,000 pages, from interested parties. Special Joint Committee of the Senate and House of Commons appointed to Consider and Report upon Bill C-136, an Act to Establish a Comprehensive Program of Old Age Pensions and Supplementary Benefits in Canada Payable to and in Respect of Contributors, *Minutes of Proceedings and Evidence* (Ottawa: Queen's Printer, 1964–65), subsequently referred to as 1964–65 joint committee, *Proceedings*.

5. The role of pension organizations is discussed in chap. 9, sec. 2.

6. *HC Debates*, 1963, p. 2344.

7. Ibid., p. 2363.

8. Ibid., pp. 2388, 2778, 2859, 2992–99. LaMarsh called Knowles "a real master at this art" (of harassing the government). *Memoirs of a Bird in a Gilded Cage* (Toronto: McClelland and Stewart, 1969), p. 84.

9. These comments are based on news reports appearing in the *Toronto Globe and Mail* and *Toronto Star* between mid-Aug. and mid-Sept., 1963, and on LaMarsh, *Bird in a Gilded Cage*, pp. 83–85.

10. *HC Journals*, 1963, p. 389; *HC Debates*, 1963, pp. 3036–38.

11. The old age security tax was not changed when the Diefenbaker government increased the pension from $55 to $65 a month immediately before the 1962 election. The 1963 budget broadened the base of the sales tax component incidentally by extending the general sales tax to building materials and production machinery and equipment. This, however, was far from enough to cover even the cost of the increase in the pension to $65 a month, much less the further increase to $75.

12. *HC Journals*, 1963, p. 451.

13. *Bird in a Gilded Cage*, p. 85.

14. *HC Debates*, 1963, p. 3053.

15. *HC Journals*, 1963, pp. 398–99. At this point in time the split of the Créditistes from the Social Credit party had just occurred.

16. For the minutes and a verbatim report of that meeting, see 1964–65 joint committee, *Proceedings*, pp. 2051–57, 2059–112. The final report of the committee appears at pp. 2041–43.

17. Simultaneously, a $500 income tax exemption which had previously been claimable by all taxpayers of sixty-five and over was removed for those receiving the universal pension before seventy. The exemption was claimable at age seventy. The new Income Tax Act of 1971 restored the qualifying age to sixty-five and raised the exemption to $650 effective Jan.

1, 1972. This raise was superseded later in the year when the exemption was raised to $1,000, also effective from Jan. 1, 1972.

18. "Report of the Minimum Financial Needs Investigation" (mimeo.), Jan., 1966.

19. *HC Journals*, 1964–65, pp. 1178–80, 1184–87.

20. *HC Debates*, 1965, pp. 39–41.

21. For a succinct yet comprehensive critique of that approach, see the Canadian Welfare Council's policy statement of 1958, *Social Security for Canada* (Ottawa: Canadian Welfare Council, 1958).

22. *HC Journals*, 1966–67, p. 29.

23. *Sen. Journals*, 1963, pp. 413–14. The committee was reconstituted in the three succeeding sessions, and it tabled its final report on Feb. 2, 1966. Ibid., 1964–65, pp. 15–16; 1965, pp. 18–19; 1966–67, pp. 28–29, 54.

24. Sen. Special Committee on Aging, *Final Report*, chaps. 2, 9.

25. *HC Debates*, 1966–67, pp. 11333–37.

26. Dated Aug. 30, 1963, and Nov. 6, 1964. The first is Sess. Paper 214A (1963); the second, Sess. Papers 202L, 202M (1964–65). The second also appears in 1964–65 joint committee, *Proceedings*, pp. 485–551, and was published separately as *Canada Pension Plan Actuarial Report, Nov. 6, 1964* (Ottawa: Queen's Printer, 1965).

27. The basic exemption meant that the annual contribution of an employee earning $1,350 a year would be $13.50 (1.8 percent of $750) or precisely 1 percent of total earnings. The percentage of earnings contributed would be progressively less for earnings below $1,350, and progressively more for higher earnings until the progression was reversed by the effect of the ceiling.

28. See LaMarsh's speech introducing the resolution on Bill C-136 and her introductory statement to the joint committee. *HC Debates*, 1964–65, p. 9900; 1964–65 joint committee, *Proceedings*, p. 17.

29. See, e.g., the executive committee's report to the 1964 convention on its submissions to the government on Mar. 14, 1962, and Dec. 11, 1963. *Convention Proceedings*, 1964, pp. 36, 69.

30. 1964–65 joint committee, *Proceedings*, pp. 1645–46.

31. No official proceedings were published of the July, 1963, conference, which was called on an emergency basis following unanimous adoption by the Quebec Legislature of a resolution condemning the federal government's proposed municipal development and loan fund. Proceedings of the other two conferences were limited to formal statements of the various government leaders and the official communiqués. As a result, they are unilluminating on the extensive but informal discussions which took place on the Canada Pension Plan.

32. Sess. Papers 202, 202A, 202C, 202H, 202J (1964–65).

33. This generalization is basically true of the Pearson years of office, notwithstanding so egregious an exception as the municipal development and loan fund announced in the 1963 Speech from the Throne, which was not discussed in advance with the provinces even though it impinged directly on their jurisdiction. The ill will engendered by the federal government's unilateral action in that case, as well as provincial dissatisfaction with the sharing of revenues, complicated negotiations on the Canada Pension Plan, but the plan itself was discussed at great length with the provinces.

34. LaMarsh, *Bird in a Gilded Cage*, pp. 86–89.

35. Written representations received by ministers from the public appear in Sess. Papers 214C, 214D (1963), 202B, 202I (1964–65), all of which are bulky and consist mainly of communications from the insurance industry and its supporters. Interviews indicated that private members also received many written and oral representations.

36. See Canadian Chamber of Commerce, *Statement of Policy*, 1963–64, pp. 29–30; 1964–65, pp. 30–31. See also its presentation to the government of Dec. 6, 1963. *Labour Gazette*, 1964, p. 22.

37. See, e.g., Ontario Committee on Portable Pensions, "Public Hearings" (mimeo.), vol. 3 (Sept. 24, 1962), pp. 107, 108.

38. See Sess. Papers referred to in n.35.

39. Bill C-75 had not actually been introduced at the time but its main provisions had been made public in mid-Jan.

40. This paragraph is based on the relevant files of the CLC Political Education Department, supplemented by explanations by the director.

41. *Bird in a Gilded Cage*, p. 96.

42. A convenient source of information on the positions of these organizations is the 1964–65 joint committee, *Proceedings*.

43. The most systematic statement of the Créditiste position was given by party leader Réal Caouette in committee of the whole. *HC Debates*, 1964–65, pp. 12698–701. He branded the plan "a devious method" of extracting money from the people which would depress the economy, increase the power of government bureaucracy, and undermine the free enterprise system. He expounded the orthodox Social Credit position that there was a purchasing power deficiency in Canada which should be offset by payment of a national dividend. An appropriate first step, he argued, would be to increase the universal pension to $100 a month and to reduce the qualifying age immediately to sixty-five or even sixty.

44. 1964–65 joint committee, *Proceedings*, p. 1300.

45. *Toronto Globe and Mail*, July 29, 1963.

46. Except as otherwise indicated, the balance of this section is based on private interviews.

47. See Jean Lesage, "The Quebec Pension Plan," in *Pensions in Canada:*

A Compendium of Fact and Opinion, ed. Laurence E. Coward (Don Mills, Ont.: CCH Canadian, 1964), pp. 11–13; Claude Morin, *Le Pouvoir Québécois . . . en Négociation* (Québec: Éditions du Boréal Express, 1972), pp. 19–21.

48. The committee's findings were presented in the spring of 1964. Interdepartmental Study Committee on the Quebec Pension Plan, "Report" (mimeo.), 2 vols. Volume 1, which outlined a provincial earnings-related plan in detail including an actuarial report, was dated Apr., 1964. Volume 2, which was concerned with the administration and economic effects of the plan and its relationship to private plans, was dated May, 1964.

49. See "Report," vol. 1, p. v.

50. *Que. Journals*, 1963 2d sess., p. 16.

51. Ibid., p. 17.

52. *Ont. Journals*, 1960, pp. 15, 165, 204.

53. Ibid., pp. 29, 30, 203.

54. *Ont. Debates*, 1960, p. 2534. Actually the committee was set up early in Jan. and was referred to in the Speech from the Throne (*Ont. Journals*, 1960, p. 8), but Frost's statement of Apr. 7 greatly enhanced its status. There was no formal instrument establishing it. It offered its first recommendations in outline form in Feb., 1961, and elaborated on them in Aug. Ontario Committee on Portable Pensions, "Summary Report" (mimeo.); *Second Report* (Toronto: Queen's Printer, 1961). The committee discussed the ideas contained in its "Summary Report" with interested members of the Legislature on Feb. 15, 1961. "Meeting of the Special Committee of the Whole House on Portable Pensions" (mimeo.). The committee also produced a draft bill which the government introduced with some modifications in the 1962 session of the Legislature for discussion purposes. In Sept., 1962, the committee held public hearings on the draft. "Public Hearings" (mimeo.), 4 vols. It then continued to advise the government in formulating the final legislation.

55. For an outline of those conditions, see chap. 2, sec. 3.

56. The positions of the three parties were set forth in the debate surrounding Frost's announcement of Apr. 7, 1960, and in the debate on the 1963 bill. *Ont. Debates*, 1960, pp. 2525–42; 1962–63, pp. 1878–85, 2085–96, 2852–61, 2867–70.

57. Bohumil V. Dymes, "Principles of a Graduated Old Age Security Scheme for Ontario" (typescript). Dymes was the department's research director at the time.

58. The other joint chairman was D. G. MacGregor, an economics professor at the University of Toronto who wrote most of the *Second Report*. Other members were R. M. Clark, author of *Economic Security for the Aged in the United States and Canada*, referred to in chap. 7, sec. 2; J. A. Tuck, general counsel of the Canadian Life Insurance Officers

Association; C. E. Hendry, director of the University of Toronto School of Social Work; and R. E. G. Davis, executive director of the Canadian Welfare Council. Clark had carefully refrained from injecting his personal views into *Economic Security*, but subsequent writing left no doubt that he was in favour of leaving earnings-related pensions in the private sector, at least under contemporary Canadian conditions. See "Some Reflections on Economic Security for the Aged in Canada," in *Canadian Issues: Essays in Honour of Henry F. Angus*, ed. Clark (Toronto: University of Toronto Press, 1961), pp. 325–66; summary of address to annual meeting of Canadian Chamber of Commerce, *Canadian Business*, Nov., 1963, pp. 83–84; oral and written submissions to the 1964–65 joint committee, *Proceedings*, pp. 1500–1521, 1535–62, 1589–96, esp. pp. 1536–39. Davis, while not dissenting in public, argued behind the scenes that the committee should confine its attention to regulating and increasing portability in private plans, but he was unable to persuade either the committee or the government.

59. "Summary Report," pp. 4–5, 19.

60. For an informed account of the development of the portable pension committee's thinking and its interaction with the government, see Robert M. Clark, "The Pension Benefits Act of Ontario and Its Relation to the Federal Pension Proposals," in *Pensions in Canada*, ed. Coward, pp. 27–44.

61. *Toronto Globe and Mail*, July 27, 1963.

62. Ibid., July 27, 29.

63. LaMarsh, *Bird in a Gilded Cage*, pp. 89–90.

64. Sess. Paper 202A (1964–65).

65. Lloyd to Pearson, Jan. 17, 1964. Sess. Paper 202H (1964–65).

66. Robarts to Pearson, Feb. 13, 1964. Sess. Paper 202A (1964–65).

67. Federal-Provincial Conference, Nov. 26–29, 1963, *Proceedings* (Ottawa: Queen's Printer, 1964), p. 49.

68. *Toronto Globe and Mail*, Apr. 2, 1964.

69. A number of not entirely consistent accounts of these negotiations have been published. See especially Richard Simeon, *Federal-Provincial Diplomacy: The Making of Recent Policy in Canada* (Toronto: University of Toronto Press, 1972), pp. 56–60; Peter Newman, *The Distemper of Our Times: Canadian Politics in Transition, 1963–68* (Toronto: McClelland and Stewart, 1968), chap. 22; Peter Desbarats, *The State of Quebec* (Toronto: McClelland and Stewart, 1965), pp. 128–32.

70. The other provinces were also canvassed about the constitutional amendment, but this was merely a matter of protocol since there was no doubt about their assent. The amendment reenacted section 94A of the BNA Act as follows: "The Parliament of Canada may make laws in relation to old age pensions and supplementary benefits, including survivors' and disability benefits irrespective of age, but no such law shall affect the

operation of any law present or future of a provincial legislature in relation to any such matter."

71. Sess. Paper 202E (1964–65). This communication was also printed as an appendix to Hansard. *HC Debates*, 1964–65, pp. 2388–89.

72. Sess. Paper 202J (1964–65).

73. The actual aggregate (employer and employee) annual contributions at different earnings levels would have been:

	Aggregate Contributions	
Annual Earnings	*Federal*	*Quebec*
$1,000	$20.00	$ 0
2,000	40.00	40.00
3,000	60.00	80.00
4,000	80.00	120.00
4,500 (federal ceiling)	90.00	140.00
5,000	90.00	160.00
6,000 (Quebec ceiling)	90.00	200.00

74. The Quebec committee had envisaged that in the immediate future disability benefits would not be paid before sixty. The final formulation agreed to by Ottawa and Quebec made them payable at any age to a beneficiary with a specified minimum contribution record. The Quebec committee's approach to disability benefits was cautious because the committee believed that the inherent difficulty of calculating the risks involved was, for a variety of reasons, considerably more complex in Quebec. It went so far as to recommend that three-quarters of a point of the overall 4 percent contribution rate should be segregated in a special disability fund and that a more mature policy decision on disability benefits should be deferred until there had been three years of experience with the fund. "Report," vol. 1, chap. 5.

75. Under the Quebec formulation, the aggregate annual contribution for a person earning $5,000 a year would have been 4 percent of $4,000, or $160. In the final formulation agreed to by Ottawa and Quebec, this contribution was 3.6 percent of $4,400, or $158.40. The corresponding figures at an earnings level of $4,000 a year are $120 and $122; at $3,000, $80 and $86.40; at $2,000, $40 and $50.40; at $1,000, nil and $14.40.

76. The Quebec committee made a strong restatement of Lesage's claim for jurisdiction over the universal plan, arguing that the province could achieve proper balance in the overall program only if it controlled both segments. "Report," vol. 1, pp. 116–17. One of the Quebec committee's arguments was that adjustment of the universal pension was desirable to complement the adjustment it proposed for the earnings-related pension. The federal government accommodated the province on that point.

77. *Ont. Debates*, 1963–64, pp. 3017–18.

78. CIPO release, July 15, 1964. The question was: "In a Canadian

portable pension plan, who do you think should run it—the federal government in Ottawa or the government of this province?" The percentages of respondents favouring federal or provincial administration were:

	Federal	Provincial	No Opinion
National	52	31	17
Quebec	25	58	17
Ontario	58	25	17
West	72	16	12

79. *Ont. Debates*, 1965, pp. 23–26. For a brief but vivid account of the soul-searching that preceded the Ontario decision to cooperate, see Simeon, *Federal-Provincial Diplomacy*, pp. 63–64.

80. 1964–65 joint committee, *Proceedings*, pp. 1682–1742, 1778–84.

81. *Nat. Fin.*, 1972–73, p. 111.

82. Figures derived from DBS, *Income Distributions by Size in Canada, 1971* (Ottawa: Information Canada, 1973), table 59. See also *The Aging: Trends, Problems, Prospects* (Toronto: Social Planning Council of Metropolitan Toronto, 1973).

83. *Unemployment Insurance in the 70s* (Ottawa: Queen's Printer, 1970); *Income Security for Canadians* (Ottawa: Dept. of National Health and Welfare, 1970). The following page references to *Income Security* are to the six-by-nine-inch edition.

84. *Income Security*, p. 2.

85. The white paper was tabled in the House of Commons on Nov. 30, 1970, and the next day the bill to amend the Old Age Security Act was introduced. Priority was given to this bill so that it passed before the end of the year. *HC Journals*, 1970–72, pp. 163, 165, 243.

86. *Toronto Globe and Mail*, June 23, 1971.

87. Commission of Inquiry on Health and Social Welfare, *Income Security*, 3 vols. (designated as vol. 5 of the commission's *Report*) (Quebec Official Publisher, 1971).

88. *Montreal Gazette*, May 10, 13, 1972.

89. The amending bill was introduced on June 16, 1972, and passed on July 4. *Que. Journals*, 1972, pp. 207, 255.

90. Hon. Marc Lalonde, *Working Paper on Social Security in Canada* (Ottawa: Dept. of National Health and Welfare, 1973). The paper was tabled in the House of Commons and commented on briefly on Apr. 18. *HC Debates*, 1973, pp. 3403–9.

91. *Income Security*, p. 79.

92. *Working Paper*, pp. 17–30. Proposals relating to the CPP are on p. 21.

93. Conference of Welfare Ministers, "Communiqué" (mimeo.), Oct. 11, 1973.

94. *HC Votes and Proceedings*, 1973, pp. 585, 730.

Notes to Chapter 9, Public Pensions and the Policy Spiral

1. Abraham Holtzman, *The Townsend Movement: A Political Study* (New York: Bookman Associates, 1963), found that "the Townsend movement arose primarily as a depression phenomenon" (p. 201) and that "with the enactment of the Social Security Act, the basic validity of the Townsend plan was undermined and a wedge driven between the movement and the great mass of its potential supporters, the aged and those already approaching this stage in life" (p. 200).

2. See chap. 5, sec. 1.

3. David B. Truman, *The Governmental Process: Political Interests and Public Opinion* (New York: Alfred A. Knopf, 1951), p. 34.

4. Ibid., pp. 511–12.

5. See chap. 2, sec. 2.

6. See Angus Campbell et al., *The American Voter* (New York: John Wiley & Sons, 1960), chap. 8.

7. See, e.g., chap. 4, sec. 3; chap. 5, secs. 1, 2; chap. 6, sec. 3; chap. 7, sec. 2; chap. 8, sec. 1.

8. Releases of Nov. 23, 1946, Apr. 15, 1950, and Oct. 14, 1950, reported as follows on questions asking if the respondents favoured pensions to "old people with no other means of support" or "to everyone who reaches old age":

	Nov. 1946	Apr. 1950	Oct. 1950
	%	%	%
No other means of support	58	50	43
All old people	34	38	55
Qualified or undecided	8	12	2

Publication of the joint committee's report intervened between the Apr. and Oct. polls in 1950. The majority in favour of a universal pension shown in Oct. became a huge majority when the old age security bill was before Parliament. A CIPO release of Oct. 24, 1951, showed 81 percent answering affirmatively and 17 percent negatively to the question, "Next year, every Canadian 70 years of age and over will start getting a pension of $40 a month, regardless of their [*sic*] financial position. Do you approve or disapprove of this?"

9. Gad Horowitz, *Canadian Labour in Politics* (Toronto: University of Toronto Press, 1968), chap. 1.

10. See Martin Robin, *Radical Politics and Canadian Labour, 1880–1930* (Kingston, Ont.: Queen's University, Industrial Relations Centre, 1968).

11. Except for J. S. Woodsworth and A. A. Heaps, information about the M.P.'s mentioned was gleaned from *Canadian Parliamentary Guide* and *HC Debates* for appropriate years, and from newspaper obituaries. There

are two full-length biographies of Woodsworth, namely, Grace MacInnis, *J. S. Woodsworth: A Man to Remember* (Toronto: Macmillan Company of Canada, 1953); Kenneth McNaught, *A Prophet in Politics: A Biography of J. S. Woodsworth* (Toronto: University of Toronto Press, 1959). There is also Leo Heaps, *The Rebel in the House: The Life and Times of A. A. Heaps, MP* (London: Niccolo Publishing Company, 1970).

12. See H. A. Logan, *Trade Unions in Canada: Their Development and Functioning* (Toronto: Macmillan Company of Canada, 1948), pp. 45–47, 62–70, 399–520, 550–54.

13. Membership figures are from Dept. of Labour, *Annual Report on Labour Organization in Canada*, 1926 (Ottawa: King's Printer, 1927), p. 8. The total number of voters on the list for the 1926 general election was 4,665,381. Chief Electoral Officer, *Report, Sixteenth General Election, 1926* (Ottawa: King's Printer, 1927), p. vi.

14. See chap. 4, sec. 2.

15. *HC Debates*, 1926, p. 1972.

16. Social Crediters and Créditistes tended to be ambivalent because of the strong disposition of many of them to regard financing through the Bank of Canada as overcoming cost and redistributional problems. Thus, they supported both the market ethos and expansive policies on public pensions.

17. For data on the financial operations of the old age security fund, see *Nat. Fin.*, 1961–62, p. 89; 1972–73, p. 111. The years from the inception of the plan to 1960 are covered in the first of these volumes and subsequent years in the second.

18. The debates relating to the tax are recorded in *HC Debates*, 1951 2d sess., pp. 386–90, 397–400, 404, 405–6, 415–16, 423–24, 609–10, 614–18, 620–21, 627, 629, 634–37, 824–39.

19. The tax was identical in absolute terms ($60 a year) for all taxpayers with taxable incomes of $3,000 a year or more. The result was an inverse correlation between incomes beyond that level and the percentage thereof taken by the tax. The point is illustrated in sec. 4.

20. The information presented on pensioners' organizations is based on interviews with the presidents of the National Pensioners and Senior Citizens Federation and of Pensioners Concerned (Canada) Inc., on unpublished records gathered from a variety of sources, and on the following three periodicals: *Bulletin*, published by the United Senior Citizens of Ontario, Inc.; *The Elder Statesman*, published by the Federated Legislative Council of British Columbia; *Pensioners' and Senior Citizens' Magazine*, published by the Pensioners' and Senior Citizens' Organization of Saskatchewan.

21. See chap. 5, sec. 3.

22. Dept. of National Health and Welfare, file no. 208-3-5, Pub. Arch., RG 29, vol. 128.

23. Ibid., file no. 208-5-9, vol. 144.

24. The information presented on the Canadian Welfare Council was derived from private interviews, CWC publications, and unpublished briefs and other written representations to governments.

25. *Social Security for Canada* (Ottawa: Canadian Welfare Council, 1958), and *Social Policies for Canada, Part 1: A Statement of the Canadian Welfare Council* (Ottawa: Canadian Welfare Council, 1969).

26. See, e.g., *Canadian Welfare* 14, no. 6 (Mar., 1939): 2; 16, no. 3 (July, 1940): 23. The conventionality of its views in that period is also illustrated by the following editorial comment in *Child and Family Welfare* 11, no. 4 (Nov., 1935): 45: "The assumption of whole or partial state responsibility for the parents should not relieve children of filial obligations."

27. Letter dated Sept. 3, 1963.

28. Letter to Pearson dated May 24, 1966, and attached memorandum.

29. The plans required employers to contribute to accident funds out of which benefits were disbursed to disabled employees. The Judicial Committee held that this requirement imposed "a statutory condition on the contract of employment" and thus fell under the "property of civil rights" clause of the BNA Act. *Workmen's Compensation Board* v. *Canadian Pacific Railway Company*, 1920 AC 184; *McColl* v. *Canadian Pacific Railway Company*, 1923 AC 126.

30. *HC Journals*, 1925, p. 457.

31. Dominion-Provincial Conference on Reconstruction, *Dominion and Provincial Submissions and Plenary Conference Discussions* (Ottawa: King's Printer, 1946), pp. 246–47.

32. See chap. 5, sec. 3. Administrative discretion became unimportant after 1951. The means test was continued for the sixty-five to sixty-nine age group but by then administration had become substantially more routine than in the earlier period. Moreover, the universal program for those of seventy and over was much the more important part of the program. The provinces were not involved in that at all and, in any case, rules governing the payment of a universal pension can be stated precisely enough to permit only minimal scope for administrative discretion.

33. Though the point is not indispensable for the argument, it is of interest that the governing statute requires payment of benefits whether or not there is money in the fund to cover them and that, in the first decade of actual operation, the accumulated excess of annual shortfalls over surpluses was about $550 million or 12 percent of the total benefits paid. See *Nat. Fin.*, 1961–62, p. 89; 1972–73, p. 111. The annual shortfalls, however, were not carried on the books as a charge against the fund but were "provided for by budgetary expenditure" or in one case "written off." The terminology in itself indicates the unreality of the operation. From 1959 on, on the other hand, successive ministers of finance went out of their way to reinstate the myth in order to justify increases in the old age security tax. In the 1959–60 fiscal year, the annual shortfall was for the first time "financed by a loan

from the minister of finance" (a sleight-of-hand provided for in the statute). This was also done in the only two subsequent years when shortfalls occurred. Because of the tax increases, however, shortfalls ceased to be the order of the day in the 1960s. On the contrary, the total tax revenues credited to the fund during the decade greatly exceeded total benefits.

34. See Antal Deutsch, *Income Redistribution through Canadian Federal Family Allowances and Old Age Benefits*, Queen's University Papers on Taxation and Public Finance, no. 4 (Toronto: Canadian Tax Foundation, 1968), esp. chap. 5.

35. Ibid.

36. See table 10, chap. 2, sec. 4. Eighty-five percent of the nonfarm population of sixty-five and over had incomes of less than $3,000 a year. The universal pension was not at that time payable until seventy. The percentage of the seventy-and-over age group in the under $3,000 cell was certainly much larger than the 85 percent shown for the sixty-five-and-over group. Inclusion of the farm population would undoubtedly have increased the percentage still further.

37. See Allan M. Maslove, *The Pattern of Taxation in Canada*, Economic Council of Canada (Ottawa: Information Canada, 1973), pp. 74, 94–95, 114–15; W. Irwin Gillespie, *The Incidence of Taxes and Public Expenditures in the Canadian Economy*, Studies of the Royal Commission on Taxation, no. 2 (Ottawa: Queen's Printer, 1966), pp. 40–43, 65, 203, 204; James A. Johnson, *The Incidence of Government Revenues and Expenditures: A Study prepared for the Ontario Committee on Taxation* (Toronto: Queen's Printer, n.d.), pp. 25–27, 38. Maslove found the general sales tax to be regressive over its entire range and especially at the lowest income level. Gillespie's study indicated steep regressivity for the under $2,000 family income group, mild regressivity between $2,000 and $5,000, mild progressivity between $5,000 and $10,000, and moderate regressivity thereafter. Johnson's study suggested slight progressivity up to $5,000, proportionality between $5,000 and $10,000, and some regressivity thereafter, but his study dealt with incidence in Ontario only. An earlier study supported Finance Minister Abbott's argument of 1951 that the tax was progressive at the lowest income range and proportional thereafter. Irving Jay Goffman, *The Burden of Canadian Taxation: Allocation of Federal, Provincial and Local Taxes among Income Classes*, Canadian Tax Paper, no. 29 (Toronto: Canadian Tax Foundation, 1962), pp. 41–44.

38. John Bossons, "Economic Overview of the Tax Reform Legislation," in *1971 Conference Report* (Toronto: Canadian Tax Foundation, 1972), p. 60.

39. It is assumed that the taxpayer's entire income consists of earnings, up to the ceiling at least. If it does not, then the percentage of his income taken by the earnings tax will be less than shown here.

40. See Gillespie, *Taxes and Public Expenditures*, p. 56; Johnson, *Government Revenues and Expenditures*, pp. 33–34.

Index